ENTERTAINING CRIME

SOCIAL PROBLEMS AND SOCIAL ISSUES

An Aldine de Gruyter Series of Texts and Monographs

SERIES EDITOR

Joel Best

Southern Illinois University at Carbondale

ENTERTAINING CRIME

Television Reality Programs

Mark Fishman and Gray Cavender

Editors

ALDINE DE GRUYTER
New York

About the Editors

Mark Fishman is Associate Professor of Sociology, Brooklyn College, City University of New York. Dr. Fishman is the author of *Manufacturing the News,* and numerous journal articles related to crime news.

Gray Cavender is Professor, School of Justice Studies, Arizona State University. Dr. Cavender is co-author of *Corporate Crime Under Attack: The Ford Pinto Case and Beyond.*

ALDINE DE GRUYTER
A division of Walter de Gruyter, Inc.
200 Saw Mill River Road
Hawthorne, New York 10532

This publication is printed on acid free paper ∞

Library of Congress Cataloging-in-Publication Data
Entertaining crime : television reality programs / Mark Fishman and
    Gray Cavender, editors.
        p.   cm. — (Social problems and social issues)
    Includes bibliographical references and index.
    ISBN 0-202-30615-1 (alk. paper). — ISBN 0-202-30616-X (pbk. :
    alk. paper)
        1. Reality television programs—History and criticism.   2. Crime
    in television.   I. Fishman, Mark, 1947–   .   II. Cavender, Gray,
    1947–   .   III. Series.
    PN1992.8.R43E58   1998
    364—dc21   98-11941
                                                          CIP

Manufactured in the United States of America

10   9   8   7   6   5   4   3   2   1

For Pam, Laura, and Nancy

Contents

IV.   CRIME, CRIMINALS, AND VICTIMS

I

Introduction

1

Television Reality Crime Programs:
Context and History

GRAY CAVENDER and MARK FISHMAN

Beginning in the late 1980s, a new trend appeared on television that has continued to the present: reality programs. There are a variety of these programs. Some, like "Geraldo," feature angry confrontations between former lovers or children who claim to be satanists. "Unsolved Mysteries" features segments on UFOs, the outlaw Billy the Kid, and crime. Others, programs like "America's Most Wanted," are only about crime. The chapters in this volume are about television reality crime programs

Television programming can be divided into various genres or categories. For example, TV programs could be categorized as situation comedies, police shows, science fiction series, news, talk shows, or game shows. A simpler way of categorizing programs is to make a distinction between fact and fiction. Programs like "The X-Files" or "Seinfeld" are fictional, while "The CBS Evening News" and news magazines like "60 Minutes" claim to present information about real people and events. Other programs are somewhere between TV fiction and the reality of the news. Game shows and late night talk shows (e.g., Letterman and Leno) are not fiction, but neither are they the news; they are entertainment programming.

Television reality programs are especially hard to categorize because they blur the line between news and entertainment; some even blur the line between fact and fiction. Programs like "Hard Copy" cover real people; often these are celebrities, although occasionally, as in the coverage of the O. J. Simpson trial, stories are about celebrities and crime. Programs like "Rescue 911" and "America's Most Wanted" reenact actual events.

Perhaps the defining feature of reality television is that these programs claim to present reality. The TV reality crime programs that are the subject of this volume claim to present true stories about crime, criminals, and victims. In this, they are a hybrid form of programming: they resemble aspects of the news, but, like entertainment programs, they often air in prime time; some even show as reruns. Moreover, as we will see in this and in other chapters, some of these programs mimic certain forms of crime fiction. The entertaining aspects of these programs are designed to make them more exciting and to increase their ratings.

Two primary formats are used by TV reality crime programs. Each format bolsters reality claims in different ways. Programs like "America's Most Wanted" present a series of vignettes in which actors reenact actual crimes. The vignettes feature interviews with victims, their family and friends, the police, and film and photographs of suspects. Viewers are urged to telephone the police or the program with information about crimes or suspects. The programs update previous broadcasts, for example, with film of a captured fugitive or a follow-up if a fugitive is still at large.

Programs like "Cops" use a second type of format: The TV camera "rides with" the police and films a story as it unfolds. There is actual footage of the police in action—breaking down a door in a drug bust, or chasing and wrestling a suspect to the ground. The audience sees and hears what the police see and hear. While this approach is touted as "the real thing," the programs are edited to air the most action-packed sequences. Typically, hundreds of hours of footage are edited each week to produce a single half-hour episode. Editors delete uninteresting video and add clips from a program's file of stock footage (Seagal 1993).

Most of the chapters in this volume discuss U.S. reality crime shows. However, these programs are not just a U.S. phenomenon: They are popular all over the world. They exist in England, France, Germany, the Netherlands, Australia, Mexico, Brazil, and probably in many other countries we are not aware of. Not surprisingly, the programs vary from country to country, although there are similarities as well. Three chapters in this book examine European reality crime shows: Brants looks at the Netherlands, Dauncey examines French shows, and Dobash et al. consider a British program.

In the remainder of this introductory chapter, we will discuss why these programs have become so popular at this time. The programs have a history of their own: they draw upon other kinds of crime shows and other tabloid-type productions that have been a part of popular culture for years. After discussing this history, we will show how, notwithstanding reality claims, these programs differ markedly from the sort of journalism that characterizes the news. Finally, we will examine changes in technology that facilitated the rise of TV reality crime programs.

IDEOLOGY AND REALITY CRIME PROGRAMS

Two obvious questions are generated by the recent proliferation of television reality crime programs: Why have these programs emerged at this time? Where did they come from?

In terms of the Why now? question, we begin with what is a standard assumption for social scientists: the social context in which we live informs and shapes everything from what we think about to the nature of our institutions and the policies that drive them. Television reality crime programs have flourished, in part, because of the social context. To put this another way, crime policy, ideological notions about crime, and television crime shows are interrelated; they occur within a particular social context.

Newspaper headlines, politicians, and public opinion surveys reflect a common view about crime today: crime is a serious problem that is getting worse; people are angry and afraid; something has to be done. This view of crime is supported by ideological dimensions that define what we perceive to be the crime problem and the solutions that we consider. To better understand the connections between our view of crime and television depictions of crime, we will consider recent U.S. crime policy since the 1960s. We will examine the links between these policies, the social context in which they arose, and media presentations about crime.

The decade of the 1960s was marked by civil disobedience and opposition to authority. The civil rights and women's movements demanded equal rights, and protested laws and policies that blocked those rights. Widespread civil disobedience was common in the opposition to the Vietnam War. In terms of criminal law, the U.S. Supreme Court condemned aspects of the criminal justice system such as brutal police interrogation techniques and the prison system's almost total control over inmates' lives. To correct abuses within the criminal justice system, the Court emphasized the legal rights of the accused and of prisoners. Rehabilitation was a central tenet of U.S. crime policy. The rehabilitative ideal entailed the belief that factors beyond the individual's control cause criminality. Criminologists said that we could identify the factors, treat them, and cure the criminal of criminality like a doctor cures a patient of a disease. Treatment—on probation, in prison, or on parole—was the order of the day.

Things changed in the 1970s. Politicians and citizens grew concerned about crime. Richard Nixon, who had campaigned on a "law and order" platform, was elected president in 1968 and again in 1972. The U.S. Department of Justice increased federal funding for state criminal justice systems and extended what had started as President Lyndon Johnson's "war on crime" into the mid-1970s. Criminology also changed its emphasis. Some criminologists criticized the search for the causes of crime: they said that society could not remedy deep-seated social causes of crime. Scholars and politicians advocated policies that vented retributive feelings and that promised to make punishment a more effective deterrent (Wilson 1975). Although some scholars advocated reduced prison sentences, state legislatures increased them in a "get tough" approach in the 1970s (Cavender 1984).

Ideologically, the 1980s were a repeat of the 1970s. U.S. President

Ronald Reagan and British Prime Minister Margaret Thatcher epitomized the continuing shift to the political right. In the United States, people feared that their country, their communities, their values, and their safety were slipping away. Those anxieties helped to produce the "war on drugs," the missing children issue (Best 1990), the satanism scare (Richardson, Best, and Bromley 1991), and an increasing fear of crime. Some of these anxieties and concerns have continued into the 1990s.

The prevailing crime policies and ideologies about crime have changed, but what about the media and how it presents crime? Media critic Steven Stark elaborates the links among the social context, ideology, and media depictions of crime. Stark notes that during the 1960s movies with anti-authority themes were common, and lawyer programs were popular on television. However, in the 1970s TV lawyers were replaced by TV cops, and a concern with civil rights gave way to plots wherein the police violated the law to produce justice (1987:264). Stark concludes that, as the public in the 1980s endorsed a crime control model of law enforcement, television crime shows came to be more about order than about law (1987:280–82).

Other scholars agree. Michael Ryan and Douglas Kellner analyze movies in terms of political ideologies. They argue that movies like *Dirty Harry* (1971) and its sequels attacked a 1960s liberal view of criminal justice that "prevents good cops from doing their job, and . . . lets criminals go free to commit more crimes" (1988:42). *Dirty Harry* and its progeny were conservative law and order thrillers that meshed with the times; they also were box office successes. Even comedy crime movies like *Beverly Hills Cop* (1984) suggested that bureaucratic rules hamstring the police.

Of course, there is not a simple cause and effect relationship between the social mood and media crime depictions. For example, in the early 1980s when the mood of the country had moved further to the right, television executives experienced mixed results when they responded to the shifting political winds. Programs like "Today's FBI" and "Strike Force," which were inserted in the TV schedule to tap that conservative mood, had low ratings and were canceled. "Hill Street Blues," which also aired in 1981, had low ratings at first, but survived and became a popular program. "Hill Street Blues" was the "first postliberal cop show" (Gitlin 1983:308). According to Gitlin, the point of the program was that people suffer and our institutions cannot stop it; the best that those in authority can do is to try to maintain order (1983:313).

Studying the related topic of war, Gibson (1991:376) notes that the United States entered the 1970s dazed and demoralized over the conflict in Vietnam. To many, the United States failure to win in Vietnam symbolized the beginning of a decline. Gibson argues that movies in the 1980s like *Uncommon Valor* (1983) and *Rambo: First Blood, Part II* (1985) revitalized a traditional "paramilitary culture" (1991:388–89). Simultaneously, President

Ronald Reagan demonstrated in Grenada that citizens would support and draw pride from "small wars." President George Bush continued that trend in Panama, and escalated it in the Persian Gulf War. The outcome of that war prompted President Bush to declare that the United States had beaten the post-Vietnam malaise. Not only did citizens support the war, they enjoyed it as a media event: "smart bombs" and other media-war technologies gave the TV viewer a ringside seat, what Gibson calls, "[t]he fantasy of becoming personally empowered through vicariously killing the enemy" (1991:394; see Bennett and Palatz 1994).

Thus, the United States entered the last decade of the twentieth century with some renewed pride. The Persian Gulf War suggested that the country was still a strong nation, at least militarily. At the same time, anxieties persist about stagnant wages, job insecurity, and a future that sometimes seems uncertain, maybe even dangerous. Media depictions of crime reflect both the pride and the anxieties.

Television reality crime programs, which appeared in the late 1980s and flourished in the 1990s, reflect the hopes for and the uncertainties about the future. These programs are a display of the worst in us. Drugs, crime, and threats to the family and to safety generally are the stock-in-trade of these shows. However, programs like "Cops" depict the police as the front line of defense against such threats. "America's Most Wanted" gives viewers a sense of empowerment as they fight back with telephone calls that help to capture dangerous criminals. The programs accomplish these ends through the sort of media technology that Gibson (1991) discussed in relation to the Persian Gulf War. Instead of "smart bombs," the TV viewer rides with the police on "Cops," or prowls through a fugitive's abandoned hideout on "America's Most Wanted."

Television reality crime programs are informed by the conservative ideologies that support current crime policies. Crime is seen as a serious problem, and longer prison sentences, not probation and parole, are offered as the solution. These programs reaffirm Gitlin's (1983) notion that, for now, we have abandoned any hope of improving the human condition. Instead, the state is simply trying to maintain order. Three chapters in this volume deal with issues of ideology, order, and control. Gray Cavender's chapter analyzes the ideological dimensions, especially in terms of symbols and language, of "America's Most Wanted" and "Unsolved Mysteries." Pamela Donovan argues that TV reality crime programs reconstruct a law and order ideology in the United States by making a spectacle of crime and criminal justice, one in which the audience participates. Aaron Doyle considers how "Cops" reinforces a law and order ideology through various techniques that prompt the audience to identify with and share the point of view of the police.

These reality programs and the ideologies they endorse reinforce prevailing views about crime, criminals, and victims. Two chapters in this volume address these programs' stereotypic views of criminals, especially regarding racial or ethnic minorities. Paul G. Kooistra, John S. Mahoney, and Saundra D. Westervelt show that "Cops" features stories about white police officers, white victims, and nonwhite criminals. Mary Beth Oliver and Blake Armstrong find that the audience for "Cops" overestimates the prevalence of crime in society, especially crime by African Americans. A third chapter by Dianne Cyr Carmody addresses stereotyping in terms of the presentation of domestic violence on these programs.

REALITY CRIME PROGRAMS:
THE HISTORICAL BACKDROP

But where did reality crime programs come from? There is no single, agreed-upon history behind the recent proliferation of these television shows. In large part, this is because different scholars focus on different aspects of the background of these programs. Our history will consider the contributions of a variety of media to the current trend in television reality crime programming. We begin with radio.

Most histories of the media note that television copied much of its programming style from radio (Barnouw 1990). Crime drama was popular on radio; it was dramatic, inexpensive programming (MacDonald 1990). Stark (1987:240) points out that, at first, many radio crime shows were based upon novels, short stories, and even comic books that featured private eye heroes. However, a new type of radio crime program appeared in the 1930s. Beginning with "True Detective Mysteries," which described an actual wanted criminal at the end of each program, shows like "Homicide Squad," "Calling All Cars," and "Treasury Agent" dramatized real police cases as radio crime entertainment (1987:241).

Movies are the second link in the chain. Crime films were popular in the 1940s. Although we most often remember Humphrey Bogart movies like *The Maltese Falcon* (1941) or *The Big Sleep* (1946), which were based on private eye novels, a series of films appeared from the mid-1940s into the 1950s that were called "police procedurals." These semidocumentary thrillers drew upon FBI and police files or newspaper accounts of actual crimes. Movies like *The House on 92nd Street* (1945—FBI uncovers a Nazi spy ring), *The Naked City* (1948—tabloidlike film about a murder in New York), and *Dragnet* (1954—LA Police Department solves a brutal murder) used a narrative style that copied newsreels and World War II documentaries (Krutnik 1991:202). Filmmakers achieved their documentary look—a gritty realism—by abandoning the Hollywood sound stage in favor of location shooting. The films compromised between a documentarylike emphasis on law enforcement agencies and the more standard detective-centered drama (1991:202–3).

Although the movie *Dragnet* appeared in 1954, the television series "Dragnet" aired in 1951 and ushered in an era of TV crime shows. Like the police procedural movies, "Dragnet" relied on actual cases and used location shooting and police jargon to create a sense of realism (Stark 1987:245). Its success generated a series of TV clones in the 1950s, including "Highway Patrol," "Treasury Men in Action," and "Night Watch," which used actual tapes recorded by a police reporter who rode with the police. Another 1950s crime show, "The Untouchables," evoked a kind of realism because it was about Eliot Ness, a real G-man; it was narrated by newspaper columnist Walter Winchell (1987:247). Robert Stack, who starred as Ness, would later host "Unsolved Mysteries," a television reality crime program.

In the 1960s and 1970s, programs like "Adam-12" and "Police Story" continued TV's emphasis on law enforcement, and a claim of realism that came from episodes that were based on actual cases. One such program, "The FBI," profiled wanted criminals at the end of each show. "Hill Street Blues" (1981) perfected the gritty look that movie and television police procedurals had begun years earlier. According to Gitlin (1983:290–95), the goal of the producers was to make a show with a realistic texture of sound and visuals. Unusual angles shot with hand-held cameras gave it a nervous look of controlled chaos. Actors said their lines as they moved toward or away from the microphone, and purposefully overlapped their dialogue. An improvisational comedy troupe was hired to generate realistic background hum. "Hill Street Blues" was influenced by *The Police Tapes,* a 1976 documentary film that focused on the police in New York City (1983:293).

In the mid-1970s, a rather different antecedent appeared. The "Crime Stoppers" series entailed a brief dramatization of an actual crime followed by a request to help the police to solve it. Journalists and police worked together to produce the "Crime of the Week," which was usually aired as a part of a local news broadcast. Crime Stoppers International started the series in Albuquerque, New Mexico in 1976. By 1988, there were 700 programs in U.S. cities, and 29 Canadian programs; they also appeared in England, Sweden, Australia, and Guam (Carriere and Ericson 1989:1–2). They still exist.

Finally, the direct ancestors of shows like "America's Most Wanted" appeared in Europe. The earliest of these started in the Federal Republic of Germany in October 1967; it had audiences in Switzerland and Austria. According to Schlesinger and Tumber (1994:251–52), "Aktenzeichen XY . . . Ungelöst" ("Case XY . . . Unsolved") combined live action, documentary, and fiction. It frequently emphasized political crime, e.g., the hunt for the Baader-Meinhof gang. The German program influenced "Opsporing Verzocht," a Dutch reality crime show, and "Crimewatch UK," a British program (1994:248).

While we have been discussing the social context in which the American reality crime shows have arisen, it is interesting to note that in rather different circumstances (different media systems, different criminal justice systems) reality crime shows have arisen and prospered in Germany, Britain, Holland, France, and elsewhere. Clearly, America's experience is not unique nor are the specific conditions surrounding the growth of U.S. reality crime shows the only ones possible. Two chapters in this volume discuss how reality shows have developed in other countries. Chris Brants's chapter discusses "Opsporing Verzocht" in the context of a shift in the politics and structure of the media in the Netherlands. Hugh Dauncey's chapter describes the history of reality crime TV in France in terms of public concern over crime and criminal justice, programming changes, and French culture. In addition, a third chapter considers the British show "Crimewatch UK." R. Emerson Dobash, Philip Schlesinger, Russell Dobash, and C. Kay Weaver analyze that program in terms of the different ways women viewers interpret the program's depictions of crime.

U.S. reality crime television started in 1987 when "Unsolved Mysteries" appeared as a pilot episode. Raymond Burr, who was famous for two TV crime shows, "Perry Mason" and "Ironside," hosted the pilot. Karl Malden, known for "The Streets of San Francisco," hosted several follow-up specials. "Unsolved Mysteries" became a regular show in the 1988–1989 television season, with Robert Stack as host (Breslin 1990:360). "America's Most Wanted" aired on the new Fox network in January 1988. Its creators were familiar with the British and European predecessors, and wanted to Americanize them. The look of "America's Most Wanted" was a combination of 1940s films, MTV music videos, and a gritty realism (1990:93–94). "America's Most Wanted" was fairly successful; it was the first Fox program to beat any of its other network competition.

"America's Most Wanted" and "Unsolved Mysteries" quickly generated clones, including, "Cops," "Crimewatch Tonight," "True Stories of the Highway Patrol," "American Detective," "Untold Stories of the F.B.I." and "Rescue 911." These programs focus on crime or emergencies, which typically fall within the scope of the news. As we noted, in some ways television reality crime programs make newslike claims. However, such programs diverge from the traditions of journalism.

NOT THE NEWS

At times, reality crime programs borrow from the vocabulary of journalism. For instance, on "America's Most Wanted," interviewers and presenters are described as "correspondents" or "reporters"; cases may be introduced with the phrase, "And now the news. . . . " Moreover, a large proportion of the audience seems to perceive these programs as news (Breslin 1990).

Nevertheless, the genre of reality crime is a long way from journalism. Program producers repeatedly step outside the bounds of accepted journalistic practice when they mix interviews of real victims and investigators with reconstructions of events using actors, when they film reconstructions from subjective camera angles, when they use music to heighten tension, and so on. To be sure, some of these techniques have found their way into local television news programs, but they are controversial among journalists, and are usually seen, at best, as a debasing of the professional standards, and at worst, as a gross violation of the rules of journalistic objectivity.

Reality crime programming eschews the watchdog role of the press—the notion that on behalf of civil society the press should keep an eye out for governmental abuse and incompetence. Instead of maintaining an independent and critical posture, reality crime programs invariably take a supportive role vis-à-vis law enforcement.

Reality-based crime programming, is, in fact, a collaborative product of media organizations and law enforcement agencies (a point discussed at length by Doyle and Donovan in their chapters on "Cops" and "America's Most Wanted"). For instance, the producers of "America's Most Wanted" depend on the FBI to learn of cases involving fugitives and for the details of those cases. Similarly, the producers of "Cops" need permission to ride in patrol cars and to film in station houses. In order to get high-quality video or rich details in a pending case, cooperation between media and police is absolutely necessary. In exchange for this cooperation, those who produce reality programs cannot or will not exercise independent and critical judgment of law enforcement agencies. The producers of reality crime shows identify with the police, viewing their role as one of combatting crime, aiding law enforcement, and showing police work in a positive and engaging way.

Now it is an oversimplification to think that newspaper and television crime reporters are entirely different. They, too, are dependent on law enforcement, cover crime through the eyes of the police, and are inclined to see their role as one of aiding law enforcement. They, too, need to cooperate with police: the police are routine sources for their first knowledge of crime and for details about a case (Fishman 1978, 1980; Ericson, Banarek, and Chan 1989). The real difference between crime reporters and the producers of TV reality crime shows is that *some* newspaper and television reporters (in particular, the "quality press") are careful to maintain independence from the police and stand ready to expose corruption, incompetence, or brutality. Ericson et al. (1989:104–10) note that the police generally distinguish between reporters who can be trusted to protect the reputation of the law enforcement agencies and reporters who may at any time publish unfavorable articles. The former, who usually work for tabloids, comprise an "inner circle," which maintains a close relationship with law enforcement agencies and is privy to details of pending cases and other police work. The latter, who usually work for quality papers, comprise an "outer circle," from which is hidden many of the details of cases. As Doyle points out in his chapter on "Cops," the producers of reality crime programs are clearly an example of "inner circle" crime reporting.

Although television reality crime programs claim to present a newslike reality, they violate journalistic traditions, and, in many ways, resemble crime fiction. These TV reality crime programs also resemble another media trend that blurs the distinction between informational and entertainment programming: infotainment.

INFOTAINMENT

Reality programming blends information and entertainment. It is about actual events and real people, but often it portrays them using reenactments that mix actors with real participants. It emphasizes action, sets events to music, compresses time, speeds up action, and uses camera angles typical of horror films, action movies, or *cinéma vérité*. In new ways, reality programming exploits the possibilities of crime and punishment as spectacle.

The tendency of some mass media to make information as entertaining as possible dates back at least as far as the rise of yellow journalism and tabloid newspapers in the nineteenth century (Kooistra and Mahoney 1996; Schudson 1978:91–106). Reality crime programming is really part of a recent resurgence of tabloids. For the past twenty-five years, U.S. television has been moving steadily toward more tabloidlike programming. Beginning in the early 1970s, the "happy talk" and "action news" formats of local TV news spread throughout the United States. In the early to mid-1980s, television talk shows appeared ("Donahue," "Geraldo," "Oprah"), featuring sensational topics like transsexuals, polygamists, and UFO abductions. In the late 1980s, there arose tabloid news magazine programs ("A Current Affair," "Entertainment Tonight," "Hard Copy"), focusing on celebrities and scandals. Finally, also in the late 1980s, there emerged reality crime programs like "America's Most Wanted" and "Unsolved Mysteries." All of these are commonly referred to as reality programs, as infotainment, or, less flatteringly, as "trash TV" (see Surette 1998:70–71).

It seems quite possible that, like the print tabloids of the nineteenth and early twentieth centuries, reality programs attract lower-middle-class and working-class audiences (Kooistra and Mahoney 1996), but, at this point, this is speculation. Research concerning the nature of the audience of reality programs has only just begun. In this volume, three chapters address different aspects of this issue. Oliver and Armstrong present the results of a survey of reality crime viewers, examining whether they are more likely to perceive the world around them as crime-ridden and, particularly, to believe that criminals are African-Americans. Dobash, Schlesinger, Dobash, and Weaver, using focus groups and interviews with women viewers, show us how ethnic background and personal experience as a victim can subtly shape viewers' interpretations of what they see in reality crime programs. Mark Fishman's chapter considers what Nielsen ratings reveal about the popularity of reality crime shows and who is watching them.

TECHNOLOGICAL CHANGE

The increase in tabloid TV shows is not the only trend underlying the development of reality crime programs. In the same time period in which infotainment has grown, new technology has developed enabling new kinds of coverage of events in the world. Smaller, cheaper, more portable video cameras made electronic news gathering more cost effective and more immediate. By the late 1970s, geostationary satellites made it possible to instantly transmit high-quality video to any media organization with a satellite dish. By the early 1980s portable uplinks (relatively inexpensive satellite dishes mounted on vans) allowed not only TV journalists from networks and local stations, but also "stringers" and freelance private companies to send live video material anywhere in the world. As increasing numbers of electronic journalists roam the urban landscape, it has become more likely that "breaking events" such urban riots, large fires, earthquakes, hostage situations, and high-speed police chases will be transmitted live to the world via satellite. This kind of coverage has become routine in the 1990s.

Meanwhile, the spread of new technology in the rest of society, particularly new products in consumer electronics, has had other consequences. By the mid-1980s camcorders became commonplace in the general population, as did surveillance cameras in private businesses and small stores. This has increased the likelihood that someone will catch crimes, accidents, and natural disasters on videotape. As such material has become more available, the television industry has incorporated it into existing programs (e.g., the news and news magazine shows) and into new types of programs (e.g., "America's Funniest Home Videos"). Reality crime shows like "Cops," "American Detective," and "Real Stories of the Highway Patrol" would not exist were it not for the portable camcorder. And, of course, other shows such as "Unsolved Mysteries" and "America's Most Wanted" incorporate videos, photos, and other "actualities" whenever they are available.

CONCLUSION

In this introductory chapter, we have defined the topic for study in this volume: television reality crime programs. We noted that the defining feature is their claim to present reality in terms of crime, criminals, and victims. However, the programs present these "realities" in an entertaining way that draws upon traditions of crime fiction and tabloid journalism. These programs are not the news. They often violate basic journalistic practices, including an attempt at objectivity.

We have presented the context and the history of these programs. They are grounded in law and order ideologies that emphasize crime control and authority. Historically, they reflect a long fascination with crime—on radio, in film, and on television. The popularity of television reality crime programming is now a worldwide phenomenon. In part, this is due to significant technological improvements in electronic equipment and satellites. However, even technological innovations are never ends unto themselves; they, too, are always embedded in a larger socioeconomic context (Williams 1974).

The authors in this volume expand upon and go beyond many of the points that we have introduced in this chapter. As you read these chapters, you will gain an in-depth appreciation of how these programs operate, in the United States and elsewhere. You will learn more about the format and narrative structure of these programs, and see how they generate their reality claims. You also will learn about the ideological dimensions of these programs, and what they portend for crime policy and for the media, especially television.

REFERENCES

Barnouw, Eric. 1990. *Tube of Plenty: The Evolution of American Television,* 2nd rev. ed. New York: Oxford University Press.

Bennett, Lance and David Palatz (Eds.). 1994. *Taken By Storm: The Media, Public Opinion, and U.S. Foreign Policy in the Gulf War.* Chicago: University of Chicago Press.

Best, Joel. 1990. *Threatened Children.* Chicago: University of Chicago Press.

Breslin, Jack. 1990. *America's Most Wanted: How Television Catches Crooks.* New York: Harper & Row.

Carriere, Kevin and Richard Ericson. 1989. *Crime Stoppers: A Study in the Organization of Community Policing.* Research Report of the Centre of Criminology, University of Toronto.

Cavender, Gray. 1984. "A Critique of Sanctioning Reform." *Justice Quarterly* 1:1–16.

Ericson, Richard, Patricia Banarek, and Janet Chan. 1989. *Negotiating Control: A Study of News Sources.* Toronto: University of Toronto Press.

Fishman, Mark. 1978. "Crime Waves as Ideology." *Social Problems* 25:531–43.

———. 1980. *Manufacturing the News.* Austin: University of Texas Press.

Gibson, William. 1991. "The Return of Rambo: War and Culture in the Post-Vietnam

Era." In Alan Wolfe (Ed.), *America At Century's End* (pp. 376–95). Berkeley: University of California Press.

Gitlin, Todd. 1983. *Inside Prime Time*. New York: Pantheon.

Kooistra, Paul and John Mahoney. 1996. "The Historical Roots of Tabloid TV Crime." Paper presented at the Southern Sociological Society. Richmond, Virginia.

Krutnik, Frank. 1991. *In a Lonely Street: Film Noir, Genre, and Masculinity*. London: Routledge.

MacDonald, Fred. 1990. *One Nation Under Television*. Chicago: Nelson-Hall.

Richardson, James, Joel Best, and David Bromley (Eds.). 1991. *The Satanism Scare.* Hawthorne, NY: Aldine de Gruyter.

Ryan, Michael and Douglas Kellner. 1988. *Camera Politica: The Politics and Ideology of Contemporary Hollywood Film.* Bloomington: Indiana University Press.

Schlesinger, Philip and Howard Tumber. 1994. *Reporting Crime: The Media Politics of Criminal Justice.* Oxford: Clarendon.

Schudson, Michael. 1978. *Discovering the News: A Social History of American Newspapers.* New York: Basic Books.

Seagal, Debra. 1993. "Tales from the Cutting-Room Floor: The Reality of 'Reality-Based' Television." *Harper's Magazine,* November, p. 50.

Stark, Steven. 1987. "Perry Mason Meets Sonny Crockett: The History of Lawyers and the Police as Television Heroes." *University of Miami Law Review* 42:229–83.

Surette, Ray. 1998. *Media, Crime, and Criminal Justice: Images and Realities,* 2nd ed. Belmont, CA: Wadsworth.

Williams, Raymond. 1974. *Television: Technology and Cultural Form.* New York: Shocken.

Wilson, James Q. 1975. *Thinking About Crime.* New York: Basic Books.

II

The Audience for Reality Crime Programs

2

The Color of Crime:
Perceptions of Caucasians' and African-Americans' Involvement in Crime

MARY BETH OLIVER and G. BLAKE ARMSTRONG

Home security systems, handguns, self-defense courses, and even "lifelike" male mannequins that ride along in the passenger seats—these are but a few of the hundreds of safety measures that are now routine in our crime-apprehensive culture. Despite continued decreases in the national crime rate, fear of crime and support for harsher criminal penalties are widespread (Lacayo 1994; "Crime Count" 1996). According to national polls, more than half of Americans (55 percent) report worrying about being a victim of crime, more than half (54 percent) believe that crime has increased in their area of residence, over one-third (37 percent) name crime as the most important problem facing the country, and the overwhelming majority of individuals (85 percent) believe that the courts are too lenient with criminals (Warr 1995). Furthermore, the sources of fear do not appear to be uniform across demographic categories. Rather, many studies report that fear of crime, especially among whites, is particularly directed toward African-Americans (Moeller 1989; Anderson 1990; St. John and Heald-Moore 1996).

The obvious question that arises from these national figures, particularly given decreasing crime rates, is What *explains* the public's attitudes and beliefs about crime? Although some attitudes may reflect unfortunate, first-hand experiences with crime victimization, most individuals report that the media serve as their primary source of crime information (Russell 1995). What sort of media provide viewers with information about crime? In the recent past, it is likely that television coverage of actual crime took the form of local and national newscasts. Today, however, "real-life" crime permeates the television environment in the form of entertainment. As one media critic described,

> Conspiracies, unsolved mysteries, horrible accidents, missing children, America's most wanted criminals, and, now, real-life beatings, shootings, and violent

deaths. When it comes to prime-time entertainment today, these are a few of our favorite things. (Zurawik 1992:E1)

Obviously, violence, crime, and mystery have been the focus of many books, films, and television programs predating reality-based programming. However, never before has the viewer been invited along in the squad car or into the scene of a drug bust in the manner encouraged by reality-based programming. In addition, traditional forms of crime-related entertainment do not claim to depict actual crimes in the same way advertised by programs like "Cops," when the narrator proclaims that the show features "the actual men and women of law enforcement."

Indeed, reality-based police programs are a new and unique genre that blurs the distinction between news and entertainment. Viewers are provided with actual video footage or reenactments of true crimes, and in some instances viewers are encouraged to participate in the capture of criminal suspects by phoning into the program with information that may lead to an arrest. The irony of this new "reality-based" genre, though, is that it differs considerably from reality in many ways, and particularly in terms of the extent to which it overrepresents the frequency of crime. In addition, reality-based programs tend to paint a picture of crime in which African-Americans, in particular, are cast as the "evil" criminals, whereas Caucasians are cast more frequently as the "good guys" or police officers. Consequently, the purpose of the present research was to examine Caucasians' perceptions of the prevalence of crime among African-Americans and Caucasians as a function of reality-based viewing.

ENTERTAINMENT AND DEPICTIONS OF CRIME

Many researchers have noted that media portrayals of crime do not accurately represent crime in the real world. For example, in his essay on entertainment portrayals of crime, Livingston (1994) observed that movies and television programs tend to glorify the private detective as the primary crime fighter and to overrepresent the number of police officers hurt or killed in the line of duty.

One of the most frequently reported differences between media depictions of crime and real instances of crime concerns the media's overrepresentation of violent crime. Content analyses of news broadcasts, of fictional police programs, and of reality-based police programs report that violent crimes such as murder, assault, and robbery are the most frequent types of crimes portrayed, with property crimes receiving very little attention (Graber 1980; Estep and Macdonald 1983; Potter and Ware 1987; Danielson et al. 1996). In a striking tabulation of the frequency of media violence, the National Coalition on TV Violence reported that by age sixteen, the typical U.S. child will view an average of approximately five hundred thousand murders on television (as cited in Van Evra 1990).

In terms of reality-based police programs specifically, Danielson et al.'s (1996) recent content analysis of reality-based programming reported that *every* police program included in its sample featured visual displays of violence. This is consistent with Oliver's (1994) content analysis of reality-based police programs, which found that 49.7 percent of the FBI Index crimes featured on the 57.5 hours of programs in her sample consisted of murder, compared to less than 1 percent of actual crimes recorded for the same time period.

Although the world of media entertainment portrays violent crime at a rate that far surpasses the amount of crime in the real world, media portrayals also feature an arrest rate that is more promising than actual criminal statistics suggest (Livingston 1994). In an early analysis of prime-time, fictional entertainment, Dominick (1973) noted that almost nine out of ten crimes were portrayed as "solved" on television entertainment (see also Estep and Macdonald 1983). Similar sorts of portrayals are common in reality-based programs. For example, Newman noted that the overly dangerous images of crime in these programs are counterbalanced by an overly successful portrayal of law enforcement: "The overall message of reality TV is that real life can be pretty bad—but help is on the way" (1992:22). Similarly, Oliver (1994) reported that 61.5 percent of all crimes portrayed in her sample of reality-based programs were depicted as solved compared to FBI reports of an 18.0 percent arrest rate. Ironically, Oliver also reported that the portrayals of "successful" resolutions on reality-based police programs also often featured police officers employing aggression in the process of making arrests. In fact, 51.0 percent of police officers were shown using at least one form of aggression toward criminal suspects, whereas only 19.4 percent of criminal suspects were shown using aggression toward victims or the police.

The final characteristic of media portrayals of crime pertinent to the present research concerns the ways in which race is presented. In general, analyses of *fictional* programs tend to report that African-Americans are *underrepresented* as criminal suspects or as perpetrators of serious violence in comparison to actual criminal statistics (see Potter et al. 1995). In contrast, analyses of more realistic content including both news and reality-based police programs report that portrayals of African-Americans are much more troublesome. For example, Sheley and Ashkins (1981) reported that blacks accounted for 93 percent of the robbery suspects featured in a New Orleans newspaper and over 80 percent of robbery suspects shown on local New Orleans television stations. Similarly, in an analyses of local television news in Chicago, Entman (1990, 1992) found that almost half of all news stories featuring African-Americans concerned violent crime. Furthermore, in an analysis of network news, Entman (1994) reported that 77 percent of crime stories concerning black criminal suspects pertained to violent or drug crimes compared to only 42 percent of crime stories concerning white criminal suspects. Entman (1992) also reported that television images of black criminal suspects were more likely to show the suspects handcuffed, poorly dressed, and nameless than were images of white criminal suspects.

Analyses of reality-based police shows, like television news, also report that blacks and whites are portrayed in different ways. Perhaps the most striking difference in portrayals concerns the roles that are occupied by black and white characters. In Oliver's (1994) analysis of reality-based police shows, the race and gender of all police or criminal suspects was noted. Among African-American characters, 77.0 percent were criminal suspects rather than police officers, whereas among Caucasian characters, only 38.4 percent were cast as criminal suspects. These findings are similar to Kunkel et al.'s (1996) large-scale content analysis of aggression across 2,500 hours of television programming. Overall, these researchers reported that 5 percent of all perpetrators of aggression were African-American. However, in reality-based programming, the percentage of African-Americans portrayed as perpetrators of aggression jumped to 17 percent. Because this analysis coded only for characters who were portrayed as violent, it is impossible to tabulate the percentage of characters who were portrayed as aggressive within racial groups.

Before leaving this discussion of aggression, it is worth noting that portrayals of aggression in reality-based police programming may not necessarily be a strong indicator of the "morality" or "immorality" of a given character. In other words, a character's use of aggression in this genre does not suggest, necessarily, that the character is "bad," particularly given the frequency with which police officers are shown using aggression (Oliver 1994). What this means in terms of analyses of race is that one needs to go beyond simply noting the race of aggressive perpetrators to including information concerning the perpetrator's role, the victim of aggression, or the extent to which the aggression may be portrayed as warranted or justified. Consistent with this reasoning, Danielson et al.'s (1996) analysis of reality-based programming found that among white characters, the most common perpetrator of aggression was a police officer, but that among African-American or Hispanic characters, the most common perpetrator of violence was a character with no official standing:

> This matters, too, for 80% of police-officer perpetrators of violence are depicted as justified in acting violently (i.e., their motivations are self-defense or protection of others), while 70% of non-police perpetrators are depicted as having non-justifiable motives. (Danielson et al. 1996, p. II-26)

In a similar analysis of the aggression portrayals in reality-based programming, Oliver (1994) reported that police officers were significantly more likely to employ physical aggression toward African-American and Hispanic criminal suspects than toward Caucasian criminal suspects. In her sample, one-third (33.3 percent) of black criminal suspects were the recipient of unarmed physical aggression by the police (i.e., shoving, pushing), whereas only 13.2 percent of white criminal suspects endured similar violence.

In summary, the depiction of crime in media entertainment contains several patterns of portrayals that are worthy of note. First, both fictional and reality-based programs feature inflated frequencies of crime in comparison to actual statistics. In addition, both genres appear to overrepresent the successful capture and arrest of criminal suspects, though in reality-based programs these arrests are often accomplished through the police's use of aggression. Finally, portrayals of race tend to differ between fictional police programs and reality-based shows. In fictional programs, African-Americans tend to be underrepresented as criminal suspects in comparison to actual criminal statistics. The opposite is true of reality-based programs, where the vast majority of African-American characters are cast in roles of criminal suspects where they are also shown as recipients of police aggression.

CRIME SHOW VIEWING AND BELIEFS ABOUT CRIME

Because reality-based programming is a recent addition to television's entertainment lineup, research on the effects of this specific genre is very limited. However, studies on general viewing, news viewing, and viewing of fictional crime-related media suggest several predictions concerning potential effects of reality-based exposure on viewers' estimates of crime prevalence.

Cultivation and Perceived Reality

In all likelihood, the theoretical perspective most frequently employed by prior research in this area has been *cultivation*. This perspective suggests that the repeated patterns of portrayals found *throughout* television programming can influence or shape viewers' conceptions about the real world (Signorielli and Morgan 1996). Although the specific explanatory mechanisms involved in cultivation are unclear at this point, some researchers have suggested that the media may play an influential role by providing viewers with highly salient examples of a given phenomenon such as crime (Shrum and O'Guinn 1993). Based on prior research on the "availability heuristic" (i.e., the idea that salient examples have an inflated influence on perceptions), it is reasoned that salient examples of crime should be more readily accessible in memory and should therefore serve to increase estimates of the prevalence or frequency of the phenomenon in question (Tversky and Kahneman 1974; Fiske and Taylor 1984).

In terms of crime-related beliefs specifically, many studies of cultivation effects have reported that heavy television viewers report higher levels of distrust and alienation as measured by the "Mean World Index" than do light television viewers (Gerbner and Gross 1976; Gerbner, Gross, Morgan, and Signorielli 1980; Signorielli 1990). Consistent findings have been reported by many researchers who have examined correlates of *specific* programming types such as news or crime dramas. For example, Jaehnig, Weaver, and Fico (1981) reported that fear of crime among the individuals in their large-scale survey was more strongly correlated with newspaper reports of crime than with actual crime statistics. Carlson's (1985) survey of adolescents found similar results for viewing fictional crime dramas; higher viewing was not only associated with greater fear of crime, but also with less understanding of the legal system, less support for civil liberties, and greater perceived effectiveness of law enforcement officials.

Importance of Perceived Reality

In addition to examining simple correlates of media viewing, many researchers have explored additional moderating variables that may help predict or explain the relationship between media consumption and viewers' attitudes and beliefs. Perhaps more than any other variable examined, the perceived reality of media portrayals is thought to play a crucial role in moderating the strength of media influences. Specifically, media content that is perceived by the viewer as real or realistic is thought to have stronger effects on attitudes, beliefs, and behaviors than is media content that is understood to be fictional (Potter 1988; Van Evra 1990).

Research exploring the role of perceived reality has operationalized this variable in a number of different ways. Some researchers have operationalized perceived reality in terms of the viewer's orientation or interpretation of media portrayals. For example, Potter (1986) reported that television viewing was positively correlated with estimates of crime such as murder, robbery, and assault, but particularly so among respondents who scored high on measures of "magic window" reality (i.e., seeing media portrayals as accurate, unbiased, and realistic). Similarly, Slater and Elliott (1982) had teenagers complete a survey measuring their perceptions of personal safety and their beliefs concerning crime and law enforcement. These authors reported that the best predictor of respondents' beliefs concerning crime was the degree to which they perceived television's portrayal of law enforcement as realistic (see also O'Keefe 1984).

Other researchers have operationalized realism not in terms of the viewer's orientation but in terms of the portrayals themselves. For example, Tamborini, Zillmann, and Bryant (1984) found that viewing a documentary concerning crime had long-term effects on viewers' concerns about crime, whereas fictional portrayals showed no long-term impact. O'Keefe and Reid-Nash (1987) reported comparable results in their survey, which found that respondents' fear of crime was positively related to attention to television news, but unrelated to general television exposure or to fictional crime-related entertainment.

SUMMARY AND PRESENT RESEARCH

The present study employed a telephone survey to examine viewers' estimates of the prevalence of crime as a function of media exposure to fictional and reality-based police programming. Prevalence was operationalized in terms of the estimated percentage of Caucasians and African-Americans who have or will be involved in violent or drug-related crime. Based on prior research reporting that media portrayals vastly overrepresent the occurrence of crime compared to actual crime statistics, it was hypothesized that exposure to crime-related entertainment would be related to higher estimates of crime prevalence. However, because of the theoretically important role that perceived reality is thought to play in media effects, it was also hypothesized that exposure to reality-based programming would be more strongly associated with estimates of crime prevalence than would exposure to fictional police-programming.

H1: *Estimates of crime prevalence will be positively associated with exposure to crime-related entertainment, but particularly so for exposure to reality-based rather than fictional police programming.*

In addition to examining perceptions of crime prevalence per se, this study also examined differences in estimated prevalence for Caucasians versus African-Americans. Although analyses of fictional police programming suggest that African-Americans are underrepresented as criminal suspects, analyses of reality-based programming paint a very different picture. In reality-based programs, the majority of African-American characters appear as criminals. Consequently, the following hypothesis was examined:

H2: *Exposure to reality-based programming will be more strongly associated with estimates of African-Americans who are perpetrators of crime than with estimates of Caucasians who are perpetrators of crime. Crime estimates as a function of fictional programming will not be differentiated on the basis of race.*

METHOD

Telephone surveys were conducted in November and December 1992 in two regions of the country: Dane County, Wisconsin, and Montgomery County, Virginia (see Oliver and Armstrong 1995). Both of these counties contain large state universities surrounded by rural communities, both counties have a low incidence of violent crime compared with national statistics (U.S. Department of Justice 1992), and both counties have a very small minority population (less than 8 percent; U.S. Census Bureau 1990).

A random sample of phone numbers was developed by generating random pages, columns, and rows corresponding to the phone books for each area. Because both surveys were conducted in areas associated with large universities, only adults who were not enrolled as full-time college students were asked to participate in the survey.

RESPONDENTS

A total of 697 eligible respondents were contacted, and of those respondents, 54 percent agreed to participate in the survey.[1] Because the primary interest in this study concerned possible detrimental effects of reality-based viewing on Caucasian viewers, data from white respondents only (representing 95.5 percent of the sample) were employed in the analyses. In addition, respondents who failed to answer any of the items examined in the analysis were excluded from the sample. The resulting sample size was 325 (46 percent of the original sample), with approximately half of the sample (50.8 percent) residing in Virginia and half (49.2 percent) in Wisconsin at the time of the interview. Slightly more females (58.2 percent) than males (41.8 percent) were included in the sample, and almost half (42.5 percent) reported having received at least an undergraduate college degree.

MEASURES

Control Variables

The control variables employed in this survey included the respondent's gender, age, residence (Montgomery or Dane County), and average daily amount of fictional television viewing.

Beliefs about Crime

Respondents were asked a series of questions concerning their beliefs about crime prevalence in the United States. For one set of questions, respondents were asked to estimate the percentage of people in various demographic categories (i.e., males, females, whites, blacks) who have committed or will commit, at some point in their lives, a violent crime such as murder, rape, armed robbery or assault. For the second set of questions, respondents were asked to estimate the percentage of people who have had, currently have, or will have a serious drug addiction problem with illegal drugs. From these questions, estimates of African-American crime prevalence were computed by averaging respondents' estimates of violent crime and drug crime for blacks ($M = 29.46$, $SD = 19.92$, Cronbach's alpha = .86), and estimates of Caucasian crime prevalence were computed by averaging estimates of violent and drug crime for whites ($M = 23.41$, $SD = 17.54$, Cronbach's alpha = .85).[2]

Media Use

To measure reality-based exposure, this survey first asked respondents to indicate their frequency of viewing five specific shows: "Cops," "American Detective," "America's Most Wanted," "Top Cops," and "FBI, The Untold Story." Responses ranged from 0 (never) to 3 (regularly). Respondents then reported the number of reality-based episodes that they viewed in an average week. Exposure to fictional programs was measured in the same way. Respondents first reported their frequency of viewing "Commish," "Law and Order," "Matlock," "Heat of the Night," and "Reasonable Doubts," and then reported the number of fictional crime episodes they viewed in an average week.

A factor analysis using varimax rotation was conducted on the six reality-based and six fictional police show items. This analysis revealed two factors explaining 54.4 percent of the variance. The six reality-based items loaded highly on the first factor, and the six fictional items loaded highly on the second factor. Consequently, two separate exposure measures were constructed by summing the Z-scores for the reality-based exposure items (Cronbach's alpha = .83) and by summing the Z-scores for the fictional police show items (Cronbach's alpha = .84). Because both of the resulting exposure measures were positively skewed, natural logarithmic transformations were employed (Kruskal 1968).

The perceived realism of reality-based and fictional programs was assessed by having respondents report how realistic they believed that these programs are in their "depiction of crime and law enforcement." Scores on these measures could range from -3 (very unrealistic) to 3 (very realistic).

RESULTS

Perceived Realism

This study predicted stronger effects of reality-based rather than fictional police programming partially on the basis of the perceived realism of the program types. To explore the validity of the assumption that viewers evaluate reality-based programs as more realistic than fictional police programs, a paired t-test was conducted on the perceived realism scores. This analysis revealed significantly higher realism scores for reality-based programs ($M = 0.47$; $SD = 1.73$) than for fictional police programs ($M = -0.74$; $SD = 1.74$), $t(324) = 11.23$, $p < .001$.

Estimates of Crime Prevalence

Multiple regression for mixed-model designs was employed to analyze estimates of crime prevalence for African-Americans and Caucasians (Cohen and Cohen 1983). This type of analysis is conducted using two separate tests. The first test explores the between-groups variance and is accomplished through multiple regression, using the average responses of the within-group treatments as the dependent variable. In this study, this average within-group response used as the dependent variable was the average crime estimate for African-Americans and Caucasians. Control variables were entered in the first step of the equation, reality-based exposure and fictional police show exposure were entered on the second step, and the product of reality-based and fictional exposure was entered on the third step to test for a possible interaction between these two program types.

The second test of multiple regression for mixed-model designs explores the within-groups variance.[3] After accounting for between-groups variance (variance due to respondents), the race for the crime estimates (African-American, Caucasian) was entered on the first step of the equation as a test for the main effect. The next step analyzed Race × Reality-Based Exposure and Race × Fictional Police Exposure interactions. The final step in the analysis tested for a possible Race × Reality-Based Exposure × Fictional Police Exposure interaction.

Between-Groups Variance in Estimates of Crime Prevalence.   The results of the first regression equation examining estimates of crime prevalence are reported in Table 1. In terms of the control variables employed, all variables were significantly associated with crime estimates. Females reported significantly higher estimates ($M = 29.77$, $SD = 17.98$) than did males ($M = 21.80$, $SD = 17.90$), and Virginia residents reported significantly higher

Table 1   Analysis of Between-Groups Variance in Estimates of Crime Prevalence

	r^a	t	R^2 Change
Controls			.24****
Sex[b]	.14	2.51*	
Residence [c]	−.15	−2.81**	
Education	−.31	−5.90****	
Television exposure	.18	3.27**	
Exposure to crime programs			.04***
Reality-based	.21	3.89***	
Fictional	.00	0.00	
Interaction between programs			.00
Reality-based × fictional		.00	0.07

Note: The total regression equation is association with $F(4, 320) = 24.66$, $p < .0001$, $R^2 = .24$.
[a]Partial correlation coefficients.
[b]Males = 0; Female = 1.   [c] Virginia = 0; Wisconsin = 1.
*$p < .05$.   **$p < .01$.   ***$p < .001$.   ****$p < .0001$.

estimates ($M = 30.10$, $SD = 18.18$) than did Wisconsin residents ($M = 22.65$, $SD = 17.80$). In addition, lower levels of educational achievement and higher levels of television viewing were associated with higher estimates of crime prevalence. In terms of exposure to police programs specifically, this analysis found support for Hypothesis 1. Reality-based exposure was a significant predictor of higher crime estimates, but fictional exposure was not a significant predictor. However, a strong correlation between reality-based and fictional viewing ($r = .50$) may have obscured their independent associations with estimates of crime. Separate analyses for each exposure item (with the control variables employed) revealed that crime estimates were significantly associated with higher levels of reality-based exposure ($r = .24$, $p < .0001$), but were only marginally associated with fictional exposure ($r = .10$, $p < .06$).

Within-Groups Variance in Estimates of Crime Prevalence.   Table 2 reports the results of the regression equation that examined within-groups variance in estimates of crime prevalence among African-Americans and Caucasians. First, this analysis revealed a very strong effect for race, with respondents reporting significantly higher estimates for African-Americans ($M = 29.46$, $SD = 17.54$) than for Caucasians ($M = 23.41$, $SD = 17.54$).

In addition, consistent with Hypothesis 2, this analysis revealed a significant Race × Reality-Based Exposure interaction. To further examine the nature of this interaction, mean crime estimates were computed for infrequent and frequent reality-based viewers (i.e., the lower and upper third of reality-based viewers). These means revealed that estimates of Caucasian crime prevalence differed by 12.7 percentage points between low viewers ($M = 17.05$, $SD = 14.40$) and high viewers ($M = 29.77$, $SD = 19.80$).

Table 2 Analysis of Within-Groups Variance in Estimates of Crime Prevalence

	r^a	t	R^2 *Change*
Main effect			.37****
Race of estimate[b]	.61	13.90****	
2-Way interactions			.01+
Race × reality-based	.11	2.05*	
Race × fictional	.00	0.02	
3-Way interactions			.00
Race × reality-based × fictional	−.00	0.87	

Note: The total regression equation is association with $F(7, 318) = 28.48$, $p < .0001$, $R^2 = .39$.
[a]Partial correlation coefficients.   [b] Caucasian = 0; African-American = 1.
*$p < .05$.   **$p < .01$.   ***$p < .001$.   ****$p < .000$.

However, estimates of African-American crime differed by 15.7 percentage points between low viewers ($M = 21.65$, $SD = 16.91$) and high viewers ($M = 37.35$, $SD = 22.01$). No interactions involving fictional programming were statistically significant.

DISCUSSION

This study supports the idea that exposure to reality-based police programs is associated with higher estimates of crime prevalence, and particularly so for estimates of crime prevalence among African-Americans. Although exposure to fictional programs was marginally related to estimates, fictional exposure was not differentially associated with estimates for Caucasians versus African-Americans. These results are consistent with prior research concerning racial portrayals of reality-based and fictional police programs, with prior research on cultivation effects, and with prior research on the importance of perceived reality. In sum, reality-based programs appear to embody many characteristics that point to the likelihood of several harmful influences: these shows portray a world that is much more crime-infested than is actually the case, they cast people of color in the role of the villain, and they are perceived as realistic by many of their viewers.

Although this research employed cultivation as a theoretical framework and therefore adopted one interpretation of a causal relationship between media exposure and viewer attitudes, it is worth noting that alternative causal orders are possible and reasonable. In other words, though this study examined the idea that exposure to reality-based police programs influences viewers' beliefs, an alternative interpretation may be that viewers' beliefs influence media selection.

Zillmann's disposition theory offers one possible explanation for why crime-related entertainment may be particularly appealing to some audience members (Zillmann 1991; Zillmann and Bryant 1975). This theory suggests that viewers experience the greatest gratification from media entertainment when liked characters are portrayed as "winning" (i.e., experiencing positive outcomes) and disliked characters are portrayed as "losing" (i.e., experiencing negative outcomes). Applied to crime dramas, this theory implies that viewers who harbor intense fear or hatred of criminals should be most likely to enjoy media entertainment that features the capture and arrest of criminal suspects.

Consistent with this hypothesis, Oliver and Armstrong (1995) reported that higher levels of punitiveness about crime, authoritarianism, and racism were significantly associated with greater viewing and enjoyment of reality-based police programming. Similarly, in an experimental study, Oliver (1996) reported that authoritarianism was positively associated with enjoyment of reality-based scenes portraying police aggression against criminal suspects, but only if the criminal suspect was an African-American rather than a Caucasian. These studies, which have examined predictors of enjoyment of this programming genre, in combination with the present research, suggest that the relationship between exposure and viewer beliefs may be circular. That is, these studies together point to a possible scenario where exposure to reality-based programs may create attitudes and beliefs that then lead to greater enjoyment of the portrayals featured in this genre.

In terms of future research in this area, subsequent studies may benefit from examining more diverse samples than the one employed here. The respondents in this study were Caucasians from areas with small minority populations and low crime rates. Because prior research suggests that media should have the strongest influence on viewers when there are few informational alternatives (Van Evra 1990; Weaver and Wakshlag 1986), the present sample may represent the audience for whom this genre is likely to have the greatest impact. However, future studies on reality-based programming and on crime-related media more broadly defined would benefit from employing samples from urban locations, from areas with higher crime rates, and from places with larger minority populations.

Finally, the results of this study strongly suggest that additional attention needs to be given to media influences on racial perceptions and stereotyping. Although some researchers have begun to suggest that portrayals associating African-Americans with crime (such as those commonly found in newscasts) can lead to higher levels of racism (e.g., Entman 1990, 1992), systematic explorations of the mechanisms by which this may occur have yet to be examined. However, research that can shed light on why and how the media may be influential in shaping viewers' attitudes about crime and race is crucial at this time when these concerns are playing key roles in shaping public policy on issues such as the death penalty, criminal punishment, and prison reform. By examining the ways in which media portrayals such as those contained in reality-based programs may have *harmful* effects, perhaps future researchers will be in a better position to explore ways in which the media may help shape attitudes that foster racial harmony rather than fear and distrust.

NOTES

1.   Although some people may consider this response rate relatively low, Babbie (1990) reports that a response rate of at least 50 percent is considered adequate. In addition, the purpose of this survey was not to describe population parameters but rather to examine relationships between variables. As Lavrakas explained, "If a survey is not meant to estimate the level to which a variable exists in the population but rather to study interrelationships *among* variables, pure random sampling may be less important. . . . A sampling design that ensures a heterogeneous sample but not necessarily a random one may well suffice" (1987:30).

2.   This paper analyzed the *average* estimates of violent crime and drug crimes because these two variables were very strongly correlated. Separate analyses of violent crime versus drug crime yielded no major differences from analyses of the combined estimates.

3.   This is accomplished by first rewriting the data matrix such that each within-groups observation is recorded as a separate data entry. For example, a design including 20 participants and 3 repeated measures would result in a new data matrix including 60 observations (20 × 3). Subsequently, the regression is conducted by first removing between-groups variance by entering the average response across the within-groups treatments on the first step of the equation. Subsequent steps of the regression equation test for the effects of the within-groups factors and interactions between within-groups and between-groups factors. Although this analysis produces correct regression slopes (and therefore correct contrast functions), the significance tests that are produced use an incorrect error term and must be adjusted. See Cohen and Cohen (1983) for the formulas that are used in these adjustments.

REFERENCES

Anderson, Elijah. 1990. *Streetwise: Race, Class and Change in an Urban Community.* Chicago: University of Chicago Press.

Babbie, Earl. 1990. *Survey Research Methods,* 2nd ed. Belmont, CA: Wadsworth.

Carlson, James M. 1985. *Prime Time Law Enforcement: Crime Show Viewing and Attitudes Toward the Criminal Justice System.* New York: Praeger.

Cohen, Jacob and Patricia Cohen. 1983. *Applied Multiple Regression/Correlation Analysis for the Behavioral Sciences,* 2nd ed. Hillsdale, NJ: Lawrence Erlbaum.

"Crime Count." 1996. *U.S. News & World Report,* 120, May 13, p. 13.

Danielson, Wayne, Dominic Lasorsa, Ellen Wartella, Charles Whitney, Shannon Campbell, Saam Haddad, Marlies Klijn, Rafael Lopez, and Adriana Olivarez. 1996. "Television Violence in 'Reality' Programming: University of Texas, Austin Study." Pp. II-1–II-55 in *National Television Violence Study: Scientific Papers, 1994–1995*. Studio City, CA: Mediascope, Inc.

Dominick, Joseph. R. 1973. "Crime and Law Enforcement on Prime-time Television." *Public Opinion Quarterly* 37:241–50.

Entman, Robert M. 1990. "Modern Racism and the Images of Blacks in Local Television News." *Critical Studies in Mass Communication* 7:332–45.

———. 1992. "Blacks in the News: Television, Modern Racism and Cultural Change." *Journalism Quarterly* 69:341–61.

———. 1994. "Representation and Reality in the Portrayal of Blacks on Network Television News." *Journalism Quarterly* 71:509–20.

Estep, Rhoda and Patrick T. Macdonald. 1983. "How Prime-time Crime Evolved on TV, 1976 to 1983." *Journalism Quarterly* 60:293–300.

Fiske, Susan T. and Shelley E. Taylor. 1984. *Social Cognition*. New York: Random House.

Gerbner, George and Larry Gross. 1976. "Living with Television: the Violence Profile." *Journal of Communication* 26:173–99.

Gerbner, George, Larry Gross, Michael Morgan, and Nancy Signorielli. 1980. "The 'Mainstreaming' of America: Violence Profile No. 11." *Journal of Communication* 30:10–29.

Graber, Doris. A. 1980. *Crime News and the Public*. New York: Praeger.

Jaehnig, Walter. B., David H. Weaver, and Frederick Fico. 1981. "Reporting Crime and Fearing Crime in Three Communities." *Journal of Communication* 31:88–96.

Kruskal, Joseph. B. 1968. "Special Problems of Statistical Analysis: Transformations of Data." Pp. 182–92 in *International Encyclopedia of the Social Sciences*, edited by David. L. Sills. New York: Macmillan.

Kunkel, Dale, Barbara J. Wilson, Dan Linz, James Potter, Ed Donnerstein, Stacy L. Smith, Eva Blumenthal, and Timothy Gray. 1996. "Violence in Television Programming Overall: University of California, Santa Barbara Study." Pp. I-1–I-172 in *National Television Violence Study: Scientific Papers, 1994–1995*. Studio City, CA: Mediascope, Inc.

Lacayo, Richard. 1994. "Lock 'em Up." *Time* 142, February 7, pp. 50–54.

Lavrakas, Paul. J. 1987. *Telephone Survey Methods: Sampling, Selection, and Supervision*. Newbury Park, CA: Sage.

Livingston, Jay. 1994. "Crime and The Media: Myths and Reality." *USA Today Magazine* 122, May, pp. 40–42.

Moeller, Gertrude. L. 1989. "Fear of Criminal Victimization: The Effect of Neighborhood Racial Composition." *Sociological Inquiry* 59:208–21.

Newman, Judith. 1992. "Reality Check." *Adweek*, May, p. 22.

O'Keefe, Garrett J. 1984. "Public Views on Crime: Television Exposure and Media Credibility." Pp. 514–37 in *Communication Yearbook 8*, edited by R. N. Bostrom. Thousand Oaks, CA: Sage.

O'Keefe, Garrett J. and Kathaleen Reid-Nash. 1987. "Crime News and Real-world

Blues: The Effects of the Media on Social Reality." *Communication Research* 14:147–63.

Oliver, Mary Beth. 1994. "Portrayals of Crime, Race, and Aggression in 'Reality-based' Police Shows: a Content Analysis." *Journal of Broadcasting & Electronic Media* 38:179–92.

———. 1996. "Influences of Authoritarianism and Portrayals of Race on Caucasian Viewers' Responses to Reality-based Crime Dramas." *Communication Reports* 9:141–50.

Oliver, Mary Beth and G. Blake Armstrong. 1995. "Predictors of Viewing and Enjoyment of Reality-based and Fictional Crime Shows." *Journalism and Mass Communication Quarterly* 72:559–70.

Potter, W. James. 1986. "Perceived Reality and the Cultivation Hypothesis." *Journal of Broadcasting & Electronic Media* 30:159–74.

———. 1988. "Perceived Reality in Television Effects Research." *Journal of Broadcasting & Electronic Media* 32:23–41.

Potter, W. James, Misha Vaughan, Ron Warren, Kevin Howley, Art Land, and Jeremy Hagemeyer. 1995. "How Real Is the Portrayal of Aggression in Television Entertainment Programming?" *Journal of Broadcasting & Electronic Media* 39:496–516.

Potter, W. James and William Ware. 1987. "An Analysis of the Contexts of Antisocial Acts on Prime-time Television." *Communication Research* 14:664–86.

Russell, Cheryl. 1995. "True Crime." *American Demographics* 17:22–31.

Sheley, Joseph F. and Cindy D. Ashkins. 1981. "Crime, Crime News, and Crime Views." *Public Opinion Quarterly* 45:492–506.

Shrum, L. J. And Thomas C. O'Guinn. 1993. "Processes and Effects in the Construction of Social Reality: Construct Accessibility as an Explanatory Variable." *Communication Research* 20:436–71.

Signorielli, Nancy. 1990. "Television's Mean and Dangerous World: A Continuation of the Cultural Indicators Perspective." Pp. 85–106 in *Cultivation Analysis: New Directions in Media Effects Research*, edited by Nancy Signorielli and Michael Morgan. Newbury Park: Sage.

Signorielli, Nancy and Michale Morgan. 1996. "Cultivation Analysis: Research and Practice." Pp. 111–26 in *An Integrated Approach to Communication Theory and Research*, edited by Michael. B. Salwen and Don W. Stacks. Hillsdale, NJ: Lawrence Erlbaum.

Slater, Dan and William Elliott. 1982. "Television's Influence on Social Reality." *Quarterly Journal of Speech* 68:69–79.

St. John, Craig and Tamara Heald-Moore. 1996. "Racial Prejudice and Fear of Criminal Victimization by Strangers in Public Settings." *Sociological Inquiry* 66:267–84.

Tamborini, Ron, Dolf Zillmann, and J. Jennings Bryant. 1984. "Fear and Victimization: Exposure to Television and Perceptions of Crime and Fear." Pp. 492–513 in *Communication Yearbook 8*, edited by Robert N. Bostrom. Beverly Hills, CA: Sage.

Tversky, Amos and Daniel Kahneman. 1974. "Judgment Under Uncertainty: Heuristics and Biases." *Science* 185:1124–31.

U.S. Census Bureau. 1990. *1990 U. S. Census Data* (On-line). Available at http://www.census.gov/.

U.S. Department of Justice. 1992. *Crime in the United States, 1991: Uniform Crime Reports.* Washington, DC: U. S. Government Printing Office.

Van Evra, Judith. 1990. *Television and Child Development.* Hillsdale, NJ: Lawrence Erlbaum.

Warr, Mark. 1995. "The Polls-Poll Trends: Public Opinion on Crime and Punishment." *Public Opinion Quarterly* 59:296–310.

Weaver, James B. III and Jacob Wakshlag. 1986. "Perceived Vulnerability to Crime, Criminal Victimization Experience, and Television Viewing." *Journal of Broadcasting & Electronic Media* 30:141–58.

Zillmann, Dolf. 1991. "Empathy: Affect from Bearing Witness to the Emotions of Others." Pp. 135–67 in *Responding to the Screen: Reception and Reaction Processes,* edited by Jennings Bryant and Dolf Zillmann. Hillsdale, NJ: Lawrence Erlbaum.

Zillmann, Dolf and Jennings Bryant. 1975. "Viewer's Moral Sanction of Retribution in the Appreciation of Dramatic Presentations." *Journal of Experimental Social Psychology* 11:572–82.

Zurawik, David. 1992. "Reality TV: Hot Programming Trend Is Changing How Viewers See the World." *Roanoke Times and World News* (Virginia), April 23, p. E1.

3

"Crimewatch UK":
Women's Interpretations of Televised Violence

R. EMERSON DOBASH, PHILIP SCHLESINGER, RUSSELL DOBASH,
and C. KAY WEAVER

What do we see on reality TV? What do we think and feel about what we see? How do viewers relate to the representation of violence on television and to "real-life" experiences of violence? More specifically, how do women who have experienced rape and physical abuse respond to the depiction of such crimes on reality TV? Do they differ from women who have had no such experiences of violent crime?

One of the best known reality programs in Britain is "Crimewatch UK." Our study of this program formed part of a wider investigation of women's responses to the representation of violence against women on television reported in *Women Viewing Violence* (Schlesinger, Dobash, Dobash, and Weaver 1992). This study examined audience interpretations of a soap opera, a television play, a feature film, and "Crimewatch." We examined the differing interpretations of women who had experienced violence and those who had no such experience, and considered differences based on sociocultural locations such as social class and ethnicity. The research of the respective authors, focusing on the lived experience of violent crime (Dobash and Dobash 1979, 1992, 1988; Dobash, Dobash, Cavanagh, and Lewis 1995) and on media politics of crime and criminal justice (Schlesinger, Tumber, and Murdock 1991; Schlesinger and Tumber 1994), provided a unique combination of knowledge about "real-life violence" and "media representation of crime." Here we consider (1) how women compare property crimes and violence against the person; (2) the discourses used to describe and "explain" a rape-murder; (3) the portrayal of the police on television and as experienced in real-life; (4) the "mission" of "Crimewatch" to engage the public as assisting the police; and (5) how such programs might articulate with the fear of crime.

"Crimewatch" aims to mobilize the audience to assist the police in catching criminals. It was an early instance of a new genre that also includes

"Crimestoppers" and "Crime Monthly" and programs in other countries such as "America's Most Wanted" (see Schlesinger and Tumber 1994:Chapter 9). Once a month, "Crimewatch" attracts an average audience on the BBC's main channel, BBC1, of more than eight million viewers (1996 figures). At its peak in 1993, the audience was more than twelve million. The audience share remains higher than that of some of the less popular soap operas, and greater than that of the national main nightly news. Compared to the average profile for its timeband on BBC1, the audience is downmarket and biased toward women. It has a loyal viewership and a high audience appreciation score (BBC Broadcasting Research 1996). It is distinguished from comparable reality crime programs by its appeal to a national audience rather than to regional ones. It also raises interesting questions about the use of drama-documentary techniques in its "reconstructions," and has been the subject of substantial discussion and controversy, particularly with respect to fear of crime.

The success of the "Crimewatch" reconstructive formula has doubtless encouraged the growth of similar programs as part of the increasingly unstable boundaries between fact and fiction, information and entertainment, that constitute what Umberto Eco (1995) has labeled "neo-TV." In an analysis of these shifting relations, Corner argues that any study of reenactment on British television with its "novel mix of reportage, interview and dramatization" (1995:20) would need to refer to the instance of "Crimewatch," which remains an exemplar. This ill-defined line between fact and fiction is clearly acknowledged by the program's production team. As the principal presenter has observed in the preface to a popular book on "Crimewatch": "Most of us tend to feel powerless about crime, but here is an opportunity to do something about it. Television is usually a passive experience—here is a chance to participate. Fictional detective work has always held a fascination, but here is the real thing. 'Crimewatch' combines the excitement of cops 'n' robbers with the grittiness of real life and personal involvement" (Ross 1994:11).

"Crimewatch" first achieved popularity in a period of law and order politics, a growing concern about fear of crime, and a new wave of "participative" television. Research suggests that the television audience tends to group it with a consumer/public watchdog function and distinguish it from documentary programs and police fiction (BBC Broadcasting Research 1988:7). While intended to mobilize audiences to help the police solve crimes, it also entertains, using crime stories with murder, armed robbery with violence, and sexual crime as staple items. Corporate crime and political crime are not included. The style is fast-moving and visually varied (see Ross and Cook 1987; Schlesinger and Tumber 1994). Sexual assaults on young children and rapes of adult women figure routinely in both national and local newspapers and in "Crimewatch." There is a close relationship between the production team and the police, who provide access to the details of the crimes; while both are identified with a fight against crime, the producers insist on editorial independence from the police, while the police have a right of veto (not used to date) over the material in the "reconstructions." Like the police, the television team also places particular importance on having a good clearance rate for the crimes presented. This functions as a measure of its value to the public and is a defense against critics who accuse it of sensationalism, gratuitous violence, or provoking public fear of crime.

Programs such as "Crimewatch" express a novel set of relations between the criminal justice system, the media, and the audience. There seems to be a fascination with the process of detection and inquiry, the role of the police, and the chase after the criminal, which has some considerable success in mobilizing audiences. Partly, it is linked with the venerable traditions of crime reporting as a form of popular culture. Perhaps it is also linked to disillusionment with the realities of policing, the failures of law and order, and a kind of correlative rise in fictive success. The more the failures of law and order become evident, the greater the interest in a resolution of these problems on television (Schlesinger 1996). We shall return to this question of "resolution" on and off the screen in the discussion of violent crimes against women, particularly violence in the home and rape. Here, the factors of gender and of crimes against the person, rather than against property, complicate the theme of successful resolutions to crime on television compared to failed resolutions by police in real life. Again, we shall witness the novel set of relations between criminal justice, the media, and the audience as they are filtered through the lived experiences of different audiences of women.

THE STUDY

The Women Viewing Violence study examined women's interpretations of and responses to the portrayal of violence against women on television. We were interested in how the lived experience of violence and sociocultural locations shape interpretations and responses to televised violence. While our primary focus was on audiences with differing experiences of violence in their personal lives, other differentiating factors (ethnicity and class) proved important. Groups included women with and without experience of violence, those from the middle and working classes and Afro-Caribbean, Asian (Indian, Pakistani, Bangladeshi), and white women.

Based on previous research (Dobash and Dobash, 1979, 1988), we speculated that experience of violence might bring a knowledgeable and nuanced realism to interpretations of violence presented for viewing consumption. It would be reasonable to expect that those who had actually experienced violence in real life would be more knowledgeable about and sensitive to its representation on television. Consequently, those with such experience might be expected to be more astutely observant of such representations and to bring an extra dimension to their responses to the television programs. Such programs form a real and painful part of the lives of some of the viewing audience but are only a fiction in the lives of others. "Crimewatch" is particularly interesting in this respect because the program presents that which is "real" to audiences, some of whom have actually lived through similar events or have personal knowledge of them and, at the same time, others whose only source of information may be popular representations and beliefs presented in media.

Does it matter if one has experienced violence when that is what is being represented? Does it matter if one is Black or from an ethnic community when viewing the representation of such individuals or groups? Similarly, does membership of a given social class inform responses to media representation of such groups? The fundamental question is, Does lived experience inform the interpretations of media representation of such experience? If so, how? In order to address these questions, we designed a study containing viewing groups who represented the different life experiences delineated above (violence, ethnicity, and class) and examine their responses to different programs depicting violence against women. With "Crimewatch," the world of fact and fiction as depicted in reality TV engages closely with the real world of fact as informed by the direct personal experience of some of the viewers and, for others, more with the "fiction-fact" of popular knowledge of such experiences, which is itself heavily informed by the popular media of Umberto Eco's "neo-TV."

VIEWING GROUPS

Using a comparative research design, ninety-one women were divided into fourteen different viewing audiences ranging in size from five to nine women per group. The relatively small size of the groups was meant to encourage discussion. Just over half (fifty-two) had been subjected to some form of violence, usually at the hands of a male partner, and were recruited through organizations such as shelters for abused women and rape crisis centers. The other half of the sample had no experience of violence and were recruited through a polling agency. The violent attacks on the women who participated in this study are similar to those reported in other studies (Dobash and Dobash 1979, 1988, 1992; Russell 1982; Stanko 1985; Kelly 1988; Edwards 1989; Johnson 1996). Women experienced a range of violent acts including being slapped, punched, kicked, and beaten up; sexual assault; rape; and having weapons used against them. Whether the violence occurred in the home or in public, most of the women who had experienced violence (80 percent) reported that they had been attacked and/or raped by men known to them, especially a husband or boyfriend; only a few reported an attack by a stranger.

Women across the entire sample were not completely "violence free" and reported experiences such as obscene phone calls and men exposing themselves in public (McNeill 1987:93–109; Kelly 1988; Johnson 1996; Gardner 1995). These results agree with other research that a sizable proportion of women have been subjected to a wide range of abusive forms of behavior by men.

SCREENINGS AND FOCUS
GROUP DISCUSSIONS

Each of the fourteen viewing groups spent one day, about seven hours, viewing and discussing the selected programs. In order to make participants feel as relaxed as possible, chairs were comfortable, refreshments were available throughout the day, and a buffet lunch was provided. Although we sought to create a comfortable atmosphere, these conditions do not recreate normal viewing in the home. All research creates a unique reality and alters the "natural" setting. We saw the setting as somewhere between the tightly controlled artificiality of the psychological experiment and the naturalness of the domestic setting. The screenings were interrupted only for lunch and tea breaks. Before each day's viewing, women were told they would be viewing scenes of violence and that if they felt the need to leave during any particular scene they should. Information was also available for the researcher to refer women to local organizations such as rape crisis centers and shelters for abused women. Participants were shown entire programs and then asked to fill in a short questionnaire aimed at assessing their immediate reactions. This was followed by a tape-recorded discussion of the program and a second opportunity to fill in the same questionnaire in order to capture any changes in interpretations arising from the discussions. Discussions of each program ranged in length from thirty to ninety minutes, with an average of one hour (Schlesinger et al. 1992).

In a distinctive approach to audience research, we combined both qualitative and quantitative methods. Quantitative data were obtained from the individual questionnaires about personal backgrounds and individual responses to the screenings, and qualitative information from group discussions of the selection of programs. This method provided over one hundred hours of taped discussions and 546 completed questionnaires.

The group discussions (see Merton, Fiske, and Kendall 1991) concentrated on a number of themes in "Crimewatch" and focused on the presenters, the victims, and the perpetrators of three reconstructed crimes (see Schlesinger et al. 1992:200–2). During the discussions of specific scenes, women were asked about their reactions and evaluations and why such scenes might have been included in each program. They were invited to consider the motivational contexts associated with crimes, particularly those including violence, and to consider the programs' value for women. Discussions involved a funneling process designed to allow groups to begin with their own concerns and comments before focusing on specific issues identified by the researchers.

WHAT THEY SAW

Opening to a punchy drumbeat, a series of crimes is briefly introduced, followed by telephone calls to the police. The "Crimewatch" logo takes shape, then the music and the logo fade as a dimly lit studio appears with two presenters seated in the front and a number of people working at desks behind. Running for forty minutes, the broadcast is live and contains reconstructions of selected crimes, usually two or three, interspersed with shorter descriptions of other crimes. The public is asked to watch, recall events, and call the police in the studio if it has information that might help solve the crime. "Crimewatch Update" lasts for ten minutes and is aired later the same evening to inform the public about progress with the cases shown. The woman presenter begins:

> Good evening, and welcome to the program where once a month instead of just hearing about crimes you can perhaps actually do something about them. As always we're live, and the detectives here from all round the country are waiting for your call.

The telephone number is given, and the man presenter then briefly lists the case that will follow.

The first reconstruction, a bank fraud, runs for seven minutes and is a complex tale of a man who poses as a cleaning contractor in order to steal company stationery and signatures to use to cash checks against a company. The con man is described, a "substantial reward" is mentioned, an appeal is made for public help and telephone numbers are provided. Brief outlines are then given of several cases throughout the country including the disappearance of a couple, an assault on two young girls by a man armed with a putty knife, an armed gang's unsuccessful hold-up and ramming of a security van, and the theft of a van load of toys.

The second reconstruction concerns the theft of Mercedes cars. Set in an expensive residential street, a wealthy-looking woman is beside her disabled red Mercedes as the owner of an old broken-down brown car approaches and suggests that his "mechanic" friend could check her car. The "mechanic" explains that the Mercedes needs a spare part and says the owner of the brown car will take her to buy one while he starts work on her car. She agrees and hands him her car keys. She is then driven to several garages before being abandoned by the man in the brown car. The "mechanic" has driven the Mercedes off. "Photo Call" follows, described by the presenter as "television's version of the Wanted Poster." Closed-circuit camera recordings of crimes are screened, including black youths committing an armed robbery at a jeweler's, white men suspected of robbing a bank, a burglary in which a woman is violently attacked, and a black man who has committed a number of raids on banks.

The final reconstruction begins and the presenter describes it as "yet another that highlights the dangers of hitchhiking." The five-minute-long reconstruction uses an actress and a male voice-over to tell the story of Rachel Partridge, a young apprentice dental assistant who lived with her parents and three sisters in the English countryside. Rachel is shown at her boyfriend's house in a village several miles from her home. They plan a trip to Italy and laugh at passport photos. Rachel's mother arrives and offers her a ride home. Rachel wants to go to a friend's to use her sun-bed. This poses a problem because her mother cannot give Rachel a ride later. Rachel catches another ride to her friend's house, where we see her in mid-shot, wearing a bra and using the sun-bed. We see Rachel leaving her friend's and thumbing a ride. The reconstruction then shows a white van at a spot where she had been seen talking to the driver. The presenter explains that, "Rachel was frightened of the dark, and there were six miles of country lanes between Rachel and her home." The final scene shows an isolated barn and the voice-over states:

> Next morning, . . . two and a half miles from Rachel's home . . . two farm workers saw someone lying in the corner of the barn. They'd discovered the naked body of a young woman. There was blood around her head and neck. Rachel was struck heavily on the face, sexually assaulted, and asphyxiated.

In the studio the presenter introduces "the man who is seeking Rachel's killer," a detective inspector who provides details about time and place, the white van, and a plaster cast of a male's footprint taken from the barn. Telephone numbers are given for viewers to call. In the customary ending of each program, the presenter stresses that such crimes are unusual and urges the viewers, "Don't have nightmares, do please sleep well." The program ends, and the credits roll to the sound of the theme music.

The "Crimewatch Update" later the same evening provides brief accounts of the crimes shown earlier, states that there has been a good response, and provides information about the bank fraud, the Mercedes thefts, and the rape-murder, including short clips of the girl and her boyfriend on the sofa in his house, of her lying on the sun-bed in her bra, and of her hitchhiking. We are told that there have been a large number of telephone calls to the program about the murder, and some details are provided. The cases covered on "Incident Desk" and "Photo Call" are reported as well as the current state of progress in apprehending the perpetrators. The "Crimewatch Update" closes with a final appeal to viewers to contact the program or the police if they have any information. The woman presenter states:

> Remember, the sort of serious crimes that we show on this program really are much less common than a lot of us might think they are, and the whole purpose of "Crimewatch" is that with your help we can perhaps make them even more rare.

Before the closing credits and theme tune, the male presenter repeats the familiar injunction not to have nightmares.

HOW VIEWERS REACTED

We examined how the viewing groups evaluated the different types of crime covered, how they assessed crimes involving property compared to those of violence, and how they viewed the different types of violence presented, especially the rape-murder. Discussion also covered the representation and general orientation to the police, the educational and entertainment value of the television program, its portrayal of women and ethnic groups, and, finally, the issue of fear of crime. The findings show that women viewers drew a clear distinction between crimes against property and those against the person, with the latter defined as far more serious. There was some skepticism about the police and differing views about their representation on "Crimewatch" compared to "real-life" responses to the public. Views were mixed about "Crimewatch" itself, and, from all women, there was an expression of some fear of crime, particularly rape. Those who had experienced violence were even more likely to express such fears.

Of the entire sample of women in the study, 69 percent were occasional or regular viewers of "Crimewatch," and the vast majority found it "believable" and "realistic," treated it seriously, and endorsed it as important. It was rated as "entertaining" or "very entertaining" by nearly half of those with no experience of violence while only one quarter of those with experience of violence rated it as such. The entertainment value also varied by ethnicity: over one-half of the Asian women said it was entertaining, while only a quarter of the Afro-Caribbean and white groups responded in this way. In addition, 44 percent of Asian women, but only 6 percent of the white and 7 percent of the Afro-Caribbean women felt the program was "exciting" or "very exciting"; an overwhelming majority of those with and those without experience of violence indicated that it was "not exciting."

The most salient items in the program were the three featured crimes in the reconstructions. When asked to name the three crimes they recalled, all but four women listed the rape-murder of the young woman, believed it to be the most serious crime, and thought the general public would agree. Also remembered was the bank fraud (75 percent of those with experience of violence, 92 percent of those with none) and the car thefts (73 and 94 percent, respectively). Women who had experienced violence were more likely to mention the assault of the child, a crime that was covered briefly on the Incident Desk. Other crimes were less likely to be remembered.

Crimes Involving Property

The audiences were amused at the "stupidity" of Mercedes owners who handed over their keys, and some felt a certain admiration for the audacity of the bank con men. Most were unmoved by the victimization of an institution by comparison to their responses to the victimization of individuals: "It's the middle and upper class that's going to own a Mercedes. They're the only ones stupid enough to give somebody their car keys" (Afro-Caribbean woman with experience of violence).

There was a note of admiration for an ingenious "sting" in the case of the bank fraud. There were some points of identification with the victims based on similar personal experiences of theft. Here, lived experiences articulate with what is seen on television. The tone ceases to be dismissive of the stupidity of the victim and is more understanding—it could happen to me.

Crimes of Property Compared to Crimes against the Person

Crimes of violence were never taken lightly. All agreed that crimes against property were less serious than violence against the person: "Money can be replaced. Cars can be replaced. Toys can be replaced. Lives can't." It was noted that the importance of persons above property was not reflected in the time given to the different items in the program or to the perceived concern of the presenters: "I [wrote] it down, 'most time given to offenses against property'" (white women with experience of violence).

This view was reiterated with respect to one of the items covered on the "Incident Desk," a knife assault on two young girls. Despite only brief coverage, this item was defined by most as the second worst crime shown and, for some, it was equal to the rape-murder. This demonstrates the potential divergence of values between the audience and the program. Many had strong views about crimes against children, and the notion that the item had been underplayed was especially strong among women with experience of violence, but not exclusive to them.

> I just felt that the beginning of the program was put on to the materialistic things. . . . And the Mercedes car, it's very distressing, it's very upsetting to have anything stolen from you, but it can be replaced. But that little girl can't be. (White woman with no experience of violence)

The reconstruction of the rape-murder of the young woman hitchhiking home was centrally important in the group discussions of the viewers. This type of story—the "woman in peril"—is a prototypical "Crimewatch" narrative. In a media discourse analysis of "Crimewatch," Fairclough (1995) echoes our own approach by concentrating on the killing of a young woman walking home from a friend's at night. Fairclough's textual analysis emphasizes the dual nature of the program—its blurred boundaries between information and entertainment. He argues that entertainment values must be muted in order to play up a public service message (1995:159–60). However, we question the imputation from a discourse analysis *alone* that "Crimewatch" and its ilk are "reconstructing a relationship of trust and co-operation on a new basis" between the public and the police (1995:167–68). As we demonstrate, the evidence is much too ambiguous to claim this with any certainty. Indeed, Fairclough, writing after the findings from our study were published, agrees that he cannot draw conclusions about legitimization of the police's efforts confidently from a linguistic analysis. He observes that "it would be fascinating to know what audiences make of this program" (1995:168). It is precisely the reception approach reported in this and our earlier publication that addresses this question.

There was an important difference in *when* the reconstruction of the rape-murder entered the group discussions: women with experience of violence turned to it almost immediately, while women with no such experience responded according to the sequence of the program and the structured questioning of the researcher. The lived experience of violence and consequent sensitivity to this issue were illustrated in the urgency in discussing this reconstruction. Women with experience of violence could draw upon their experiences of assault, whether physical or sexual. This provided a strong identification with the victim. Others drew upon their general experiences as women in relation to men, and many drew upon their experience as parents of daughters. At one level, some women identified as mothers; at another level, most women identified as women expressing commonly held

views about the perils faced from men. Based on their lived experience
and/or a view of their cultural context, women offered a critique of mas-
culine privilege and aggressiveness and social arrangements that make public places dangerous for women and limit the scope of their daily lives.

> Why should women be restricted? [Men are] privileged. They're privileged to
> walk about wherever they like, at whatever time of the night, at any time, it
> doesn't matter. Nobody says you shouldn't be doing it, he shouldn't be doing
> it, if anything happens to him. (Asian woman with experience of violence)

Women criticized media messages that reinforce limitations on their lives in
the name of safety, while not addressing the men who act violently. This also
embodies a critique of the police in stopping such crimes of violence:

> [W]hat they actually said about the hitchhiking was wrong. . . . Why should
> we be the ones to stop hitchhiking? They should be catching the people that
> are murdering these people that are hitchhiking. (White woman with experi-
> ence of violence)

DISCOURSE ABOUT VICTIMS AND CAUSES

Discussions of violent crimes against women tend to focus on the victim,
not the criminal, which has the effect of implicitly making women the
"cause" of their own victimization (Dobash and Dobash 1979:27–30, 133–
37, 195–99; 1992:213–50). Such discourse either directly or indirectly
"blames the victim" for the violence while the perpetrator remains a shad-
owy figure left undiscussed or completely overlooked as the focus increasingly turns to the woman victim. Explanations sometimes excuse male
violence by citing the actions of others, often women in their roles as mothers or wives. This discourse about crimes of violence against women is
expressed throughout our culture. It is learned to varying degrees by everyone, including women who simultaneously accept it and, at the same time,
find it problematic based on their lived experience.

These tensions were evident in the discussions about the role of the
mother in the rape-murder. Since no clear suspect was identified, little mention was made of the possible perpetrator during the program or in the group
discussions. Instead, the focus was on the victim and her mother. Judgments
were offered concerning the young woman's behavior, the perils of hitchhiking, parental responsibility, and the young woman's appearance. Specula-
tions were made about what should have been done by the young woman
and/or by her mother to avoid the crime. Women wondered what they
might have done in similar circumstances. Many drew attention to Rachel's
nonprovocative way of dressing and underlined that she was not "asking for

it": "I think it probably highlights that even though you're not wearing provocative clothes or anything, the dangers are still open to you" (Asian woman with no experience of violence).

The victim was repeatedly described as "respectable," "normal," and not "suggestive," leaving unsaid the idea that women defined otherwise might be blameworthy. With a particular cultural slant, some Asian women linked modesty in dress to other norms in their communities and highlighted the positive value—in terms of personal safety—of restrictions on women's freedom of movement. Other Asian women expressed the view that restrictions should be placed on perpetrators of violence, not on women: "I don't think it's fair that she should be restricted" (Asian woman with experience of violence).

There was a tendency among some to blame the mother of the victim, while others reflected on their personal experience and acknowledged the difficulties of protecting children from violence. For some, Rachel's actions were put down to youth and inexperience; others thought alternative arrangements should have been made such as asking her boyfriend to drive her home, taking a taxi, or staying overnight at her friend's house. Such comments seem to represent a desire to "will away" the awful event, to suggest a means by which the extraordinary outcome of this otherwise ordinary set of events could have been avoided.

There were diverse reactions to the scene (repeated in the "Update") in which the young woman is shown in her underwear in a sun-bed. Some saw it as irrelevant to the "Crimewatch" mission of "helping to find criminals and solve crimes." They speculated about the "entertainment" value of this gratuitous display of near nakedness; others did not consider the scene to be problematic:

> You don't need to see the fact that she was in her underwear on a sun-bed. I think that was a bit of titillation, which you don't need.
> She was trying to get herself a tan . . . and it's just that extra personal thing to show. (White women with no experience of violence)

SHOWING REAL-LIFE VIOLENCE

Many women with experience of violence said that the program ought to be more explicit about the real horrors of violence and the impact of rape. They felt that this would educate others about violence, and would serve a purpose for the general viewer and particularly for the perpetrators of violence. The thrust of such comments was that if the representation of violence was, in fact, truer to the lived experience of violence, i.e., harsh, cruel, and consequential rather than neutralized, entertaining, and even glamorized, it might educate the population about their own lived experiences. More specifically, it might help deter those who would use violence:

> One minute it was green fields and the next minute there was a body in the barn and that was it.
> They portrayed the violence in the hold up thing, the guys with the guns. And they portrayed a lot of the action by the perpetrators in the other crimes, but in the one in the rape and murdered girl, there was no attempt at reconstruction of anybody actually doing anything to her. . . . I mean, because it would be so offensive wouldn't it, to actually show that?
> It's like watching a film with no ending, you [add your own]. That girl could've gone through hell . . . if it's gonna upset you. . . . Well the TV have to say what can be put on and what can't.
> I thought it could've been stronger.
> I agree but they won't put it on. (White women with experience of violence)

Such views are similar to those of Martin Bell, a BBC war correspondent in a series of programs for BBC Radio 4 on violence and the media in May 1997. He asks if responding to public sensitivities about depicting violence in its true form is problematic. Again, what the women wanted was a realistic depiction of the horrors of violence and its negative consequences, not a depiction of violence as exciting, entertaining, and inconsequential. They hoped that realism would educate and enlighten the public, and raise understanding and sympathy for the victims of violence, while impressing upon perpetrators the true nature of their actions.

BELIEVING IN THE POLICE?

The program's requests to assist the police and help solve crimes received mixed responses: about half indicated a willingness to report someone to the police while a quarter were unsure. This varied by ethnicity, with three-quarters of Asian and white women saying they would report known perpetrators (15 percent said they would not) while only one-quarter of Afro-Caribbean women indicated a willingness to report someone, although most sympathized with the victims portrayed on the program (79 percent saying they felt sorry for them—the highest figure for any group). "Crimewatch" failed to increase the women's confidence in the police, with only a quarter of all the women indicating greater confidence in the police. Again, ethnicity made a difference with most Afro-Caribbean and white women (about 85 percent for both groups), indicating the program did not increase their confidence while nearly half of the Asian women (42 percent) said it did. Obviously, not all viewing groups shared an identical view of the police; skepticism was most likely among Afro-Caribbean women and those with experience of violence. The source of skepticism was, for the most part, related to the experience of various forms of contact with the police. For some, this rested on personal observations about police effectiveness in solving crimes and catching criminals, the same image as that portrayed on "Crimewatch:"

> In reality, when you do try to help the police, the police never turn up until the crime's been committed. (Asian woman with experience of violence)
> But they don't catch them, do they? (Afro-Caribbean woman with experience of violence)
> I have actually seen them standing in shop doors, calls coming through and they totally ignore them. I've actually seen it. (White woman with experience of violence)

Comments based on experience with the police also came from professionals who worked with women victims, and from people with other forms of personal experience. Of course, bad experiences travel further and last longer than good ones, and little or no experience often leaves individuals neutral or without views. Our findings from this and previous studies show that victims of violence who are supported by positive police responses are grateful and appreciative of such support (Dobash and Dobash 1979; Dobash, Dobash, Cavanagh, and Lewis 1995). Thus, the viewing audiences offered varying interpretations of police practice, with the greatest correspondence between perception and media representation occurring among those with no experience of violence or of the police. There was skepticism among some women, particularly those with experience of violence and those from ethnic communities.

PLACING THE PROGRAM

"Crimewatch" was discussed in a variety of ways: in terms of its education and entertainment value, its public service role, police-public relations, and its depiction of women and ethnic minorities. It is presented as having an educational and motivational intent, and its format, style of presentation, and call to action are meant to increase empathy for victims of crime and lead to greater cooperation between police and the public. Members of our viewing groups, however, responded in a mixed and ambivalent manner. Few felt the program sensationalized crime; six out of ten thought it increased their knowledge of crime. The program did generate empathy: three-quarters said they felt sorry for the victims and a similar proportion (76 percent of women with experience of violence, 65 percent with none) said it made them angry about crime.

There was a pronounced ambivalence among the viewing groups about whether "Crimewatch" should be categorized as entertainment. While expressing the view that a public service program must be taken seriously, they discussed its attention-grabbing qualities or entertainment value, drawing analogies with television drama. Some said that the desire to know how the crimes are solved is what makes the "Update" interesting to an audience.

For the most part, "Crimewatch" was seen as a specialized television program aiming to help the police, and not a piece of police public relations. However, questions were raised about police effectiveness; some were concerned about the guarantee of confidentiality for callers that seemed to be compromised by televised comments identifying them as "neighbors" or "former girlfriends," or giving other identifiable characteristics. However, some women who had experienced violence simply dismissed the program's public service claims. Some of these women said that "Crimewatch" engaged in trivializing for the purposes of amusement, or that it lacked sensitivity and glamorized crime.

Some viewers said that "Crimewatch" presented women as weak, stupid, and in supporting positions, while men, including the criminals, were clever and in authority:

> The men were all in suits and looking very formal, and the woman presenter was in a pretty dress and . . . the women in the background were doing . . . side issues . . . answering the phone and the men were looking very serious. [In] the reconstruction of the fraud they were focusing on the women a lot. . . . [The women] were all presented as very soft and sweet and powerless and easily conned. And they're presenting these men as being quite clever. . . . And another thing I noticed was that the woman police officer had no jacket on, she just had this white shirt on. The men were in jackets.
> I thought the whole program made the general public, but particularly women, look like absolute idiots. . . . And the hitchhiker, she was made to look the fool for leading herself into a situation where she gets murdered. (White women with experience of violence)

Ethnicity played a major role in influencing the interpretation of "Crimewatch." Some stressed that the program was biased against blacks, a view coupled with an intensely hostile perception of the police and their relationships with black people:

> When you get a program like that, and you're also seeing black people being associated with the crime, it doesn't make me feel very comfortable . . . if you were a white person and you were watching that, you would zoom in more on the things that have been done by black people. (Afro-Caribbean woman with experience of violence)
> I thought they were very racist as well. When they were talking about the suspects, one of them referred to a black man and they hadn't already referred

to anybody else by color apart from when it was a black man. (White woman with experience of violence)

Because only a few audience members are likely to have "been there" or to have "seen something suspicious," very few television viewers can respond to an appeal for relevant information. Thus, in reality, the reason for watching "Crimewatch" is less likely to be one of "stopping crime" than one of "watching crime." All but a few individuals are spectators rather than active participants in the cooperative fight against crime.

"CRIMEWATCH" AND FEAR OF CRIME

Finally, there is the general issue of fear of crime and "Crimewatch" itself. Over half of all the women said that "Crimewatch" "increased" their fear of crime; about a third said it had "no effect." Only five of the ninety-one women said it made them feel safe. There has been some official concern in Britain about whether such programs cause fear of crime. Program producers have responded with reference to the "payoff," the final statement stressing the statistical infrequency of the crimes featured and asking viewers not to have nightmares. Some women spontaneously mentioned that "Crimewatch" increased their fear of crime and indicated that they were not convinced by the "payoff":

> More or less they say, "Don't go to bed and have nightmares. You've got nothing to worry about if you don't let your children sit outside shops, if you don't go hitchhiking and if you remember to lock your car. . . . Then nothing will happen to you". . . . That's the kind of the ethos . . . they're putting a lot of the blame for the crimes on the people who are actually the victims of them.
> The ending of the program really annoyed me, you know, "Don't have nightmares or anything." Ha, ha, ha, let's joke about this. Somebody's just been violently murdered, but you can still go to bed and sleep. I thought it was disgusting. (White women with experience of violence)

Television seems to articulate with fear of crime in complicated ways that are integrated into a preexisting complex of daily experiences, risks, and anxieties about safety. Does the depiction of relatively rare crimes create an anxiety among the viewers that these crimes occur much more frequently, which in turn increases anxieties about becoming a victim of such crimes? Does one truth (that a real-life crime such as murder or rape actually occurred and is being reconstructed on television) lend itself to the creation of a falsehood (that rape-murder occurs with some frequency and is likely to happen to me)?

The issue is about the occurrence of unusual events and the frequency and patterning of these events. That is not to say that all fear of crime is unfounded and based solely on anxieties caused by television. Certain categories of individuals experience greater risks of being victimized than others. Those who must use public transportation, who live in high-crime areas, who must move about in public spaces at night, and who live alone are at greater risk than others. For some crimes (rape and certain kinds of murder), women are at greater risk than men; for others (public order violence), young males are more likely to be both the victims and the perpetrators. The view that fear is unfounded or that rare crimes are equally unlikely for us all is not warranted by crime data. It is true that most individuals are far more likely to be afraid of crime than they are to experience it personally; for some, however, the risks are higher than for others, and this may be borne out by the experience of victimization. The following quote illustrates the complex intersection between the lived experience of being victimized and the fear of further victimization punctuated by a disbelief in the rarity of the events depicted on "Crimewatch" and in other media:

> I didn't like the bit where she says the cases are rarer than—what?. . . . You get it in the papers day in and day out. You get it on the telly day in and day out. I don't know how they can say it . . . if that was true why do they have that program? Because it's not a rare occasion. I mean, none of those things are rare occasions, they're happening every day. So how are they rare? (White woman with experience of violence)

A government study, *Report of the Working Group on the Fear of Crime,* expressed concern about media coverage and fear of crime. It noted that "Crimewatch" did issue a "health warning" that the crimes it featured are uncommon (Home Office 1989:32–34; Schlesinger and Tumber 1994:251). One BBC study found that women were more likely to mention fear than men (BBC Broadcasting Research 1988:18), and of the five discussion groups (three composed of women and two of men) some of the women, but none of the men, said they were frightened by the program. Women who mentioned fear were more likely to live alone or to view alone. It would seem that gender should be considered when examining findings about the media and fear of crime. Another BBC study indicated that about one-third of viewers found the program frightening and that women are twice as likely to do so as men. At the same time, they thought that it raised their crime awareness, and the vast majority approved of the program (BBC Broadcasting Research 1994:1–2).

Research on "Crimestoppers," another British reality program, observed that while over half of the respondents said the program had not made them afraid, they thought a warning should be given before showing a reconstruction of a violent crime. One in three respondents thought that "Crimestoppers" made them feel more cautious about going out alone in the dark, or that other people had probably become more afraid of crime as a result of watching the program. A similar proportion said they were reassured that the police solve a great many crimes (Wober and Gunter 1990:ii). Unfortunately, the survey did not distinguish respondents by gender. Given our findings, it seems that future research should routinely include gender in the analysis, and also consider in more detail the complex anxieties about personal safety that we discovered among women. Even with a focus on women, however, the evidence remains complex: a crime reconstruction may cause anxiety at one level and reassure at another, and gender and life-style may differently articulate with fear of crime and the real and perceived potential risk:

> I do take "Crimewatch" seriously, because when I have watched it in the past, it's made me nervous, like when I've had to go upstairs, thinking "God, I'm not safe," because they have shown a lot of scenes where things have happened within your own home. . . . I don't like it because it makes me nervous . . . if you go outside you're not safe, and even in your own home, you're not safe. (Afro-Caribbean woman with experience of violence)

REAL-LIFE VIOLENCE AND FEAR OF CRIME

The findings from this and other studies point to a strong relationship between fear of crime and victimization (Stanko 1985:122–34, 1996; McLaughlin, Dobash, and Dobash 1990; Johnson 1996:61–90). A considerable proportion of the women studied were concerned about violent crime and personal safety. However, while almost all women were afraid of rape because of widespread cultural beliefs, the fear of domestic violence was more likely to be based on the personal experience of such violence. In addition, women who have been the victims of violence in the home are more likely to express a sense of vulnerability to crime and attack, and this extends to fear of crimes outside the home.

Concerning the fear of crime, we examined four dimensions and, for the most part, found greater fear among those with experience of violence than among those with no such experience. In brief, the findings show:

1. *Fear of violence in the home*—61 percent of the women who had experienced violence worried about physical attacks while 23 percent of women with no experience did so.
2. *Fear of crime in a public setting*—67 percent with experience and 56 percent without experience of violence were worried
3. *Going out at night in their local area*—65 percent of women who had experienced violence were worried while 63 percent of women who had not experienced violence were not worried.

4. *General concerns about crime*—90 percent of the women with experience of violence were worried as were three-quarters of the women with no experience.

Stanko (1995) notes that despite their underrepresentation as victims in victim surveys and in official crime statistics, women's sense of personal safety is conditioned by a lifetime of experience of a wide range of harassments, intimidations, and violence by men in public and private places. Supporting evidence has been found in a large national survey of twelve thousand Canadian women (Johnson 1996:61–90). Many women exist in an intimidating atmosphere punctuated with incidents that remind them that they may be in danger and that they must remain alert to and concerned about personal safety. Women may pursue strategies of avoidance by remaining alert to indicators of risk and to possible means of avoiding harm: television provides one medium that conveys messages about risk and about strategies for avoiding danger.

THE MEDIA AND FEAR OF CRIME

While fear of crime and violence are generated through many social and cultural experiences, perhaps the most important being the personal experience of violence, scholars have sought to assess the media's contribution to such fears and anxieties (Gunter 1987). When women were asked whether certain types of media increased or decreased their fear of crime, there were few discernible differences between the two categories. Over half of the women indicated that certain types of media tended to increase their anxieties about crime. When asked to choose from a list of formats most likely to increase fear of crime, women selected television news, television dramas and documentaries, television films, and the local tabloid press. Fifteen percent spontaneously named "Crimewatch." A small number of women mentioned pornographic magazines, nude photographs published in popular newspapers, and sensationalist forms of reporting. Very few indicated that their fear of crime was increased by radio news, the cinema, magazines, or quality newspapers. When queried about the role media play in reducing their fears, a small proportion of women in both categories said these could play such a role (28 percent of women who had experienced violence, 19 percent of those who had not); they mentioned television documentaries and current affairs programs. When asked if there was any specific type of television programming or newspaper reporting that reduced their fear of crime, 8 percent mentioned "Crimewatch." Overall, however, women thought the media play an important role in *increasing* their anxieties and fear of crime while playing little or no role in *decreasing* those fears.

MASS-MEDIATED VIOLENCE
AND REAL-LIFE VIOLENCE

When asked what they thought of media reporting of violent crimes against women, many women indicated that they were not sure of the impact of such reporting. However, an overwhelming majority from both categories (87 percent with experience of violence, 90 percent with none) thought that crime reporting might help make women become more aware and more safety-conscious; over three-quarters of the women thought that crime reporting might actually increase women's fear of crime. They were unsure about what impact such presentations might have on men. Of those who offered an opinion, nearly three-quarters of those with experience of violence believed crime reporting would encourage male violence while almost the same proportion of women with no experience believed the opposite. Across the sample, many women said that reporting crimes of violence against women could make some men more aware.

In summary, most women thought that reporting of violence against women would make women and men more aware of such crimes, but many also believed that it would increase women's fear of crime. On whether such reporting might encourage violence against women, our respondents were divided: among women with experience of violence, some did not know while others thought it would; women with no experience of violence did not think that reporting would increase women's fear. Again, personal experience seems to be related to notions about the relationship between media representation and behavior in real life. This also illustrates that, with respect to the media representation of violence against women, there is no single audience providing an unvaried response; rather, there are multiple audiences that appear to bring their personal experiences and cultural background to their responses.

CONCLUSIONS

The women in all viewing groups unequivocally held that violent crimes against the person were far more important than any crime against property. Most agreed that the most serious crime was the rape and murder of the young woman. The discussion focused on how the event had occurred and how it could have been prevented. The responses revealed a tension between popular forms of explanation often referred to as "victim blaming," and arguments that, by contrast, rejected women's responsibility for male violence and viewed as unjust the constraints upon women's independence and mobility. This is a common theme in debates about real-life violence against women and reappears in the discussions of the media representation of violence against women in the "Crimewatch" programs studied.

With respect to fear of crime, women who had been victims of violence were more fearful and apprehensive about crime than those who had not been victims, but all women expressed concern about crimes such as rape. The "payoff" statement about the infrequency of such crimes and urging viewers not to have nightmares was not convincing and sometimes was seen as dismissive. There is a general desire to believe in the police and in "Crimewatch's" stated purpose of helping police catch criminals. However, the program does not seem to be viewed as unambiguously as might be expected. Women with the lived experience of violence who have used the police are most critical of "Crimewatch's" presentation of the police, although skepticism was not limited to that group. Ethnicity was important in shaping responses: many Asian and Afro-Caribbean group members believed that police practices are racially discriminatory. Overall, social class seemed to have little impact on women's reactions, but ethnicity was important in varying ways. Many Asian women saw "Crimewatch" as representing an alien world to which they did not belong and, with such distance, were more likely to see it as "exciting" and "entertaining." Afro-Caribbean and white women were less likely to do so. Criticisms were made of the negative portrayal of women as victims of crime, of the perceived negative portrayal of ethnic minority groups, of the breach of confidentiality revealed in the program, and of the way that crime is sometimes sensationalized. Finally, the responses with respect to different viewing audiences were varied and changing across the many issues addressed. As a consequence, there was no single viewing audience but many different audiences who brought their lived experiences to their interpretations of what they saw on television. The points of articulation between lived experience and interpretations of the reality program were most obvious and "real" where the two corresponded most closely.

REFERENCES

BBC Broadcasting Research. 1988. *Crimewatch UK.* London: BBC Special Projects Report, SP.88/45/88/16, October.
———. 1996. *Series summary.* London: Television Group.
Corner, J. 1995. *Television Form and Public Address.* London: Edward Arnold.
Dobash, R. E. and R. P. Dobash. 1979. *Violence Against Wives.* New York: Free Press.
———. 1988. "The Nature and Antecedents of Violent Events." *British Journal of Criminology* 24(3):269–88.
———. 1992. *Women, Violence and Social Change.* London: Routledge.
Dobash, R. E., Russell P. Dobash, K. Cavanagh, and R. Lewis. 1995. "Evaluating Criminal Justice Programmes for Violent Men." Pp.358–89 in *Gender and*

Crime, edited by R. E. Dobash, R. P. Dobash, and L. Noaks. Concord, MA: Paul
and Company; Cardiff: University of Wales Press.
———. 1998. *Changing Violent Men.* Thousand Oaks: Sage.
Eco, Umberto. 1995. "A Guide to the Neo-Television of the 1980s." In *Culture and
Conflict in Postwar Italy,* edited by Z. G. Baransky and R. Lumley. London:
MacMillan.
Edwards, S. S. M. 1989. *Policing 'Domestic' Violence.* London: Sage.
Fairclough, N. 1995. *Media Discourse.* London: Edward Arnold.
Gardner, C. B. 1995. *Passing By: Gender and Public Harassment.* Berkeley: Univer-
sity of California Press.
Gunter, B. 1987. *Television and the Fear of Crime.* London: Libby.
Home Office. 1989. *Report of the Working Group on the Fear of Crime.* London:
Author.
Johnson, H. 1996. *Dangerous Domains: Violence Against Women in Canada.* Toron-
to: Nelson Canada.
Kelly, L. 1988. *Surviving Sexual Violence.* Cambridge: Polity.
McLaughlin, P., R. E. Dobash, and R. P. Dobash. 1990. *Women Thinking About
Crime: A Survey of Women's Experiences and Fear of Crime.* Available from R.
Dobash, Violence Research Centre, Williamson Bldg., University of Manchester,
Oxford Road, Manchester M13 9PL.
McNeill, S. 1987. "Flashing: Its Effect on Women." Pp. 93–109 in *Women, Violence
and Social Control,* edited by J. Hanmer and M. Maynard. London: Macmillan.
Merton, R. K., M. Fiske, and P. L. Kendall. 1991. *The Focused Interview: A Manual of
Procedures,* 2nd ed. New York: Free Press.
Ross, N. 1994. "Foreword." Pp. 11–13 in *True Crime Stories Solved,* edited by L.
Mills. London: Penguin, BBC Books.
Ross, N. and S. Cook. 1987. *Crimewatch UK.* London: Hodder & Stoughton.
Russell, D. 1982. *Rape in Marriage.* New York: Macmillan.
Schlesinger, P. 1996. *Broadcasters, Policemen and the Deregulation of Reality.
Franco-British Studies,* Special Issue: "Trial by Media" 21(Spring):28–31.
Schlesinger, P., R. E. Dobash, R. P. Dobash, and C. K. Weaver. 1992. *Women Viewing
Violence.* London: BFI, and Indiana University Press; Bloomington: Indiana Uni-
versity Press.
Schlesinger, P. and H. Tumber. 1994. *Reporting Crime: The Media Politics of Crimi-
nal Justice.* Oxford: Clarendon.
Schlesinger, P., H. Tumber, and G. Murdock. 1991. "The Media Politics of Crime and
Criminal Justice." *British Journal of Sociology* 42(3):407–8.
Stanko, E. 1985. *Intimate Intrusions: Women's Experience of Male Violence.* London:
Routledge.
———. 1995. "Women, Crime and Fear." *Annals of American Political and Social
Science* 539:46–58.
———. 1996. "Warnings to Women: Police Advice and Women's Safety in Britain."
Violence Against Women 2(1):5–24.
Wober, J. M. and B. Gunter. 1990. "Crime Reconstruction Programmes: Viewing
Experience in Three Regions, Linked with Perceptions of and Reactions to
Crime." Research Paper. London: IBA.

4

Ratings and Reality:
The Persistence of the Reality Crime Genre

MARK FISHMAN

When social scientists and media commentators discuss reality crime programs, there is a tendency to assume that the emergence and survival of this genre on prime time television in and of itself indicates that these shows are quite popular and influential (Sauter 1992; Fennel 1992). It is the purpose of this chapter to question that assumption and refine our understanding of their appeal.

Let me point out from the outset that I am *not* suggesting that reality crime shows have little appeal, nor that they are overrated as a cultural phenomenon. The mere fact that they exist on prime time television, and that they have persisted for several years as a new form of nonfiction TV, is testimony to their importance in popular culture. Obviously, many people are watching reality crime programs. But how many and which parts of the audience? And how does this compare with other kinds of television programs?

In other words, if we want to say something specific about the appeal of reality crime shows, we need to open up the matter to empirical investigation. This chapter will primarily try to answer such questions as: How widely viewed are reality crime shows? Are they among television's most highly rated programs, or do they attract relatively small numbers of viewers? Do reality crime shows attract a broad spectrum or only a specific segment of the audience? And, if these programs turn out to have only limited appeal, how and why could they spread so rapidly on television and survive so long?

RATINGS AS DATA

If we are interested in empirical evidence bearing on such questions, there is one obvious source to turn to: the ratings data of Nielsen Media Research. I will examine such data for the United States for a single week in

October 1993. This is an exploratory study; a more complete examination of ratings covering a larger time frame for both national and local media markets is a topic for future research.

Before looking at the data, however, I want to sound a note of caution. Nielsen surveys offer the most complete information available concerning nationwide television viewing patterns. That is why the television industry depends upon these data. Yet they are flawed; one must be careful which parts of the surveys one uses and how one interprets them.

Among the many criticisms leveled at Nielsen's methodology, two especially serious problems have been noted. First, there is the issue of sample selection. Nielsen has always had the problem of low cooperation rates (with less than 50 percent of those asked agreeing to allow installation of audimeters or people meters in their homes). It has been found that in the past Nielsen's field staff apparently had the habit of picking too many households with only one television set (perhaps because it was easier to install the devices in those homes), and also a tendency to pick households that watched more television than the average (Carter 1997; CONTAM 1989a; Gitlin 1985:49–52; Mayer 1966, 1970).

Second, there are problems with the data collection instruments placed in homes. Of the three instruments used—audimeters, people meters, and diaries—the latter two are the most problematic. Diaries require one member of the household to record all the television watching (what hours, what programs) for all members of the family for an entire week. This is not a trivial task, especially in large households with cable TV, multiple sets, VCRs, etc. It is widely believed that information in these diaries is questionable or incomplete. To get around the difficulties of keeping track of who is watching what, Nielsen introduced the people meter in 1987. This is an electronic device that sits on the TV set. When viewers begin watching television they are supposed to key in (using a special remote control), and when they leave, they should key out. Independent researchers have found that after a few months household members bother to do this less and less. This may explain why people meters produced much smaller ratings for TV programs than the older audimeters, which only measure whether the set is on or off, and what channel it is tuned to (Carter 1997; CONTAM 1989b).

It is important to note that of the three devices, the two less reliable ones—diaries and people meters—measure individual viewers. These make it possible for Nielsen to estimate not only how many individuals are watching a given show, but also the composition of the audience by age, gender, and other demographic variables. The third (and more reliable) device, the audimeter, only allows estimates of how many households are watching a given program, not how many people or which people in those households are watching. Since advertisers want demographic data, Nielsen continues to rely on people meters and diaries. But executives at the major networks have been unhappy, claiming that these recording devices are underestimating the size of the audience (Carter 1997).

Interestingly, despite skepticism, the entire television industry still uses Nielsen data because it allows them to do business. The ratings are crucial in deciding whether to continue a show into the next TV season, or to bargain over the price for thirty seconds of advertising time. The ratings constitute the only common standard that allows all parties to negotiate the value of particular programs.

But should *we* be using Nielsen data? The answer is that we must be circumspect when we use it to estimate who is watching a given program (by age or gender), because those data are based on people meters and diaries. However, we can be more confident about estimates of the overall size of a program's audience (in terms of households), since they are based on audimeters. Even though we may be highly interested in the demographics of the audience, that information is less reliable.

GAUGING THE SUCCESS OF
REALITY PROGRAMS

There is, however, an entirely different way we may use Nielsen data with confidence. We can view them not as a reflection of viewership, but as an indicator of the relative success of a program by the TV industry's own standards. In other words, network executives, advertising executives, and station managers treat the ratings as if they accurately reflected viewership. Thus, we may use these figures as an indicator of the relative success of reality crime programs from the point of view of those who decide whether a program will survive on television and what it is worth. Later we shall consider what Nielsen data have to say about who is watching reality crime programs.

Within the television industry, one finds Nielsen data used in a number of ways to gauge the success of a program. Four commonly used measurements of popularity are

1. a program's overall household rating,
2. a program's overall household share,
3. a show's rank in its time slot, using household rating as the basis for ranking,
4. a show's rank in its time slot, using the rating among viewers eighteen to forty-nine years old as the basis for ranking.

Table 1 shows national Nielsen data on these four indicators for reality programs appearing on network television during prime time (7 to 11 P.M.)

Table 1.   Indicators of Success: Nielsen National TV Ratings, October 11–17, 1993

	Time	Net	House-hold Rating	House-hold Share	House-hold Rank	18–49 Rank
Reality crime						
"America's Most Wanted"	9:00	Fox	5.9	9	4	4
	9:30	Fox	6.9	11	4	4
"Unsolved Mysteries"	8:00	NBC	13.6	22	2	2
	8:30	NBC	14.4	22	2	2
"Missing Persons"	8:00	ABC	9.1	15	3	3
	8:30	ABC	9.5	15	3	3
"Top Cops Special"	10:00	NBC	7.2	12	3	3
	10:30	NBC	6.5	12	3	3
"Cops"	8:00	Fox	8.4	16	2	1
"Cops 2"	8:30	Fox	8.8	16	1	1
Average			9.0	15	2.7	2.6
News						
"ABC World News"	6:30	ABC	10.2	21	1	1
"CBS Eve News"	6:30	CBS	8.2	17	3	3
"NBC Nightly News"	6:30	NBC	8.8	18	2	2
Average			9.1	19	2	2
News magazines						
"Dateline"	10:00	NBC	11.7	19	3	3
	10:30	NBC	12.3	21	3	3
"Eye to Eye w/Chung"	9:00	CBS	8.5	13	3	4
	9:30	CBS	8.8	14	3	4
"Primetime Live"	10:00	ABC	13.5	23	1	2
	10:30	ABC	13.6	25	1	2
"20/20"	10:00	ABC	13.7	26	1	1
	10:30	ABC	13.8	26	1	1
"60 Minutes"	7:00	CBS	18.2	31	1	1
	7:30	CBS	20.3	33	1	1
Average			13.4	23	1.8	2.2

Source: Nielsen Media Research, Nielsen Television Index National TV Ratings October 11-17, 1993.

in one week of October 1993. Most shows in this table have two entries because Nielsen data are given separately for each half-hour segment of a one-hour program. For the purposes of comparison, Table 1 also shows similar data for two other related kinds of TV programs: network evening news broadcasts and news magazine shows.

Household Ratings

Probably the most widely mentioned Nielsen figure is a program's household rating. A household rating is the percentage of households viewing a particular program out of the total number of households with televisions.[1] What is a good rating? During the fall of 1993 the most popular network shows ("Seinfeld," "Home Improvement," and "60 Minutes") got household ratings ranging from 17.5 to 22. At that same time the average household rating for a prime time network show was 12.0. In contrast, some of the most poorly rated prime time network shows ("Front Page," "South Central," "Brisco County," "Townsend Television," "Bakersfield, P.D.") got household ratings ranging from 3.5 to 5.0.

How did the household ratings of reality crime programs compare? Table 1 shows that the numbers are not impressive. Their average rating is 9.0, well below the 12.0 average for all network prime time programs of this same time period. Only NBC's "Unsolved Mysteries" had respectable (but not large) ratings. Even so, a rating of 9.0 means that the average reality crime show is viewed in approximately 8.7 million households. "Unsolved Mysteries," with an average rating of 14, reaches about 13.6 million households.

Table 1 also shows that reality crime shows on average get about the same ratings as the major networks' evening news broadcasts. Note that neither reality crime nor news programs are at all as popular as news magazine shows.

Another common way of judging programs is by ranking the household ratings of all prime time shows in a given week. Approximately one hundred shows air during prime time in one week. The fifteen or twenty most highly rated programs are deemed particularly successful. Checking the top twenty lists published from January 1993 to June 1997 in two major industry journals (*Variety* and *Broadcasting and Cable*), I found that reality crime programs have never achieved this kind of success. Typically, the most widely viewed reality crime programs aired by the major networks ("America's Most Wanted," "Cops," and "Unsolved Mysteries") rank anywhere between fortieth and ninetieth place.

Household Shares

A household share is the percentage of households viewing a particular program out of the total number of households tuned in to television at that time. Whereas a rating estimates the absolute size of the audience, a share gives some idea of how well a program is doing against its competition. Successful network shows during prime time typically get above a 25 share. For example, in October 1993 the very popular shows "Seinfeld," "Home Improvement," and "60 Minutes" got shares ranging from 29 to 32. The average share for a prime time program is about 18. The most poorly rated shows have shares below 12. For example, "Front Page," "Brisco County," and "Townsend Television" had shares of 5.5 to 9.

Table 1 reveals that reality crime programs have poor to mediocre shares. As a group, they average a 15 share—well below the network average. Once again, only "Unsolved Mysteries" has respectable numbers. In comparison with news broadcasts and news magazine programs, on average reality crime shows capture a significantly smaller share of the available audience during their time period.

Rank of a Show in Its Time Slot

Another common way a program is judged is to see if it comes in first, second, third, or fourth among the other network programs broadcast at that same time. Such a ranking is based either on household ratings or on the ratings for eighteen- to forty-nine-year-old viewers. Why are eighteen- to forty-nine-year-old viewers so important?

Advertisers are drawn to younger demos—and in particular adults 18–49—for a number of reasons. The arguments include more people on average per household (including higher purchasing volume), more malleable buying habits in terms of trying new products and greater responsiveness to ads. (Lowry 1993)

Analyzing advertising rates for prime time programs, Lowry (1993:33) found that shows with high proportions of viewers eighteen to forty-nine years old fetched higher prices for a thirty-second ad than programs with higher household ratings but lower ratings in the eighteen- to forty-nine-year-old group (see also Sharkey 1994).

How do reality crime shows rank among their competitors in the same time slots? Table 1 shows that only "Cops" does well (first place for both half-hours among eighteen- to forty-nine-year-olds, and first place in household ratings for its second half-hour); "Unsolved Mysteries" does acceptably well (second place for both half-hours for both types of rankings). But the rest do not do well against the competition, coming in third or fourth.[2] As a group, reality crime programs average somewhere between second and third place. Table 1 shows that, generally, news magazine shows do much better in their respective rankings.

In short, no matter how you measure it, reality crime programs are not wildly popular. They have an audience, but, by industry standards, it is neither large nor particularly lucrative. While a few such programs get reasonably high ratings ("Cops," "Unsolved Mysteries"), most do not. Over the years, many have been canceled, only to be replaced by new reality programs. One might well ask, then, Why have such programs as a group lasted so long on television? And why do they seem to be more numerous than ever?

DEVELOPMENTS IN THE TELEVISION INDUSTRY

The success of reality programs as a whole cannot be adequately understood if one only looks at their Nielsen ratings. To understand the growth of reality programming on prime time television, one must examine the larger economic and historical context of the industry that produces these programs.

Reality programming has arisen during a troubled period for broadcast television. As one recent text (Dizard 1994:82) puts it:

Broadcast television is an industry in long-term decline. The erosion in network viewing is probably irreversible. Despite the increase in television viewing households, . . . the number of viewers watching prime time programs declined from 36.9 million in 1975 to 32.7 million in 1990, according to an FCC study (Setzer and Levy 1991:19).

For the past several years Nielsen data have shown that the major networks account for a declining share of the prime time audience. Between 1980 and 1992 that share has fallen by a third. The four networks' audience share has leveled off in the 1990s to just over 60 percent during prime time, with the rest of the audience watching programs on independent stations and cable channels (Schlosser 1997; Auletta 1991:560, 1994; MacDonald 1990:224, 226; Anonymous 1987, 1989).

Even though cable television as a whole has severely cut into the audience for broadcast programs, the cable industry suffers from the same problem plaguing broadcast programs: fewer viewers per program because of the increasing number of program choices. As one industry executive put it:

The pie of total viewership is not getting bigger. What all the new [cable] networks are doing is fragmenting the market and cutting more slivers into the same basic-cable pie. (Betsy Frank, senior vice-president at Saatchi & Saatchi, quoted in Dempsey 1994)

Increased competition from cable television and independent stations (as well as the widespread use of VCRs) has divided up the existing pool of viewers into ever smaller segments. Consequently, advertising income has suffered: During the 1980s the networks' share of all television advertising revenue fell from 45 to 36 percent (Dizard 1994:84).[3] Although still profitable, by the late 1980s ABC, CBS, and NBC found themselves dealing with the problem of rising program costs and a declining audience.[4] They responded by making deep staff cuts (Dizard 1994:86; Auletta 1991). By the early 1990s, with a lingering recession exacerbating the situation, management at the three major networks was keen to further reduce program costs.

Auletta (1991:551) points out that by the end of the 1989–1990 season, it was apparent to programmers at the major networks that audiences were stagnant or declining:

> None of the 23 new series introduced by the three networks in the fall of 1989, nor of the 22 introduced in the fall of 1990, became a hit. Network programmers came to defend series that ranked in the bottom third of the ratings . . . if they had good demos. Or they defended shows that cost little to produce—like "America's Funniest Home Videos," reality shows like CBS's "Top Cops," or sometimes even news specials. . . . Slowly but perceptibly, the networks switched from a focus on mass appeal to a focus on demos and costs.

So network programmers were willing to experiment with new kinds of shows because the old formulas were not bringing in the same audiences anymore:

> Historically, networks want to program comedies and dramas as long-term solutions. In order to get a reality show developed and scheduled, you need a network with some problems. (Jim Paratore, president of Telepictures Productions, quoted in Coe 1994)

In fact, even before 1990 reality-based programs had already begun to appear in the United States. In 1987 Rupert Murdoch's Fox Broadcasting Company introduced the electronic tabloid program, "A Current Affair"; in early 1988 it aired the first reality crime program, "America's Most Wanted."[5] NBC quickly followed in the 1988–1989 season with "Unsolved Mysteries." But it was Murdoch's Fox network that really pioneered reality programming. Murdoch's publishing empire was based on American, English, and Australian print tabloids. Murdoch imported tabloid journalists from Fleet Street (and their methods) to Fox's reality programs. And it seemed to appeal to a substantial number of viewers. By the relatively modest standards of the Fox network, "America's Most Wanted" was a ratings success.[6]

Murdoch's strategy was to offer programs that attracted an audience not served by the three major networks: young, low-income, and minority viewers. At the same time, Murdoch wanted to run the Fox network, and produce programs for it, on a tight budget. As part of this strategy, Fox included in its program schedule reality-based crime programs. "America's Most Wanted" seems to have worked reasonably well in this regard. By network standards it was very cheap to produce ($140,000 to $170,000 a show) and appeared to attract the audience Murdoch was aiming for. According to a Nielsen Audience Demographic report cited in Breslin (1990:218), "America's Most Wanted" was watched more by households in more heavily populated areas, by large households (of four or more persons), and by households with incomes below $40,000. Although the show seemed to have broad appeal in terms of age and sex, it tended to do better with younger adults and less well with teens and viewers over fifty-five.

So by the end of the 1980s the Fox network had shown the rest of the television industry that there was an audience for reality-based crime shows. At the same time, on the major networks the usual programs did not seem to be working as well as they had. Programmers had every reason to experiment with newer types of shows, especially ones that were cheaper to produce. It was in this environment that reality crime programs spread on television.

PRODUCTION COSTS

One should not underestimate the importance of the low production costs of reality programs. How much cheaper are they than comedy and drama series? Even though actual production costs are secret, trade magazines like *Variety* and *Broadcasting and Cable* provide ballpark estimates.

Drama and comedy series have become quite expensive. Some recent examples: Paramount's "Star Trek: The Next Generation" (one one-hour show per week) cost from $1.5 to $1.7 million an episode. All American TV Distribution's "Sirens" (also a one-hour, once-a-week show) cost somewhat over $1 million an episode (Robins 1994; Schmuckler 1994). ABC's "Roseanne" was estimated to cost from $2 to $3 million an episode (Carter 1994).

Tabloid newsmagazine shows cost $250,000 to $600,000 per week. (A week of shows means five half-hour episodes, and sometimes a weekend hour episode.) For example, Paramount's "Entertainment Tonight" (six shows a week) costs $500,000 to $600,000; King World's "Inside Edition" costs about $400,000. Others ("Hard Copy," "A Current Affair") may be as cheap as $250,000 (Freeman 1993a).

Reality-based crime programs cost $150,00 to $250,000 per week. For example, Genesis Entertainment's "Real Stories of the Highway Patrol" (six half-hour shows per week) cost about $250,000 to produce (Freeman 1993a). Fox's "America's Most Wanted" in its early days (1989) cost $140,000–170,000 to produce its one weekly half-hour episode (Breslin 1990:180).

The astronomical costs of producing comedy and drama programs, in contrast with the low costs of cop and rescue shows and news magazines, helps explain their proliferation.

SHELF LIFE, "PUBLIC SERVICE," AND FLEXIBILITY

There are other economic advantages of reality programs besides their low production costs. Unlike conventional news programs or news magazine shows, reality crime shows can be (and are) made in such a way as to have a long shelf life. Programs like "Cops" and "Real Stories of the Highway Patrol" are filmed without dates or other temporal references that might age the programs. Episodes can be reshown. If a show lasts at least two seasons, there are enough episodes to repackage and sell as reruns in syndication to independent stations or cable networks.[7] Producers realize their greatest profits this way.

Reality programs have been attractive to the networks for other than economic reasons as well. One of these reasons has to do with the Prime Time Access Rule (PTAR), a 1971 FCC regulation that says that in the top fifty television markets the three major networks are limited to no more than three hours of programming during the prime time hours of 7 to 11 P.M. In the early 1970s the networks all chose 8 to 11 P.M. in which to provide their affiliates with programs, in effect creating an "access hour" from 7 to 8 P.M., which was (and still is) open to non-network, independent productions. The original intent of the FCC regulation was to encourage more local programming. In fact, the access hour has been dominated by a few large production companies that provide local stations with game shows and (since the late 1980s) tabloid news magazines and reality crime programs:

> The rule fails to promote the FCC goal of programming diversity. . . . 93% of all slots on all stations are served by either King World ["Jeopardy," "Wheel of Fortune," "Inside Edition"], Fox ["A Current Affair," "Cops"], or Paramount ["Entertainment Tonight," "Hard Copy"]. (Anonymous 1994)

There are two important exceptions to the PTAR. First, it does not apply to the Fox Network, because the FCC only recognizes ABC, CBS, and NBC as networks. Second, it allows the three major networks to provide their affiliates with programs during the access hour if those programs are news or documentaries. Therefore, by claiming that cop and rescue programs or tabloid news magazines are documentaries, the networks can offer programs during the access hour that compete with what independent syndicators are already selling (see Freeman 1993b).

Furthermore, because of their ambiguous relationship to news and documentaries, reality-based programs also allow the networks that produce them and the independently owned television stations that show them to claim that these are "public affairs" programs (McClellan 1994). This is important particularly to television stations concerned with renewing their broadcast license with the FCC.

So we see that reality crime programs combine some of the advantages of entertainment programs (they can be resold as reruns) without the disadvantage of high production costs. At the same time, reality crime shows have some of the advantages of news and news magazine programs (they give the appearance of serving their community with public affairs programming) without the disadvantage that they cannot be sold as reruns.

One final advantage that helps explain the persistence of reality crime programs is their flexibility. Over the years they have survived not because they have flourished in any particular time period, but because they are a "utility player" in the lineup of TV programs during the week (Littleton 1996). They can be (and have been) moved about wherever TV executives need to fill holes in a network or TV station's schedule of programs. In the early 1990s reality crime shows appeared on the major broadcast networks during the weekday "access hour" (7 to 8 P.M.) and on Saturdays during prime time (8 to 10 P.M.). But as their already low ratings sagged even lower, these programs have been slowly disappearing from prime time and from the major networks, only to spring up in the latter half of the 1990s during off hours (late afternoon and late evening) and on the cable networks. Able to put down roots wherever there is an opportunity in the TV schedule, reality crime shows appear to have evolved into the "crab grass" of television.

THE NATURE OF THE AUDIENCE

Now let us turn our attention to what Nielsen data can tell us about who is watching reality crime programs. Table 2 shows the composition of the audience for reality crime programs that aired on the major networks during prime time for the week of October 11–17, 1993. The table does not show Nielsen data in the usual form of ratings and shares. Rather, the information has been recalculated to reveal what percentage of the audience is male or female, and what age groupings are over- or underrepresented. (The particular age groupings in the table were chosen because they were the only contiguous age categories provided in Nielsen's data.) As with Table 1, for the sake of comparison Table 2 includes data for two other related types of television programs, evening news shows and news magazines. As a way of gauging the degree to which demographic groups may be over- or underrepresented, the table also presents the percentage of each category in the U.S. television viewing population (based on Nielsen Media Research 1993:131).

What does Table 2 show with respect to gender? It appears that reality crime programs are more popular with women than men. On average, 58.4 percent of the viewers are female. This is, at first blush, a curious finding. One might have expected these programs, with their emphasis on crime, violence, and action, to attract more of a male audience. Indeed, the most action-oriented of these programs, "Cops," is a notable exception. Here there is an approximately even split between male and female viewers.

Nevertheless, how can we understand the tendency for the audience to

Table 2.   Composition (%) of Audience by Age and Gender: Nielsen National TV
Ratings, October 11–17, 1993

	Women	2–11	12–17	18–34	35–64
Universe	52.3	17.6	9.8	30.4	42.2
Reality crime					
"America's Most Wanted"	56.7	10.0	5.7	24.7	59.6
	59.3	8.9	6.3	27.9	56.9
"Unsolved Mysteries"	62.3	8.5	5.0	22.1	64.3
	60.8	8.0	5.0	23.4	63.7
"Missing Persons"	63.1	9.8	5.9	18.5	65.8
	63.5	7.6	6.4	19.4	66.5
"Top Cops Special"	58.0		8.0	28.4	63.5
	58.4		7.4	31.0	61.5
"Cops"	50.9	12.7	9.2	31.1	47.0
"Cops 2"	51.0	13.5	8.7	32.2	45.6
Average	58.4	9.9	6.8	25.9	59.4
News					
"ABC World News"	57.5		3.7	24.5	71.8
"CBS Eve News"	57.9		3.4	23.8	72.8
"NBC Nightly News"	58.0		4.5	23.0	72.5
Average	57.8		3.9	23.8	72.4
News magazines					
"Dateline"	60.8	5.1	4.9	33.1	56.9
	59.2	3.3	4.1	34.0	58.6
"Eye to Eye w/Chung"	63.8			22.1	77.9
	61.2	5.2	4.9	22.8	67.1
"Primetime Live"	58.4	5.2	3.3	22.2	69.4
	56.8			24.2	75.8
"20/20"	59.9	14.1	7.1	26.3	52.5
	57.7	7.3	5.3	26.4	61.0
"60 Minutes"	45.5	5.1	4.3	27.5	63.0
	48.5	4.1	3.9	25.7	66.2
Average	57.2	6.2	4.7	26.6	64.8

Source: Nielsen Media Research, Nielsen Television Index National TV Ratings October 11–17, 1993.

be more female? Part of the answer lies in the fact that the audience for prime time television programs in general is more female than male, and that this is so particularly in the early hours of prime time when most of these reality programs aired. Almost any program during this time would have a larger female audience. In support of this, we can see that the audiences for the network evening news programs and the news magazine shows are also more heavily female. They average approximately the same percentage of female viewers (57.8 and 57.2 percent, respectively) as reality crime programs.

Even so, I do not feel confident that this entirely explains the tendency for more women than men to watch reality programs. First, this trend has been seen in other contexts, notably in the British audience for "Crimewatch UK" (as noted by Dobash et al. in this volume). Second, there are prime time programs that manage to attract much larger male audiences. We can see two examples of this in Table 2: CBS's news magazine "60 Minutes" and the reality program "Cops."

In several respects "Cops" is unlike any of the other prime time reality programs in Table 2. It is more action-oriented. Its cinema verité style invites voyeurism. It does not solicit viewer tips, and offers no pretence to catching criminals. Whether such differences in content account for the gender differences in the audience for "Cops" remains to be resolved in future research. One thing, however, is clear from the Nielsen data: all reality crime shows are not alike. "Cops" seems to represent a type that draws a different audience.

What does Table 2 tell us about the age of the audience? First, reality programs are not very popular among children and teenagers. Viewers two to eleven and twelve to seventeen are, on average, decidedly underrepresented in the audience. In contrast, older viewers (thirty-five to sixty-four) are clearly overrepresented. Why would this be?

In general, the audience of network prime time programs tends to be older than the population at large. Younger viewers tend to migrate to shows on cable and independent stations. They are more likely to be watching situation comedies and sports. Moreover, it is well-known in the media business that news, whether in newspapers, radio, or television, attracts an audience older than the general audience for that medium. In Table 2 we can see that news and news magazine shows have an even greater tendency to attract older viewers than reality crime shows do. It appears that television news magazine shows attract somewhat less of an older audience than conventional news programs, and that the newer genre of reality crime programs reduces this tendency toward older audiences even further.

Once again, the program "Cops" is an interesting exception. Its audience comes much closer to the actual percentage of these age categories in the general population. Even though the audience for broadcast network programs skews older and more female, the audience for "Cops" comes close to reflecting the actual age and gender composition of the population.

CONCLUSIONS

From one point of view, reality crime programs have had only limited success on television. They do not reach huge audiences. Their ratings and shares range from modest to poor. By no means is everybody watching them. However, even with mediocre ratings, because the television market in the United States is so large, reality crime shows attract millions of viewers. Who are those millions?

We have seen in this chapter that Nielsen data reveal that most (but not all) reality shows tend to be watched more by women and by older viewers. But these are only tendencies. There is still a sizable proportion of male and young adults in the audience. Reality programs are not like some shows, which draw a highly defined audience (for instance, the audience of older women attracted to "Murder She Wrote" or of teenage girls attracted to "Beverly Hills 90210"). Although skewed toward older and more female audiences, reality crime shows have a broad base of viewers. On the basis of Nielsen data used in this chapter, it is hard to say more.

In order to extend this analysis of the audience, future research could examine Nielsen ratings in a sample of local television markets. The data in the current study were based entirely on *national* Nielsen ratings. An examination of *local* television markets would enable us to look at a much larger number of reality crime programs, since most are not on the national networks at a fixed time, but on independent and cable stations in a variety of time slots. This would be particularly crucial in confirming whether or not the different viewer demographics for "Cops" really represents a different audience for the type of reality program that "Cops" represents. (For example, do other "Cops"-like programs—"Real Stories of the Highway Patrol," "American Detective," "LAPD"—have the same viewer demographics?)

Although the audience of reality crime programs is quite limited, from another point of view, the genre has been and continues to be a successful survivor of commercial TV in the United States. Since the late 1980s, reality crime shows rapidly spread on evening television (Battaglio 1991; Fennel 1992; Coe 1993). By the mid-1990s, however, audience ratings were declining in most reality programs and several shows were canceled. The prevailing wisdom in the television industry was that there were now too many reality programs dividing up a limited audience (Coe 1994). But by the late 1990s the prevailing wisdom seems to have changed as it became apparent that new reality crime shows were replacing those that had been canceled. Reality programs were able to survive by moving increasingly onto cable channels and into more marginal time slots. In other words, they survived by fitting into whatever time slots other (more expensive) programs could not fill (Littleton 1996).

This is an important development in light of two trends in the television industry: the tendency for the number of TV channels to increase and the tendency for the cost of producing original content for those channels to increase. If these trends hold, they create conditions for the continuing survival of the reality crime genre: a highly competitive TV market in which cable and broadcast networks need a large volume of inexpensive programs. It would seem that we can expect reality crime programs for many years to come.

NOTES

1. Nielsen estimates the television universe at 97 million households. Each household rating point (percentage point) represents 970,000 homes. Nielsen's weekly national television ratings are based on audimeter and people meter data from approximately 3,500 sample households or 8,700 individuals.

2. Since the Fox network does not program after 10 P.M., a third place from 10 to 11 P.M. means last place.

3. The networks' drop in ad revenue is not only due to increased competition from independent stations and cable networks, but also due to a shift in advertising dollars away from television into other marketing techniques: coupons, telephone marketing, and mail order catalogs (Dizard 1994:85).

4. Auletta (1991:551) points out that in 1989 for the three major networks "the combined profit margin was 10.2 percent (a low of 1 percent for CBS, a high of 17 percent for NBC); by contrast, the profit margins for cable systems averaged 42 percent, and for affiliated stations 38 percent."

5. "America's Most Wanted" was the first show of its type in the United States, but reality-based crime shows appeared first in Europe. In fact, Breslin (1990:3–4) recounts how it was these European shows (from Britain and West Germany) that gave Fox executives in 1987 the original idea for "America's Most Wanted." The most notable early reality crime programs are Germany's "Case XY . . . Unsolved," started in 1967, Holland's "Wanted," started in 1982, and Britain's "Crimewatch UK," started in 1984. The German program was apparently a model for the other two (Breslin 1990:352–57; Schlesinger and Tumber 1994:252–54).

6. In the late 1980s, the early years of the Fox network, a typical ABC, CBS, or NBC show would get a household rating between 10 and 15 during prime time hours. In contrast, most Fox shows typically got ratings between 5 and 8. For example, in the 1989–1990 season, Fox programs had an average rating of 6.6, while ABC had 13.5, NBC had 15.2, and CBS had 12.5 (MacDonald 1990:226). For the part of 1988 in which "America's Most Wanted" debuted, it averaged a 6.8 rating. These figures improved in the 1988–1989 season, with a 9.2 rating (Breslin 1990:180, 218). By the 1993–1994 season, the show had slumped to ratings around 6.5. In the 1996–1997 season those figures were about the same.

7. Syndicated programs are created by independent production companies and sold to local stations for broadcast at the discretion of the station. In contrast, network shows are produced by the network and supplied to their affiliates for broadcast during a specified time. Syndicated programs may be reruns of network shows or may be programs never shown before.

REFERENCES

Anonymous. 1987. "TV's Shifting Balance of Power." *Broadcasting and Cable,* October 12, p. 40.
———. 1989. *Variety,* January 4, p. 26.

———. 1994. "FCC to Begin Reviewing PTAR Comments." *Broadcasting and Cable,* June 13, p. 43.

Auletta, Ken. 1991. *Three Blind Mice: How the TV Networks Lost Their Way.* New York: Random House.

———. 1994. "Back in Play." *New Yorker,* July 18, p. 26.

Battaglio, S. 1991. "A Bigger Dose of Reality: Networks Cut Costs with More Shows About Police Work, Rescue Missions." *Adweek* July, p. 18.

Breslin, Jack. 1990. *America's Most Wanted: How Television Catches Crooks.* New York: HarperCollins.

Carter, Bill. 1994. "NBC Takes Aim at Tuesday Nights." *New York Times,* August 1, p. D1.

———. 1997. "Watching the Watchers: Nielsen Taking Heat for Drop in TV Viewing." *New York Times,* March 10, p. D1.

Coe, Steven. 1993. "Reality's Widening Role in the Real World." *Broadcasting and Cable,* April 12, p. 22.

———. 1994. "The Reality Is That [Some Network] Reality Bites." *Broadcasting and Cable,* May 9, p. 29.

CONTAM. 1989a. "Nielsen Procedures: Sampling and Field Implementation." New York: Television Information Office, Committee on Nationwide Television Audience Measurements, August.

———. 1989b. "Review of Nielsen People Meter: Final Report." New York: Television Information Office, Committee on Nationwide Television Audience Measurements, October.

Dempsey, John. 1994. "Wanted: Viewers for New Cable Channels." *Variety,* January 3–9, p. 1.

Dizard, Wilson. 1994. *Old Media, New Media: Mass Communications in the Information Age.* New York: Longman.

Fennel, T. 1992. "True-to-Life TV: Realistic Shows Earn Top Ratings." *MacLean's,* December, p. 48.

Freeman, Mike. 1993a. "The Economics of First-Run Reality." *Broadcasting and Cable,* April 12, p. 34.

———. 1993b. "Ratings Are Reality for Off-Net." *Broadcasting and Cable,* April 12, p. 30.

Gitlin, Todd. 1985. *Inside Prime Time.* New York: Pantheon.

Littleton, Cynthia. 1996. "Reality Television: Keeping the Heat On." *Broadcasting and Cable,* May 20, p. 24.

Lowry, Brian. 1993. "Ad Coin Rolls to Youth." *Variety,* December 27, p. 33.

MacDonald, J. Fred. 1990. *One Nation Under Television.* Chicago: Nelson-Hall.

Mayer, Martin. 1966. "How Good are Television Ratings?" New York: Television Information Office, Committee on Nationwide Television Audience Measurements.

———. 1970. "Television Ratings Revisited. . . . " New York: Television Information Office, Committee on Nationwide Television Audience Measurements.

McClellan, Steve. 1994. "Magazines Prime Earners in Prime Time." *Broadcasting and Cable,* May 9, p. 42.

Nielsen Media Research. 1993. *Nielsen Television Index: National TV Ratings October 11–17, 1993.*

Robins, J. Max. 1994. "Mutter Over Clutter." *Variety,* January 24–30, p. 1.

Sauter, Van Gordon. 1992. "Rating the Reality Shows—And Keeping Tabs on the Tabloids." *TV Guide* 40(May 2–8), p. 18.

Schlesinger, Philip and Howard Tumber. 1994. *Reporting Crime: The Media Politics of Criminal Justice.* Oxford: Clarendon.

Schlosser, Joe. 1997. "Big 4 Wrap Up Season with Fewer Viewers" *Broadcasting and Cable,* May 26, p. 14.

Schmuckler, Eric. 1994. "Profits, Reruns, and the End of the 'Next Generation.'" *New York Times,* July 24, Section 2, p. 29.

Setzer, Florence and Jonathan Levy. 1991. *Broadcast Television in a Multichannel Marketplace.* OPP Working Paper No. 26. Washington, D.C.: Federal Communications Commission, June.

Sharkey, Betsy. 1994. "The Secret Rules of Ratings." *New York Times,* August 28, Section 2, p.1.

III

Ideology and Social Control

5

In "The Shadow Of Shadows":
Television Reality Crime Programming

GRAY CAVENDER

This chapter addresses a contemporary television phenomenon: television reality crime programming. Reality programming broadcasts crime dramatizations or film footage of police and other emergency personnel at work as regular television series.

Two of the earliest and most successful reality programs, "America's Most Wanted" (AMW) and "Unsolved Mysteries" (UM), present a series of vignettes in which the participants or actors reenact actual crimes. The vignettes feature interviews with victims, their family and friends, the police, and photographs and film of suspects. Viewers are urged to telephone the police or the program with relevant information about the crimes or the suspects. The programs update previous broadcasts, e.g., with film of a captured fugitive or with information about sentencing.

AMW and UM employ an interesting hybrid television format. Like the news, these programs claim to present reality as they pursue a public service intention—capturing criminals. However, they also are prime time entertainment in the crime genre tradition of television programs such as "Dragnet," "Ironside," and "Magnum PI." Their emotional, fast-paced stories fit current programming trends (Blumler 1991:206–210), they have enjoyed large audiences, and, as a result, programs like AMW and UM have proliferated on television.

The law enforcement community lauds these programs, and some media scholars offer limited praise. Barber (1991:21) argues that, by sensitizing men and women to women's victimization, AMW contributes to a national feminine community; she calls the program a kind of "participatory democracy of law enforcement." However, she invokes Foucault, noting that, although AMW promotes a sense of community, the program facilitates widespread surveillance, and revives the spectacle of punishment (1991:24).

Cohen (1985:68), who also invokes Foucault, suggests that extant crime policies, by inviting citizen surveillance and reporting, redistribute the

79

state's control wider and deeper into society. Amid an already pervasive fear of crime, reality programming's depictions of criminals may encourage more repressive crime policies. And yet, obscuring this repressive potential are the crime genre's familiar symbolic themes and underlying ideology: crime symbolizes evil that must be condemned and stamped out to preserve the established social order (Schattenberg 1981). AMW and UM adopt this symbolism and ideological preference.

AMW's and UM's crime genre format also validates their reality claims. The crime genre has long been characterized by a realistic style: attention to even trivial detail conveys a sense of objective, almost cameralike reality (Krutnik 1991; Thompson 1993). These crime genre characteristics, when combined with overt reality claims, yield a verisimilitude for AMW's and UM's stories. Thus, these programs rationalize the deeper penetration of social control and, at the same time, foster television's deeper penetration into the audience's sense of reality.

Gitlin observes that the key to understanding television crime programs is to ask what they mean "as cultural objects and as signs of cultural interactions between producers and audiences" (1979:259). To understand their meaning, I examined these reality programs as cultural objects. I conducted a content analysis of nine half-hour-long AMW episodes and seven hour-long UM episodes broadcast during the 1989–1990 television season. The analysis is informed by critical media studies and the sociology of literature, especially the crime genre.

The crime genre is characterized by particular symbolic themes, an ideological preference for the conventional social order, and a realistic style. Accordingly, symbols, ideology, and realism frame the study's three analytic sections. Before turning to the analysis, I offer some comments on the crime genre.

THE CRIME GENRE

Television's crime genre references a long-standing tradition in literature and in film. Genres are types or kinds of literature, film, or television programs (Feur 1987:113). Genres are defined by repetitious, often formulaic plots and characterizations that yield predictability and stability in cultural production. They are not mutually exclusive, however. Literary works may combine genres, and, in television, genres are blurring or perhaps collapsing altogether (Fiske 1987:147). Thus, reality crime programs combine news, crime drama, and even elements of the horror genre.

The crime genre covers a large territory, from Sherlock Holmes short stories to Dashiell Hammett's hard-boiled detective novels, to films like *Beverly Hills Cop.* Even so, common plots and themes characterize the crime genre. Typically, it consists of simple plots in which villains commit a mysterious crime (usually murder), and the hero—a police officer, a private detective, a private citizen—solves the mystery by identifying, apprehending, or killing them (Knight 1980; Krutnik 1991). These repetitive plots, which take on a ritualistic, almost mythic quality, feature symbolic themes: evil threatens but good intervenes and, in the denouement, vanquishes evil (Schattenberg 1981).

Of course, myths are ideological, as are the genres that offer mythic plots (Barthes 1973; Blumler 1991:208). The crime genre affirms dominant interests and attitudes even as it offers the vicarious pleasure of suspense and freedom from restrictive bureaucratic rules (Cawelti 1988:126). Even in *film noir*, a subgenre wherein political institutions and the police often are depicted as being corrupt, the detective incorporates moral law as a personal code (Vernet 1993:17). The hero, although an iconoclastic outsider who seems to flaunt the conventional, nevertheless restores the social order (Winks 1988:8; Krutnik 1991:144). Indeed, the stability inherent in the crime genre rests not only in the formulaic conventions of cultural production, but in the degree to which these conventions reflect and reproduce a preference for a populist-type social order (Routley 1988:162–63; Vernet 1993:17–18).

This traditional ideology often goes unnoticed. The crime genre obscures its penchant for order and control behind a style so realistic that its ideology seems natural and appropriate (Deming 1985:18; Mandel 1984; Williams 1989:70).

In the sections that follow, I analyze the content of AMW's and UM's vignettes. I consider their symbols, their ideology, and their reality claim. I cite references to specific AMW or UM vignettes.

SYMBOLS

We represent and perceive the world through symbols. Widely used symbols affirm dominant social values and condemn threats to the social order (Durkheim 1964). In contemporary society, symbolic representations circulate as widely through the media as through personal interactions (Thompson 1990:19).

The media's symbolic predominance is apparent in the crime genre. With the bureaucratization of social control, media crime representations have virtually displaced the spectacle of public punishment as a vehicle for symbolically affirming moral sentiments and reproving their violation (Schattenberg 1981:72). The crime genre renders moralistic plots in which criminals, whose villainy symbolizes social malaise and disorder, threaten the established order. Their defeat resolves the plot's tension, reaffirming moral boundaries (Schattenberg 1981:74; Winks 1988:9).

Accordingly, to understanding their meaning, I consider AMW's and UM's symbolic use of malaise and resolution. In my research protocol, *symbols* included references to crime as a threat to the social order and to the resolution of that threat.

Social Malaise

As in the crime genre, crime on AMW and UM symbolizes the social malaise that threatens contemporary society. Crime is a vile social blight on AMW's and UM's landscape, representing the frustrations, the uncertainties, and the dangers of modern life: drugs figure prominently among victims and criminals; the family is victimized as children and spouses are kidnapped; and decent, hard-working people are devastated by despicable acts.

The programs offer a seemingly inexhaustible array of brutal, violent crimes. These crimes are characterized sensationally as "gruesome" or "bizarre," yet they appear commonplace, a disturbing, almost defining fact of modern life. Production techniques complement the symbolic message of chaos and threat. Slow-motion cinematography captures crimes' lurid, visual nature, and a soundtrack cues emotions like sorrow or fear. Some vignettes draw upon horror genre techniques to instill a sense of the uncanny (see Krutnik 1991:49).

AMW's and UM's criminals are recurring stereotypes, stand-ins for contemporary social concerns. The night teams with drug dealers and satanists, and crazy, cold-blooded killers prowl the mean streets of cities and small towns. The public fears what these criminals symbolize, and AMW and UM breathe life into this symbolism, giving their criminals a name and a face, and, in the process, evoke powerful symbols of disorder and social decay. Criminals are described in terms that connote physical ugliness. They are depicted as dangerous, depraved, unremorseful people.

In contrast to their loathsome criminals, AMW's and UM's victims are depicted as respectable, often physically attractive people, e.g., "a good-looking college kid" or "a pretty, young wife." The victims, who typify innocence and beauty, shape our sense of the crime problem as dirty and threatening (see Best 1989; Fiske 1994). The programs foster audience identification with these attractive victims. Family and friends personalize them, hosts speak as if they know them, and the camera dramatizes crimes from the victim's point of view. Victims recount their emotions during the crime, prompting the audience to share the victimization experience: "I was mad, then scared; he [an armed robber] could have hurt me, and then who would raise my children?" (UM, 12 April 1989). Sometimes the host speculates on the victim's fear, or encourages the audience to do so, e.g, what it is like to be "stalked by a killer." AMW's and UM's victims are like sacrificial lambs; they are innocent and vulnerable, but, as in the horror genre, the narrative moves inexorably toward their destruction (Carroll 1990). The symbolism is straightforward: the victim's plight should be felt by the audience, who are the "not yet victimized" (Pfuhl 1992).

The fear of victimization is at the heart of the social malaise that crime symbolizes (Stanko 1990). This fear reflects and reproduces a loss of trust in contemporary society (Bellah, Madsen, Sullivan, Swidler, and Tipton 1985; see Warr 1990). Misplaced trust is a frequent subplot in AMW's and UM's narratives. Seemingly normal situations and people turn out to be not so normal, again, in ways that reflect common contemporary concerns, e.g., a policeman, trusted by other officers and by citizens, molests children; a respected community leader is an escaped murderer. This standard crime genre device—the criminal as poseur—symbolizes larger issues of identity, trust, and disorder: nothing is as it seems (see Grella 1988:98; Marx 1990; Thompson 1993:132–33,147).

AMW and UM adopt the crime genre convention of crime as a symbol for social malaise. That sense of malaise creates a tension that the programs must resolve.

Resolution

The crime genre's mythic narrative constructs and then resolves a tension: the villain who threatens society is ritually defeated by the hero, restoring order. In AMW's and UM's version, crime disrupts the social order, but resolution comes with the criminal's condemnation, capture, or punishment.

AMW and UM create tension with crime genre–like plotting and characterizations. Shocking, tragic crimes not only offend common sensibilities, they disrupt life's normal routines. In one poignant vignette, a family is seated around a table upon which sits a birthday cake with lighted candles. But something is wrong with the picture: the birthday child's chair is empty; she was kidnapped (UM, 25 January 1989). In this and in other vignettes, families lament that they cannot get on with their lives until a victim's fate is known, an assailant's identity is revealed, or until a fugitive is captured. Crime undoes the rightful order of things, generating the vignette's tension.

Once generated, tension is converted into outrage that is focused on the criminal. Outrage, which follows "naturally" in the crime genre, is not left to chance on AMW and UM. Victims or their survivors explicitly express anger at the criminal, or the host conveys to the victim's family his outrage at their loss. Visuals and soundtracks heighten these emotions. A vignette about the wanton killing of a young police officer includes photographs of the officer and his family, and film footage of his funeral, including fellow officers firing a rifle salute and Taps playing (AMW, 5 February 1989).

Like the crime genre, AMW and UM give vent to outrage and resolve tension in a ritualistic catharsis. Of course, since most of the fugitives are "at large," the catharsis differs from the killings or captures that characterized most television crime drama. Instead, vignettes culminate in some form of denunciation or condemnation. In one vignette, a police officer denounces the criminal as someone who "doesn't belong in society" (UM, 15 March 1989). In another vignette, an officer notes that avoiding capture is just a game to the fugitive, and adds, "I don't want him to win this time; he doesn't have a right to win" (UM, 1 March 1989). The ultimate resolution comes in updates that combine film or photographs of a captured fugitive, often in handcuffs, with language like, "He's [the criminal] no longer a threat," or that announces a prison sentence.

Crime is a symbolic threat on AMW and UM, a malaise that affects individuals and society. These programs displace contemporary fears and frustrations onto the criminal, allowing viewers to vent their anger by fighting back against crime. Updates that delight in captured or imprisoned criminals offer resolution, and symbolically herald the restoration of the social order.

IDEOLOGY

The symbolic restoration of the established social order states an ideological preference. Indeed, the symbols that circulate in media crime presentations carry ideological meanings. Ideology constitutes a belief system that enables us to make sense of the world; its principal medium, the practice of language and consciousness, falls heavily within the domain of the mass media in contemporary society (Hall 1979:322, 340; Thompson 1990).

Dramatic fiction conveys ideology—in form, in content, even in the genres into which presentations are organized (White 1987:147). With their familiar formats and codes, genres provide an interpretative context that privileges some readings over others (Feur 1987:118). The crime genre privileges authority and order. Authority is located in the hero/detective who triumphs over evil, defining the "good" in terms of a preference for the social order (Krutnik 1991:6). The audience experiences ideological pleasure when it identifies with the detective, whose sense of justice reflects the dominant ideology (Knight 1980:4–5; Bennett and Woollacott 1987).

Genres are sensitive, at least indirectly, to ideological shifts in society (Fiske 1987:112; Kellner 1995:64). With the ascendancy of neoconservatism, the crime control model has emerged as the ideological foundation of U.S. crime policy (Stark 1987). This model posits crime as a serious threat to the social order, and is accompanied by *controltalk*, the language that discusses the crime problem and its solution (Cohen 1985:272–74). Controltalk is a form of political language; like all political language, it defines what constitutes the (crime) problem and what might be done about it (Edelman 1988). Thus, controltalk symbolically conveys ideology.

Controltalk imbues old words with new meanings, e.g., justice is stripped of due process connotations in favor of more punitive readings such as "full force of law" (Cohen 1985:149–51; Ericson, Baranek, and Chan 1991:294). Because television crime programming constantly relays and reproduces ideology, crime control ideology on reality programming seems so natural that it goes unnoticed (see Gitlin 1979:253).

Accordingly, to understand AMW and UM, I consider their appropriation of crime control ideology, and the language and consciousness that reinforce it. In my research protocol, *ideology* included references that constructed images of crime, criminals, and victims, and that favored some anticrime strategies and discredited others.

Crime Control Ideology

AMW and UM maintain both the crime genre's penchant for order and authority, and the tenets of the crime control model. As in the crime genre, a breach of order—crime—motivates the vignettes, and the action follows the effort to put things right (see Routley 1988:163).

AMW's and UM's vignettes typically open in a state of equilibrium. The soundtrack, the visuals, and the narrative convey a pastoral or small-town sense of equilibrium. Crime shatters this tranquility. Discordant music, jump cut editing, and lurid close-ups frame the criminal act, and interviews with devastated victims and families detail the resulting disruption.

Vignettes depict crime as out of control. Small towns that were safe havens in our collective nostalgia no longer are safe, and caution is no guarantee against horrible victimization, e.g., careful people are tortured and murdered. Crime appears to be random and pervasive, confirming the crime control model's view that crime has disrupted the rightful order of things.

Courage and worldly knowledge make the genre hero/detective an authority figure who puts things right (Jameson 1970:629; Mandel 1984:43). The police are authority figures on AMW and UM. The police may be clueless, but they are portrayed as "on the case." The program host is an authority figure, too. Like the genre detective, he narrates the story and exudes knowledge about the case and about crime in general. The hosts are seen examining evidence with the police or receiving praise from them, an apparent partnership that enhances authority for both.

The crime control model detaches crime from its social context, as do AMW and UM. However, they appear to do the opposite as they offer social histories of their fugitives. One vignette presents a criminal's life history, from the cycle of violence that attended his childhood—he and his mother were abused by his father—through his own brutality as an adult (AMW, 2 April 1989). But closer analysis reveals these social histories to be caricatures that describe a fugitive's life of crime, and deflect attention from the social milieu that contextualizes the behavior. In the cycle of abuse vignette, the fugitive is depicted as an obsessed man whose life is characterized by undifferentiated deviance.

Moreover, the fugitive is depicted as guilty though not yet convicted of a crime. This portrayal of guilt squares with the crime control model's working presumption of guilt (Packer 1968). Although the narratives often use cautious language, e.g., "alleged" or "only a suspect," the visuals tell a different story. In one vignette, a victim notes that his injury left him with no memory of the crime, yet the dramatization depicts the suspect clubbing the victim (AMW, 26 March 1989). In another vignette, the host reminds the audience that the person sought is only a suspect, but adds, "The police would like to talk to him so that *if* he is innocent, he can clear his name" (UM, 1 March 1989).

AMW and UM vilify liberal anticrime strategies and due process guarantees, and the criminals who benefit from them. Victims or the police claim to know a criminal's identity, but complain that burdensome evidentiary requirements impede their efforts. Vignettes feature criminals who commit serious crimes while free on bail or parole. After discrediting such wrongheaded strategies, AMW and UM privilege sterner crime control measures such as extremely high bail and maximum prison sentences without parole. The death penalty is indirectly endorsed, especially in vignettes about dangerous criminals who repeatedly escape from prison.

AMW and UM, like the crime genre, take a law and order stance. They circulate crime control ideology through their scripted and visual depictions of crime and criminals. They suggest that, if bolstered by ordinary people, our system of law and order will work (Fiske 1994:33).

Language and Consciousness

Like all political language, controltalk sets the agenda of public discourse, privileging some interpretations over others (Cohen 1985:157; Edelman 1988). AMW's and UM's vignettes reinforce a consciousness about criminals that justifies crime control–type outcomes.

The caricatured depictions portray criminals as being fundamentally different from the audience, with the victim standing in for the audience. Whether the criminal is "a born criminal" or someone who becomes psychotic, criminality is a totalizing characterization on AMW and UM; the criminal represents "the other." The differences appear in paired juxtapositions such as career criminal vs. respected worker, lazy vs. hard working, or ugly vs. attractive. Physical stigmata such as tatoos with deviant symbols and inscriptions, e.g., the grim reaper, visually cement the ideological barrier that separates them from us.

This "them vs. us" dichotomy speaks to a perceived cohesive social order, which the criminal threatens. AMW and UM evoke social cohesion with the language of solidarity. The hosts repeatedly use the word *we*, sometimes referencing a collective comprised of the police and the program, and punctuated by law enforcement referents such as "our task force." The audience is urged to assist the collective, e.g., "We need your help." In other vignettes, *we* situates the audience in the collective, and the host speaks for the whole, "We've been shocked and saddened to learn what happened to [a murdered son]; we can search for his killers while his family grieves" (AMW, 16 April 1989). The plural *you* also references membership in the collective, e.g., "You joined the manhunt."

AMW and UM thus differ from that form of crime genre construction that creates an atomistic society through which the detective walks as an outsider (Jameson 1970:633). Instead, AMW and UM foster a notion of community to which the audience can belong by watching the programs and by participating in the common effort to capture fugitives. The community exhibits a set of idealized shared values, including group commitment and even a kind of televised intimacy, e.g., the audience sees families struggle to maintain composure during an emotional interview. Some vignettes describe a neighborliness grounded in religion: the host says, "We sympathize with you and what you're going through tonight; our prayers are with you" (AMW, 26 March 1989). In other vignettes, the hosts reference the audience as a community, e.g., "Thanks for caring, thanks for helping," or, appealing to both community and patriotism, "Thanks America."

Justice is an idealized value of a moral community, although such an ideal is imbued with ideological readings (Young 1981). Justice on AMW and UM connotes the punitive outcomes of crime control ideology, e.g., "Help bring [the fugitive] to justice," or "Put him back behind bars." This sense of justice is rationalized by the language of controltalk, which casts crime as a kind of Hobbesian war (see Williams 1989:190). War imagery depicts criminals as the enemy who must be defeated if the social order is to be preserved.

REALISM

Raymond Williams characterizes television's simple tales of crime and the social order as "crude propaganda" (1989:82). With their relatively low budgets and less-than-subtle crime control ideology, AMW and UM could be dismissed as the crudest of the crude but for one important fact: they claim to present reality.

AMW and UM stake their reality claim on television formats that suggest realism: they appropriate the realistic style of the crime genre, and the televisual empiricism of the news. Accordingly, to understand their meaning, I consider AMW's and UM's reality claim in relation to the crime genre's realism, and the notion of television's visual images as an unmediated reality. In my research protocol, *reality* included references that appealed to the realism of the crime genre, or that made reality claims.

A Genred Reality

Interestingly, AMW's and UM's adherence to the crime genre format bolsters their reality claim. The crime genre adopts a seemingly realistic naturalism, which AMW and UM mimic in production style, in story construction, even in their hosts.

AMW and UM feature the sort of violent, sensational crimes that are a staple of television crime drama (Cavender and Bond-Maupin 1993). These crimes attract an audience—viewers have learned to enjoy the vicarious experience of suspense—and also maximize television's visual capabilities (Fiske 1987:147). Narratives about "real" crimes combine with the visuals to lend a sense of objective, empirical reality to their vignettes.

AMW's and UM's story construction mirrors a standard crime genre plotting device: the story opens as the detective addresses the audience, narrates the tale in flashback, and addresses the audience at the story's end (Krutnik 1991:27). An UM vignette about a murder on an isolated highway opens as host Robert Stack emerges from the shadows. Stack epitomizes the detective/storyteller as he recounts the victim's past, the dramatized murder, and addresses the audience at vignette's end (UM, 12 April 1989). AMW's vignettes open and close with host John Walsh, in the studio, addressing the audience. Walsh also plays the detective/storyteller, using argot that could be drawn from the pages of a hard-boiled detective novel, e.g., "hit the safe," "the take," and "face the music." This narrational form gives the teller and the tale the ring of authenticity (Knight 1980:140; Fiske 1987:51–53).

AMW's and UM's hosts enjoy a form of credibility that is based on audience familiarity with their prior television crime genre credits. UM's host, actor Robert Stack, played a tough federal cop on the television drama "The Untouchables." John Walsh, AMW's host, gained recognition in "Adam," a television docudrama about the tragic kidnapping of his young son. Their television credentials allow Stack and Walsh to play the role of host/crimefighter. Story construction reinforces this role, e.g., as the credits roll in one AMW episode, Walsh and the police study a map, apparently closing in on a fugitive (AMW, 12 February 1989). His and Stacks's knowledge of exact dates, locations, and other details privileges their authority, and gives the vignettes a police blotter effect that imitates the crime genre. Realism in the crime genre is an effect produced by such attention to detail (Mandel 1984:43).

AMW and UM imitate a subgenre of crime film, the "police procedural," which was popular during the forties and fifties. This subgenre was characterized by documentarylike production techniques and plots that were drawn from actual police cases (Krutnik 1991:202).

Like those films, AMW and UM employ production techniques that produce a gritty realism (Breslin 1990:93). Lighting and camera work, e.g., freeze frame and slow-motion shots, yield a sense of intense emotional reality (see Deming 1985:8). They also achieve a careful compromise between documentary and drama. Television and film establish a documentarylike realism when characters directly address the camera and the audience; dramatic characters do not address the camera (Fiske 1987:119). When AMW's Walsh directly addresses the audience as host, he establishes the program's realism; direct address also invites the audience to share his view of reality (see Deming 1985:17). At other times, the camera might catch Walsh, in his crimefighter role, seemingly unaware that a commercial break has ended, sans jacket with shirt sleeves rolled back, examining stolen gems through a jeweler's eyepiece.

AMW and UM are constructed according to the conventions of the crime genre. However, the particular subgenre they mimic conveys a sense of reality even as it conveys the dramatic.

A Television Reality

Television has entered the rhythm of contemporary life; its visual images, its sense of "being there" at events, make television the most attended and the most believable medium (Williams 1989:4). Our reality, even our criteria for what counts as real, are mediated through television, which claims to present an unmediated picture of reality. Television's phenomenal popularity, its sense of immediate and intimate reality, have made of us what Raymond Williams (1989:4) calls a "dramatized society" (Fiske 1987:21).

Williams's characterization is especially apt for reality programming; its reality claims are based on dramatized events. Although AMW and UM note that they are not news broadcasts, they establish the "reality" of their presentations with techniques that suggest the news. The hosts often introduce vignettes with crime statistics or other public service–type material that resembles news and information programming. In their closing credits, staffers are identified as reporters or correspondents.

AMW's and UM's most significant reality claim is that they dramatize actual crimes. Frequent invocations such as "police say," or "according to the police" construct a credibility premised on official sources (Fishman 1980; Chermak 1995). Not only are the police an authoritative source, narrative statements like "the police suspect" are accompanied by visuals that confirm their suspicions. AMW deliberately establishes its credibility. Broadcast from Washington, D.C., the home of federal law enforcement agencies, AMW displays its own law enforcement–type seal, and wanted posters and seals from official enforcement agencies dot its studio set. That set was designed to resemble a police squad room to enhance credibility (Breslin 1990:112).

AMW's and UM's staccatolike pace resembles the crime genre, but also reinforces their reality claims. Vignettes appear as fast-breaking stories, generating the immediacy that makes television news credible. Hosts speculate that viewer tips might locate a fugitive "tonight," or urge viewers to call "right now." The programs seem to be "live" broadcasts (AMW says "live from Washington, D.C." although it is taped), when, for example, the host communicates directly with the police or a victim. Comments like, "We'll continue to update you as developments occur," combine with frequent updates to produce a sense of immediacy.

The claim that real cops are investigating real crimes validates the hosts' crimefighter image, enhances AMW's and UM's realism, and pulls the viewer into that reality: if a television character can work with the police, so can the viewer. The programs' hybrid format reproduces television's characteristic sense of "being there." The viewer knows what the police know, and, because of the camera's omnipotence, seemingly sees events—the criminal committing the crime—that the police only suspect. Indeed, the premise of these programs is that the viewer knows more than the police, e.g., "Detectives are eager to know what you know."

The ability to see and to know is somewhat voyeuristic on these programs. In one vignette, as the camera pans through a fugitive's recently abandoned apartment, the host urges the viewer to "take a look around, take a good look" (AMW, 19 February 1989). Such intrusions are justified by vignettes that play on fear and frustration, e.g., the police and victims complain about criminals who go unpunished, who thumb their noses at the system, or who are dangerous and still "out there," while reproducing the familiar story lines of the crime genre. Through their vignettes and through direct appeal, AMW and UM urge viewers to envision a reality that consists of themselves, the police, and television, working in a common effort to fight crime.

CONCLUSION

AMW and UM have been popular programs. Their success has generated television's ultimate compliment—a nightly schedule filled with reality crime programming. This trend suggests the obvious question: What do the programs mean?

At the outset, I noted Gitlin's (1979) observation about understanding the meaning of television crime programs as cultural objects. AMW and UM are popular cultural objects, in part, because they reference a genre that enjoys a ready-made audience. The crime genre symbolizes and simplifies issues of good and evil, order and chaos. AMW and UM draw on the crime genre as, week after week, depraved criminals brutalize innocent victims who resemble the viewer. Crime in these vignettes symbolizes such contemporary concerns as the breakdown of the family, lack of trust, and loss of community.

AMW and UM are an outlet for the audience's pent-up rage, which is vented in old-fashioned moral condemnation that targets the criminal. They also are a call to arms. Like the genre hero who takes a beating but defeats the criminal, AMW and UM urge the audience to fight back. Their hosts offer a running tab of successes—crimes solved, captures, lengthy prison terms—all credited to the audience, and accompanied by the gratitude of the host, the police, or the victim's family. AMW and UM signal empowerment and community in a society where the viewer all too often has little of either.

However, AMW's and UM's view of community is a troubling one. Using the symbols of the crime genre, they cast crime as an evil that has destroyed community in contemporary society. Such scary depictions negate a real moral community—trust is forfeit, everyone is suspect—substituting a nostalgic, televised version.

Juxtaposed against this nostalgic community are AMW's and UM's criminals. These ideological caricatures draw upon a language and evoke a consciousness that legitimates the crime control model's strategies in the war against crime. If crime is the battleground in a Hobbesian war, these programs and their viewers are the combatants. Any stranger or, worse, a friend or relative, represents a threat, and viewers must be vigilant against such threats.

AMW represents vigilance with Orwellian imagery. Episodes open as a giant eye fills the television screen. The eye's watchful, raking gaze penetrates every burrow, every disguise. Updates revel in fugitives who are run to ground or surrender because television makes escape impossible. Host Walsh sums up the futility of trying to escape AMW's scrutiny, noting that a fugitive "can run but he can't hide." No one can; television's eye sees all.

This Orwellian voyeurism masquerades behind the seemingly innocuous symbols and conventions of the crime genre. By appearing as familiar entertainment, AMW and UM effectively circulate ideology as taken-for-granted common sense (Hall 1979:325). Yet, what passes as common sense is advocacy, advocacy of a kind of "carceral archipelago," a partnership of television technology and the police and the citizenry that would disperse state control wider and deeper into the social fabric (Foucault 1979:211; Cohen 1985:76–77). Through the miracle of television, the audience, with millions of ears pricked and eyes scanning, become a panoptic citizenry.

Reality programs are designed to draw the audience into this reality. The line between television fact and fiction, already indistinct (Fiske 1987:147), becomes even more hazy on these programs. Often, it is difficult to discern if a vignette is depicting a dramatization or actual footage, a suspect or an actor playing a suspect. In several instances, viewers have turned in the actor who played the fugitive in a dramatization. The audience's confusion is no surprise. Reality programming exemplifies Williams's observation that television so permeates modern life that viewers "watch the shadows of shadows and find them substance" (1989:5). Television, especially this new hybrid genre, defines reality (see Fiske 1994:xxii).

AMW, UM, and their progeny abound on television, and their meaning is clear. These programs reinforce the public's fear of crime and sentiment toward the more punitive crime control model (Stark 1987:280). Reality programming points up television's potential either to serve the common good—capturing criminals—or to create illusions that are dangerous, not only because they confuse television and reality, but because they are a powerful tool for a repressive ideology. These programs blame crime for society's ills, ranging from loss of community to the alienation and frustration that characterize contemporary life, and pin their hopes for a better future on catching and punishing criminals. Were it that simple . . .

REFERENCES

Barber, Deborah. 1991. "Women, Televised Justice, and State Surveillance in Crime Reenactments: An Examination of the Feminine in America's Most Wanted." Paper presented at Law and Society Association meeting, Amsterdam.

Barthes, Roland. 1973. *Mythologies.* London: Paladin.

Bellah, Robert, Richard Madsen, William Sullivan, Ann Swidler, and Steven Tipton. 1985. *Habits of the Heart.* New York: Harper and Row.

Bennett, Tony and Janet Woollacott. 1987. *Bond and Beyond: The Political Career of a Popular Hero.* New York: Methuen.

Best, Joel. 1989. *Images of Issues: Typifying Contemporary Social Problems.* Hawthorne, NY: Aldine de Gruyter.

Blumler, J. 1991. "The New Television Marketplace: Imperatives, Implications, Issues." Pp. 194–215 in *Mass Media and Society,* edited by J. Curran and M. Gurevitch. London: Edward Arnold.

Breslin, Jack. 1990. *America's Most Wanted: How Television Catches Crooks.* New York: Harper & Row.

Carroll, Noel. 1990. *The Philosophy of Horror.* New York: Routledge.

Cavender, Gray and Lisa Bond-Maupin. 1993. "Fear and Loathing on Reality Television: An Analysis of America's Most Wanted and Unsolved Mysteries." *Sociological Inquiry* 63:305–17.

Cawelti, John. 1988. "The Study of Literary Formulas." Pp. 121–43 in *Detective Fiction,* edited by R. Winks. Woodstock: Foul Play.

Chermak, Steven. 1995. *Victims in the News: Crime in American News Media.* Boulder, CO: Westview.

Cohen, Stan. 1985. *Visions of Social Control.* Cambridge: Polity.

Deming, C. 1985. "Hill Street Blues as Narrative." *Critical Studies in Mass Communication* 2:1–22.

Durkheim, Emile. 1964. *The Division of Labor in Society.* New York: Free Press.

Edelman, Murray. 1988. *Constructing the Political Spectacle.* Chicago: University of Chicago Press.

Ericson, Richard, Patricia Baranek, and Janet Chan. 1991. *Representing Order: Crime, Law, and Justice in the News Media.* Toronto: University of Toronto Press.

Feur, J. 1987. "Genre Study and Television." Pp. 113–33 in *Channels of Discourse,* edited by R. Allen. Chapel Hill: University of North Carolina Press.

Fishman, Mark. 1980. *Manufacturing the News.* Austin: University of Texas Press.

Fiske, John. 1987. *Television Culture.* New York: Routledge.

———. 1994. *Media Matters: Everyday Culture and Political Change.* Minneapolis: University of Minnesota Press.

Foucault, Michel. 1979. *Discipline and Punish: The Birth of the Prison.* New York: Vintage.

Gitlin, Todd. 1979. "Prime Time Ideology: The Hegemonic Process in Television Entertainment." *Social Problems* 26:251–66.

Grella, George. 1988. "The Formal Detective Novel." Pp. 84–102 in *Detective Fiction,* edited by R. Winks. Woodstock: Foul Play.

Hall, Stuart. 1979. "Culture, the Media, and Ideological Effect." Pp. 315–48 in *Mass Communication and Society,* edited by J. Curran, M. Gurevitch, and J. Woollacott. Beverly Hills: Sage.

Jameson, Fredric. 1970. "On Raymond Chandler." *Southern Review* 6:624–50.

Kellner, Douglas. 1995. *Media Culture: Culture Studies, Identity and Politics Between the Modern and the Postmodern.* London: Routledge.

Knight, Stephen. 1980. *Form and Ideology in Crime Fiction.* Bloomington: Indiana University Press.

Krutnik, Frank. 1991. *In a Lonely Street: Film Noir, Genre, and Masculinity.* London: Routledge.

Mandel, Ernest. 1984. *Delightful Murder: A Social History of the Crime Story.* Minneapolis: University of Minnesota Press.

Marx, Gary. 1990. "Fraudulent Identification and Biography." Pp. 143–65 in *New Directions in the Study of Justice,* edited by The School of Justice Studies. New York: Plenum.

Packer, Herbert. 1968. *The Limits of the Criminal Sanction.* Stanford: Stanford University Press.

Pfuhl, Erdwin, Jr. 1992. "Crime Stoppers: The Legitimization of Snitching." *Justice Quarterly* 9:505–28.

Routley, Erik. 1988. "The Case Against the Detective Story." Pp. 161–78 in *Detective Fiction,* edited by R. Winks. Woodstock: Foul Play.

Schattenberg, Gus. 1981. "Social Control Functions of Mass Media Depictions of Crime." *Sociological Inquiry* 51:71–77.

Stanko, Elizabeth. 1990. *Everyday Violence: How Women and Men Experience Sexual and Physical Danger.* London: Pandora.

Stark, Steven. 1987. "Perry Mason Meets Sonny Crockett: The History of Lawyers and the Police as Television Heroes." *University of Miami Law Review* 42:229–83.

Thompson, John B. 1990. *Ideology and Modern Culture: Critical Social Theory in the Era of Mass Communication.* Stanford: Stanford University Press.

Thompson, Jon. 1993. *Fiction, Crime, and Empire: Clues to Modernity and Post-modernism.* Urbana: University of Illinois Press.

Vernet, Marc. 1993. "Film Noir on the Edge of Doom." Pp. 1–31 in *Shades of Noir,* edited by J. Copjec. London: Verso.

Warr, Mark. 1990. "Dangerous Situations: Social Context and Fear of Victimization." *Social Forces* 68:891–907.

White, Mimi. 1987. "Ideological Analysis and Television." Pp. 134–71 in *Channels of Discourse,* edited by R. Allen. Chapel Hill: University of North Carolina Press.

Williams, Raymond. 1989. *On Television: Selected Writings,* edited by A. O'Connor. London: Routledge.

Winks, Robin. 1988. "Introduction." Pp. 1–14 in *Detective Fiction,* edited by R. Winks. Woodstock: Foul Play.

Young, Iris. 1981. "Toward a Critical Theory of Justice." *Social Theory and Practice* 7:279–302.

6

"Cops":
Television Policing as Policing Reality

AARON DOYLE

The media are very powerful institutions, yet the nature of media influence is often too narrowly conceived. There has been massive study of how individual media products may help shape the views of audiences. While this question is very important, this chapter will also consider three other forms of influence. First, media products influence each other's meanings. People do not consume them in isolation but together. An evening's television may combine accounts of crime from news, fictional drama, advertising, and reality TV, and viewers may often make sense of them through their interplay or intertextuality as a package. If we see the O. J. Simpson trial on the news, it will probably affect how we interpret a similar fictionalized trial later that night on "Law and Order." Second, mass media shape the practices of other institutions. For example, television does not simply record events in the criminal justice system. In doing so, as we will examine, it alters the actual practice of criminal justice. Finally, some theorists argue that media are not just implicated in short-term opinion formation, but in more profound long-term social and cultural shifts. Historical shifts in our media world—such as the rise of television and the penetration of its influence into many aspects of daily life—do more than just affect individual beliefs and attitudes about particular matters. Mass media are seen to influence the very nature of our subjectivities (McLuhan 1964; Poster 1990), the boundaries of our social experience (Meyrowitz 1985), our sense of what is real (Baudrillard 1988).

This chapter argues that the popular reality TV program "Cops" displays all four types of influence. Because "Cops" takes a pioneering form, these influences occur in new ways. The first half explores how, while "Cops" purports to show "raw reality," it offers a very particular vision of criminal justice. This vision has strong political implications, fostering among audiences a "law and order ideology." The second part demonstrates that "Cops" has important influences beyond this. First, "Cops" plays a key part in the intertextual media package about crime including other reality programs, advertising, fictional

95

dramas, and news. These formats all help shape one another's meanings so that this package makes a whole that is more than the sum of its parts. Second, "Cops" helps shape events in the criminal justice system itself, for example, by prompting informal rituals of "summary justice" by police, altering the experience of criminal justice for suspects and civilians, and functioning as informal promotional and teaching footage for would-be police officers. Finally, "Cops" is part of a cultural trend toward "hyperreality." "Cops" is implicated in the blurring of different ways of representing the real, and the blurring of mediated representations and the "real" world itself.

"Cops" was ground-breaking and instantly popular when it appeared in 1989. It was the first reality TV program to use actual video footage as opposed to reenactments. "Cops" put a new spin on the fly-on-the wall or *verité* documentary form. To make the program, a video and sound team has accompanied police officers in action in dozens of American cities. Suspects and other civilians recorded must sign releases giving permission for "Cops" to show them. Otherwise, their faces are digitized to conceal their identities.

As of 1996, "Cops" remained the highest rated reality TV program (Coe 1996). "Cops" and its numerous imitators succeeded partly because they are cheap to make. A "Cops" episode cost around $200,000—about a third the cost per half-hour of a typical situation comedy (Smith 1993). Television executives also found that, unlike news magazines, which dated quickly, "Cops" had a timeless quality. Episodes retained immediacy for years. This makes "Cops" suitable for countless syndicated reruns of its three-hundred-plus episodes (Freeman 1993), even as new episodes continue to air in prime time on the Fox network. "Cops" became one of the most ubiquitous American crime shows, showing twelve times a week in some areas. Two factors came together: television executives sought innovative programming to fill the expanding range of channels, while police offered massive cooperation, part of a strong trend toward increasing self-promotion in the media (Ericson, Baranek, and Chan 1989; Schlesinger and Tumber 1994).

"Cops" and similar programs also form part of the context for increasingly punitive "law and order" policies (Scheingold 1995). These include "three strikes, you're out" legislation, a prison population explosion, the rebirth of chain gangs, and the renewed rise of punishment by death. Now we will examine how and why "Cops" promotes a law and order approach to criminal justice.

IDEOLOGY

In "law and order ideology," society is seen to be in decline or crisis because of spiraling crime, specifically violent street crime of the underclasses. The answer is tougher crime control. Due process and civil rights are part of the problem, because all right-thinking people know criminals are guilty. Police themselves are not too soft; instead they are held back by others, such as liberal politicians. The answer is partly more police, and police who can get tougher.

Intertwined with the notion of a soft system is an us and them mentality: crime is a problem of evil or pathological individuals who are a them less human than us. Police are the thin blue line between them and us. Criminals are strangers, not family members. An overt profession that crime control is efficient and utilitarian is bound up with less conscious, more affectively charged undercurrents of fear and anger, identification with powerful authority, and punitiveness and retribution. Various analysts argue this punitiveness involves the displacement of anxieties and angers from other sources (Sparks 1992; Scheingold 1995). Law and order ideology is seen to touch a chord with audiences looking for a focus for their anger.

Law and order ideology is not the official position of Western justice systems. Official discourse is somewhat diverse, but is increasingly characterized by more amoral, utilitarian risk management approaches to crime. In fact, there is wide recognition among criminal justice professionals that a simple "get tough" approach does not achieve its purported aims. Law and order ideology does, however, fit traditional media templates well, because of its simplicity, drama, emotiveness, violence, and easily identifiable villains. Thus, law and order ideology has been a key political tool of the Reagan-Bush governments in the United States, of the Conservatives in Britain and of Canada's Reform party.

Ideology is meaning that fosters relations of domination (Thompson 1990). Law and order ideology displaces a different set of meanings that links crime with structural causes such as poverty and unemployment. Law and order ideology thus has wider political implications. It is often tied with other systems of meaning that construct people as us and them, notably race. Law and order ideology may speak most strongly to white audiences. Reactions to the Simpson case dramatized stark differences between white and African-American understandings of criminal justice, differences repeatedly confirmed by survey research (Flanagan and Longmire 1996). Fear and loathing of criminals thus often means nonwhite criminals. Class is another key dimension along which law and order ideology works. For example, it focuses on crimes of the lower classes, not white-collar and corporate crime.

"Cops" offers a particular view of criminal justice that fits with law and order ideology in numerous ways. How so, if "Cops" simply depicts reality? For this analysis, thirty episodes of "Cops" aired between 1991 and 1997 were reviewed in depth, along with the "Too Hot for TV" video featuring outtakes from "Cops." Some anecdotal data about audience experiences were drawn from discussions with "Cops" viewers. Information was downloaded from the official "Cops" website, including transcripts of self-interviews with two "Cops" producers. Unless otherwise noted, quotations are from these interviews. Other data came from numerous secondary academic, journalistic, and industry sources.

According to "Cops" creator and executive producer John Langley, the program is a television version of the "ride-along" in which a curious civilian tags along in a police cruiser for a shift. Its producers call it "unfiltered" television (Katz 1993:25). Langley describes it simply as "raw reality," noting, "Reality is often ironically difficult to capture because it is unstructured, unpredictable and unscripted."

However, the "raw reality" of the video footage undergoes considerable processing before it reaches the airwaves. As Langley states:

> The process begins with production in the field with producer Bert Van Munster and his staff of cameramen and soundmen and support staff. . . . All the material comes back to Los Angeles, with the field staff tagging what looks like potential *stories* [emphasis added]. Then our editorial staff cuts together the most interesting material, whereupon I determine what goes in the shows after recutting or refinessing if needed. Basically we try to put together interesting combinations. For example, an action piece (which hooks the audience), a lyrical piece (which develops more emotion), and a think piece (which provokes thought on the part of the audience).

One may note the movement in this description from "unpredictable and unscripted" reality to ready-to-air "stories" with thematic unity. "Cops" uses a variety of mechanisms to naturalize its footage as "reality." However, to turn raw reality into "stories" for television entertainment, "Cops" also skillfully introduces narrative devices such as heroes for audiences to identify with, unambiguous story lines with resolution or closure, and often a moral or theme. Now we will examine how these naturalizing and storytelling techniques promote law and order ideology.

NATURALIZATION

An opening voice-over states that " 'Cops' is filmed on location with the men and women of law enforcement." Apart from this, there is no formal narration, nor any other artifice that suggests journalism. Instead there is simply what seems to be actuality sound. As Langley puts it, "We were certainly the first, and we are still the only reality show that has no actors, no script and no host. That's as pure as you can get in documentary filmmaking."

Various modernist factual and fictional forms of storytelling use different strategies to construct realism. News employs truth-claims largely rooted in appeal to legitimate authority and its authorized forms of discourse such as science and law. Visual evidence plays more of a supporting role (Ericson, Baranek, and Chan 1987). In contrast, the realism of "Cops" is based more in the pervasive cultural understanding that "seeing is believing," the veracity of firsthand experience "straight from the horse's mouth," and emotional authenticity (it "feels real"). News at least purportedly seeks to provide audiences with the five Ws (who, what, when, where, why); "Cops" ignores some of these questions entirely (who are the civilians present, when did the events occur) and focuses instead on creating the sense that the viewer is on scene.

Langley states that the program allows the viewer "to share a cop's point of view *in real time* during the course of his or her duties" [italics added]. "Cops" condenses footage shot over much longer periods into its seven-minute vignettes. Fifty or sixty minutes of videotape are shot for each one used. Yet most of the action aired on "Cops" unfolds in a flowing linear sequence that simulates "real time." "Real time" is also suggested by a lone subtitle flashed once in most vignettes indicating the time that a particular piece of action commences: for example, "burglary call, 6: 23 P.M." This suggests that the action flows continuously from that time, as if a stopwatch had been started.

Although "Cops" is presented as though visuals and soundtrack are captured simultaneously in the raw, often the sound has actually been recorded at other times from the visuals. This allows for a subtle, frequently used device that the casual viewer may not notice, which simulates the continuing flow of "real time": continuity in sound is edited to overlap cuts in the visuals, and vice versa. For example, the continuous sound of an officer talking, radio calls, or a helicopter overhead will overlap a cut between two different visuals. The continuous sound suggests continuity in time, as if the viewer has simply looked in a different direction in the same time and place (although, in fact, an hour's worth of action and dialogue could have been omitted between the cuts). "Real time" thus suggests continuous time; however it does not attempt to inform the viewer how far removed in time the incident actually occurred by giving the calendar date (for example, 6:23 P.M., June 22, 1995). Thus "real time" also means the programs do not date easily and are suitable for reruns. "Cops" does not recede into history; instead, cops chase, wrestle, and handcuff criminals in an eternal present. While presenting the highlights of an incident in "real time" provides a fictive immediacy or "nowness" that makes "Cops" more exciting for viewers, it also has the effect of naturalizing the footage somewhat. Events unfold in an edgy, fast-forward procession that seems disconcertingly paced, yet naturalization occurs in that the actual cuts are concealed.

Any signs of the camera crew are nearly always edited out from footage of encounters between police and civilians. As the "Too Hot for TV" video reveals, this means considerable excising of civilians reacting to the camera, often with hostility.

Each segment is most often hooked on a particular officer, that vignette's "host cop," who sets the scene. The host cop (or sometimes, cops) will talk directly to the camera, most often while driving to and from an incident. Even then, the presence of the camera crew is not acknowledged. This offers the illusion that the viewer is in the car—perhaps in the role of the partner officer.

IDENTIFICATION

Much research on crime and the media uses rather simple models of how audiences interact with media texts. Such research suggests a passive linear process whereby audiences absorb faulty information or scary representations, making them misinformed or fearful. However, consumers also interact with media texts partially by identifying with particular characters (Livingstone 1990). Indeed, *verité* documentary makers sometimes deliberately structure their films to encourage identification with particular individuals (Anderson and Benson 1991:49). Good storytelling requires such protagonists.

"Cops" similarly encourages the viewer to identify with police, while distancing them from other characters shown. This provides protagonists for the story, but also reinforces the us-them dichotomy characteristic of law and order ideology. "Cops" promotes such identification through four mechanisms. Some are intended by the producers; others are simply consequences of the program's structure.

First, various categories of people shown on "Cops" are contextualized very differently. The host officer's name, rank, and department are flashed on the screen as an introduction. Other officers are often identified by name in subtitles. On the other hand, noncops remain nameless. The host cop also often provides autobiographical information, so the viewer gets to know the host personally. The officer will talk about why he—or occasionally she—joined the force, how long he/she has been a cop and so on. One officer talked about how he had joined the military and this helped him "get some discipline and maturity." Another said, "I suddenly realized I couldn't sit behind a desk. . . . I wanted to get out and make a difference."

Sometimes the viewer even accompanies the host through his off-duty daily routine. One officer was shown making tea in his kitchen with his wife, who was also a cop. The viewer accompanied the officer to the pub after work, joining in police camaraderie there, and spent more off-duty time with him enjoying his vintage Daimler car.

Civilians shown are stripped of similar human background. The television spotlight focuses on the brief moment of police intervention, and does not provide any social context for the noncops portrayed or the alleged crimes. When any context is given, it is likely to be the suspect's criminal record. For example, after a young African-American man was arrested, an officer stated, "We've been chasing this guy around for years. He's got a drug problem. He was just arrested last week. He just got out of jail today. It just worked out pretty good. We just happened to be right there." When civilians have their faces blurred, this further depersonalizes them.

Second, "Cops" encourages identification with police through its use of point of view. The lone camera simulates a single viewpoint—that of the police officer. This resembles the point-of-view shot used in film fiction to simulate the view of a particular character. Thus, while viewers get up close and personal with the host cop, they are also positioned on scene as if they themselves were cops. For example, the viewer gets a cops-eye-view through the cruiser window of the hunt for fleeing suspects. This technique is explicitly acknowledged by the producers: "The goal is to put you (the viewer) in the passenger seat with them *so you can experience what it's like to be a cop*" (emphasis added). Thus, the "raw reality" the producers talk about elsewhere is discussed here as "reality" from a particular point of view.

Third, the officers shown describe the sensations and satisfactions of their work, encouraging the viewer to share them. Thus, viewers can identify with authorized power and its pleasures. One officer described his job as "like Disneyland." Another said after an arrest, "I enjoyed that. It's a nice way to end the night." A third said, "I suppose the best thing is you never know what's going to happen next. Occasionally you get something exciting happening and it makes all the boring bits worthwhile." Another host said, "I don't like thieves. . . . I've had two cars stolen over the last ten years. When I pop a car thief and get to chase him and catch him, that's a good high there."

Finally, identification is also bound up with the program's voyeuristic aspects. The supervising producer, Murray Jordan, suggests that "Cops" is successful because of the "inherent voyeuristic interest that most human beings have." Scholarly analysts have also pointed out a voyeuristic quality in reality crime programs (Bondjeberg 1996; Andersen 1996). Voyeurism is taking pleasure from viewing the private or forbidden. The viewer overrules the wishes of others that the object of viewing remain secreted. Viewing may thus be experienced as an act of domination. The voyeurism of "Cops" is intertwined with its authoritarian pleasures. The seductions or pleasures of one type of power—voyeuristically intruding into the private or forbidden— are meshed with the seductions of another type of power—identifying with the sanctioned authority of the police.

A warning that "viewer discretion is advised" because of the "graphic nature" of the program may contribute to this sense of voyeurism. Concealing subjects' faces also adds a frisson of voyeurism, suggesting the viewer is being allowed to see "private" incidents.

Survey research shows that viewers who report greatest enjoyment of "Cops" and similar programs tend to be young males (Oliver and Armstrong 1995). A small portion of the material on "Cops" is explicitly sexual and seems aimed at a heterosexual male viewer. One opening montage began with a close-up of a woman's bikini-clad torso, from which the camera pulled back to establish that the location was a Miami beach. The "Too Hot for TV" video marketed by "Cops" producers contains more explicit sexually voyeuristic material. This includes footage of a sting operation in which the viewer is positioned with cops hiding behind a one-way mirror, pressing against the glass to get a good view of seminaked female prostitutes with their male customers. Another televised vignette featured the arrest of a teenaged girl who allegedly led police on a drunken car chase. Tearful and not apparently resisting the police, the teenager, clad in shorts and a revealing halter top, was kept in handcuffs in the station for an extended period as the camera lingered on her body. Such sexually voyeuristic sequences are apparently included by the producers because they help sell the program. Yet the explicit interplay of police power and voyeuristic power may also contribute to viewer identification with the authoritarian pleasures of policing.

CLOSURE

A second key storytelling mechanism is closure—editing the footage to create a relatively unambiguous story line. Often this story line encourages viewers to interpret events in ways consistent with law and order ideology.

The speech of police is edited together to tell the stories, essentially using police as informal narrators. The words of the host cop and other officers, from briefings and from police radio, are subtly stitched together, overlaying various visual sequences. This spliced-together narration often imposes a story line that makes sense of a jumble of video imagery that would otherwise be meaningless or ambiguous. To understand what is going on, viewers must rely heavily on the police interpretation of events, rather than the video record itself.

For example, one episode featured a raid on an alleged drug dealer's home. Without the host cop's explanation, all the viewer would have seen would have been a short confusing set of images, featuring some figures in body armor running through the darkness, several explosions in the night, the sound of breaking glass, then men in body armor standing in a hallway, and a woman lying face down on the floor. However, on the way to the scene, an officer told the viewer that the man inside the house carried a shotgun at all times and had bragged about blowing another man's head off. The cop described the villain as "very paranoid, has a bulletproof vest, goes to the bathroom with a shotgun in his hand, has vowed to kill any law-enforcement officers that come on the property." Then there was the short burst of images described above, lasting perhaps twenty seconds. An officer narrated after the fact, "These doors were locked back here. We had to break them. We got one suspect on the ground right here. We got a shotgun (not shown). He's the dude we were thinking about." In this segment of reality TV, the reality was the narrative constructed by the officer. Only through his words did the viewer know that police had succeeded in controlling a dangerous criminal.

Good storytelling means removing confusion from the plot. Police accounts—and how they are edited—serve to partially close off alternative readings of the televised events. One officer on "Cops" said to a suspect who protested his innocence, "That's something that the courts are going to have to determine." However, in the very next vignette, "Cops" pronounced who the guilty party was in a highly ambiguous situation. A police cruiser pulled up on a suburban street to a scene where one man, brandishing a baseball bat, had beaten another man who was sitting on the road. The beaten man staggered up with one eye swollen shut, in tears and moaning, "I'm hurt bad. I need help." The bat-wielding man said the beaten man had tried to break into his house, but the other man denied it, saying he was just walking by. A foiled burglary or a brutal assault on a passerby? Police made a decision. An officer said to the man with the bat, "You want to press charges for prowler, right?" The cop directed the bat-wielding man to place the injured man under "citizen's arrest," even though the injured man was lying on a stretcher in an ambulance by then. One officer commented that the beaten man "lives in (another suburb). That's kind of a bad area." He asked, "Why is he coming down to this area? It makes no sense." Another cop was given the last word by the editors, saying the beaten man was "a prowler and a thief who got caught. A prowler with a broken jaw."

Making that the last word provided a neat wrap-up, avoiding any ambiguity that might leave the audience more troubled than entertained. The result was that the incident was constructed in terms of social class, as though it was clear that the "bad guy" was the one who came from a "bad area."

Some officers even seem to try to obtain forms of on-the-spot resolution to wrap up the stories. Another ambiguous situation arose when an African-American mother had apparently abandoned her baby: did she flee because of threatened violence from the baby's father, or was she simply guilty of neglect? The moral confusion was resolved when the host cop took the camera crew right into the woman's jail cell. He elicited from her that there was no threat of violence, thus demonstrating her guilt for the viewer, and clarifying the story line.

While "Cops" announces that "all suspects are innocent until proven guilty in a court of law," all the evidence viewers ever get says they are guilty. Events have only one story line, and it can be swiftly diagnosed and dealt with by police. Police are the ones who know the reality of events. This creates an "illusion of certainty," as Haney and Manzolati argue concerning fictional police dramas. "Police work . . . is fraught with uncertainty. . . . [T]his image of sureness and certainty may actually create in the minds of most viewers a presumption of guilt" (1988:127). Haney and Manzolati's survey found that heavy television viewers were significantly more likely than light viewers to believe that defendants "must be guilty of something, otherwise they wouldn't be brought to trial."

There is usually a closing comment or "last word" from a cop, voiced over a black screen featuring only the "Cops" logo. Some "last words" simply sum up events to create closure. Others provide a moral for the story. These morals—interpretations of the events by frontline cops—often reinforce aspects of law and order ideology. For example, after two suspected burglars would not admit their guilt, the officer's "last word" was that this was "just a sign of the times." Other morals spoke to the comfort of police protection in an uncertain world. These included: "That's it for today. Who knows what might happen tomorrow?" and "We'll be sleeping safely in the knowledge that the night shift are on." Frequently, the last word emphasizes that "lives have been saved" or "someone could have been killed." A vignette where an officer decided not to arrest a suspected drunk driver concluded with a moral about due process: "It's a pity . . . I couldn't get him off the street. He's probably going to kill someone." A similar moral concerned the need to get tough with teenagers. After some youths were arrested, a cop noted: "They'll go ahead and say 'release them to their parents'. . . . They may not spend the night in jail. That's kind of frustrating. . . . [T]hey may be kiddie crooks but they grow up to be adult crooks."

SELECTION OF EVENTS AND SITUATIONS

Other reality programs such as "America's Most Wanted" and "Unsolved Mysteries" focus on statistically rare serious crimes, notably homicides (Cavender and Bond-Maupin 1993). "Cops" tends to feature more common crimes such as burglaries, robberies, less serious assaults, street-level drug busts, domestic disturbances, and incidents involving intoxication. Nevertheless, in some ways, "Cops" offers a highly selective picture of criminal justice. Oliver's (1994) content analysis indicates "Cops" (and four other reality shows) overrepresent both violent crime and the proportion of crime solved by police. Oliver found that 69 percent of suspects on these programs were portrayed as arrested, a dramatic increase over actual arrest statistics. In these respects, "Cops" resembles most fictional portrayals of crime (Reiner 1992:Chapter 5). More generally, "Cops" tends to show cases where police apparently deal effectively with situations, swiftly diagnosing trouble and resolving it.

"Cops" also rarely airs material that would reflect negatively on police. Two factors explain this: the producers depend on ongoing police cooperation, and producers themselves internalize propolice attitudes.

Many police forces are keen to cooperate with "Cops," part of a trend toward increasing police self-promotion. However, the content of "Cops" is shaped more by the interpretations of frontline officers than it is by officialdom (although officers who appear on "Cops" are likely carefully vetted by management). These frontline officers are immersed in "cop culture" (Reiner 1992), which resonates well with law and order ideology.

The relationship between police and media in making "Cops" can be compared to police-journalist relations. Journalists often depend heavily on official police sources (Fishman 1980). Ericson et al. (1989) describe an inner circle and outer circle of police reporters in Toronto. While outer-circle reporters are more adversarial, inner-circle reporters are very friendly with police sources and internalize police ideology. They have access to more information, but also self-censor to maintain close ties with these sources. The producers of "Cops" resemble inner-circle reporters—yet their dependence on police is even greater. There is no subcultural valorization of at least some degree of critical journalistic autonomy. Nor does the "Cops" format feature any perceived requirement for balance.

The producers of "Cops" also acknowledge that, like inner-circle reporters, they have internalized pro-police attitudes. Langley said:

> If you had asked me . . . in the 60s, I would have laughed and said I would never do a show called "Cops." Maybe "Pigs" but not "Cops." Of course I was brash and immature back then. . . . I have developed a profound respect for police officers. . . . They put their lives at risk for others, and I think that's both admirable and inspirational.

One "Cops" producer said she had been approached by several police forces about signing up as a cop herself (Bernstein 1992). Debra Seagal, a former editor at a similar reality show, "American Detective," noted that the camera crews for that program "even wear blue jackets with 'Police' in yellow letters on the back. . . . The executive producer . . . frequently wears a badge on his belt loop" (Seagal 1993).

A Kansas City officer who had a "Cops" crew on his midnight shift for two weeks told *Time* magazine:

Most officers would be apprehensive to have the media ride with them. . . .
But these guys proved themselves to us. They said that they wouldn't do
anything to undermine us, and that we'd have final discretion about what ran.
(Zoglin 1992)

Time reported that "each episode of 'Cops' is reviewed by the police before
airing, in part to make sure no investigations are compromised."

Thus, "Cops" is highly unlikely to air footage that makes police look bad.
As Katz (1993:27) argued:

The cameras recording "Cops" would probably not catch a Rodney King
style beating. The officers would know better than to behave like that; even if
they didn't, it's unclear whether the broadcast's producers would show it, since
the program depends on the voluntary co-operation of the police.

For example, as reported in the *Seattle Times* (Scattarella 1992), in May
1992 a "Cops" crew recorded the scene as police on a drug raid burst into a
suburban Washington State home. They rousted a couple and their children
from sleep, and handcuffed the half-naked woman before finally realizing
they were in the wrong house. The woman complained, "They pulled me
out of bed and put a gun on me. Here I am with my butt showing, and I see
the camera." Police apparently had the wrong address on the warrant.
"Cops" decided not to broadcast any of that raid.

Seagal (1993:55) described an incident she reviewed on "American Detective" videotape:

Our cameramen, wearing police jackets, are in one of the [Santa Cruz police]
undercover vans during the pursuit [of two Hispanic suspects]. . . . One of [the
cameramen] has his camera in one hand and a pistol held high in the other.
The police don't seem to care about his blurred role. . . . [T]he suspects are
pinned to the ground and held immobile while cops kick them in the stomach
and the face. . . . Our secondary cameraman holds a long, extreme closeup of
a suspect while his mouth bleeds into the dirt. One producer shakes his head at
the violence. "Too bad," he says. "Too bad we can't use that footage." This was
clearly a case of too much reality for reality-based TV.

"Cops" is also selective in its portrayal of race. This reinforces ties between law and order ideology and racism. Oliver (1994) demonstrated that
five reality programs including "Cops" underrepresent African-Americans
and Hispanics and overrepresent whites as police officers, while overrepre-
senting minorities and underrepresenting whites as criminals. "Cops" also
omits any portrayals of overtly racist behavior by police. Management
would not let overtly racist officers on the program; officers who were filmed
would likely censor their behavior. Furthermore, even if such material was
recorded, producers would likely not air it. According to survey research (of

white viewers only), viewers who report greater enjoyment of reality programs including "Cops" also tend to show higher levels of racial prejudice
(Oliver and Armstrong 1995).

The many episodes of "Cops" reviewed for this chapter focused exclusively on "street crime," most often in poorer neighborhoods. This focus was
confirmed in a *Los Angeles Times* interview with a "Cops" coproducer:
"Most often, it's poor neighborhoods where 'Cops' goes for its stories" (Bernstein 1992). Wealthy areas, while often host to the same domestic abuse and
robbery problems that make up the program's stable of policing situations,
are disdained as not crime-ridden enough. "Traditionally, we don't go and
ride in those areas," the coproducer said. Things that happen in places like
Beverly Hills, she said, "aren't the kind of things that are stories for us on the
show" (Bernstein 1992). Thus law and order ideology is intertwined with
wider issues of class.

LAW AND ORDER IDEOLOGY AND AUDIENCES

Clearly not all audiences will simply accept that "Cops" is reality. Yet
audience research suggests many viewers largely do see it this way. A survey
of 358 television viewers in Wisconsin and Virginia by Oliver and Armstrong
(1995) showed that audiences perceive "Cops" and four similar programs as
significantly more realistic than crime fiction. Andersen (1996) notes that,
according to a 1993 *Times-Mirror* survey, viewers tend to think of reality
crime shows as informational programming rather than entertainment. Industry research also suggests that many viewers see "Cops" as very similar to
local news (Freeman 1993).

Not all viewers will take "Cops" the same way, and some will subvert its
meanings. Yet many viewers are already inclined toward law and order
ideology, and these are the people to whom "Cops" will most likely appeal.
This is confirmed by Oliver and Armstrong. Their survey found that reality
programs like "Cops" "were most enjoyed by viewers who evidenced higher
levels of authoritarianism, reported greater punitiveness about crime and
reported higher levels of racial prejudice" (1995:565). Another survey
showed that regular viewers of "Cops" and three other reality programs were
significantly more fearful than infrequent viewers of being sexually assaulted, beaten up, knifed, shot, or killed (Haghighi and Sorensen 1996:23).

The influence of crime in the media on audiences has been very extensively researched (Gunter 1987; Sparks 1992). There are repeated findings of
a strong tendency for viewers who watch large amounts of crime on television to be more afraid of crime and more inclined toward law and order.
However, the extent to which each circumstance causes the other has
proved difficult to isolate. Do people want more law and order because they

watch crime on TV, or vice versa? The relationship is most likely one of mutual reinforcement. Like many media products, "Cops" is not exactly "preaching to the converted," but more preaching to those who lean that way—reinforcing fear of crime and law and order views among people already predisposed to those views.

It is particularly hard to demonstrate empirically how media may reinforce existing viewpoints (Livingstone 1996). Nevertheless, mainstream and critical communications literature converge on one point—the strongest socializing influence of media may be precisely that: to reinforce existing views (Curran 1996).

INTERTEXTUALITY

So far, we have discussed "Cops" mostly in isolation of other media products. However, another key form of influence is that media products help shape the meanings consumers make of other media products. This notion of interplay or intertextuality is well established (Fiske 1987). However it has been little considered in specific analyses of crime in the media. Most consider either news, entertainment, or reality TV in isolation, or else treat them as discrete components of media content that may be considered in additive fashion. This ignores the extent to which these media products are intertwined and mutually constitutive.

A striking facet of Fox's Saturday night lineup is the interplay between different elements. "Cops" is repeatedly situated as part of a broader television package related to fear and loathing of street crime. Ads during "Cops" said viewers could stay tuned afterward to "help the cops catch a killer on 'America's Most Wanted'" because "it's a night of nonstop action on Q13." One segment of "Cops" immediately cut from the closing credits to a slogan saying: "Real Cops," an ad for "Top Cops," another reality program, which features reenactments of heroic police moments. Back-to-back episodes of "Cops" were followed immediately by "Front Page," a news magazine that featured segments on the kidnapping and strangling of a young girl, on "gangsta" rap music, and on "locking up drug dealers . . . how one state sends first-time drug dealers to prison—for the rest of their lives."

Ads repeatedly asked "Cops" viewers to phone in with information to help the "Greater Vancouver Crimestoppers" and "Western Washington's Most Wanted" programs track down wanted criminals. Also interspersed were repeated ads for Pepper Mace spray. Airing in the Christmas season, these suggested Pepper Mace "makes a great stocking stuffer."

"Cops" and "America's Most Wanted" are sometimes even tied together thematically: for example, they featured back-to-back episodes set in New Orleans for Mardi Gras. "America's Most Wanted" is much more overtly ideological, and "Cops" will be read in the context of this. For example, one episode of "Cops" featured vignettes of a suspected assault/child neglect case, a drug raid, and a car chase. The closing "Cops" credits ran on half a split screen. On the other half, with a backdrop of dramatic fictional crime footage, "America's Most Wanted" host John Walsh offered a monologue. This monologue encapsulated law and order ideology:

> You know what I'm sick of? Criminals who serve only a fraction of their sentences. Sexual predators who are released to live next door to you and your children and you don't even know it. Drug dealers who think they run these streets. This is a society where criminals have all the rights and victims don't have any. Well, it's going to change. You're going to make that happen. The new "America's Most Wanted." America fights back. Premieres next Saturday after "Cops" on nonstop Fox.

An immersion in the "real crime" of "Cops" offers a strong priming for this appeal.

More broadly, accounts of crime from news, entertainment, and other sources are often consumed in juxtaposition. Being viewed alongside news may add an immediacy to crime dramas like "Law and Order"; being viewed alongside such dramas may add dramatic impact to crime news. "Cops" occupies a special place in this mix. Episodes of "Cops" are often broadcast right after the six o'clock news, bridging the gap between the news and prime time crime. This bridging is both literal and figurative. Twentieth Television syndication president Greg Meidel said the interplay between "Cops" and news is key to its success in this slot:

> All our research indicates that viewers closely identify "Cops'" content with that of similar sorts of law enforcement coverage on newscasts locally. That's why "Cops" has been so compatible as a lead-in or lead-out from local news programming. It looks, feels and tastes like a first-run news program. (Freeman 1993)

Yet, if viewers see "Cops" as resembling news, its storytelling also resonates extremely well with fictional television crime. "Cops" has the simple, unambiguous narrative structure, pumped-up action, heroic police protagonists, high arrest rate, and illusion of police certainty characteristic of much fictional crime drama. Like many such dramas, the action on "Cops" also ends with closure or summary justice at the arrest stage of the criminal process. "Cops" takes place in linear "real time" in a fictional present rather than being a past-tense summary of events like news. The presence of the camera is not acknowledged on "Cops," which is also characteristic of fictional or dramatic realism. If people see "Cops" as fictional crime on television, such fiction may become more realistic for them.

More generally, viewers will draw on experience of one media format to interpret others. Thus, "Cops" and other media visions of crime together make a package that is more than the sum of its parts.

MEDIA LOGIC

"Cops" does not simply influence viewers; it also shapes practices and situations in the criminal justice system itself. Altheide and Snow (1979) explored numerous ways in which the requirements of mass media lead to the reformatting of practices in other institutions such as sports, religion, and politics. "Cops" also exerts this kind of influence, which Altheide and Snow call "media logic." Indeed, "Cops" helps constitute events in the justice system, so that criminal justice events also become media events. "Cops" does not simply offer a distorted representation of some "real world" of policing; "Cops" helps shape that world. "Cops" illustrates that "media do not merely report on events but rather participate directly in processes by which events are constituted and exist in the world" (Ericson 1991:219).

The justice system is displaying "media logic" by increasingly shaping some of its day-to-day practices to be media-friendly. For example, Altheide (1995) describes situations of "gonzo justice," where judges pass spectacular individualized sentences apparently targeted to achieve media attention. These sometimes even directly involve media in their execution, for example, forcing convicts to buy advertising shaming themselves.

As reality TV, "Cops" is the example par excellence of how media directly affect criminal justice practices. There are numerous indications that police tailor their behavior for the program. Outtakes reveal both police and camera crews giving stage directions during "real" incidents. In many cases on-the-spot interrogations of suspects or conferences between officers seem conducted for the camera's benefit. Some police operations seem ready-made for "Cops" (although there is no direct evidence they are prompted by the program's needs). In one, a Mack truck was intentionally abandoned in poor urban areas. Police and cameras were concealed in the truck. Soon, local youths, usually African-American or Hispanic, would break in to see what valuables might be contained inside. This resulted not only in ready-made arrests but also ready-made footage for "Cops."

Another example of how media logic reshapes criminal justice is the emergence of informal rituals of punishment involving the media. For example, police sometimes parade suspects in handcuffs in strategic locations so they can be photographed by the news media—a kind of shaming ritual sometimes called the "perp walk" (Doyle and Ericson 1996). Parallel practices are evident on "Cops." Police sometimes seem to try to produce an on-the-spot resolution to meet the storytelling needs of "Cops." One way this happens is that some suspects are subjected to police lectures that are like informal shaming rituals. These offer summary justice, providing a wrap-up and/or a ready-made moral for the vignette. Of course, police often engage in such lectures even without the camera, but the camera's presence re-defines the situation dramatically, making the punishment something more than it would be (whether or not the footage is eventually aired). For example, a man driving to a funeral with his family was pulled over by police, and caught with a small amount of marijuana. Instead of being charged, he was given instant informal punishment: a roadside lecture by police in front of a television camera.

More generally, "Cops" reshapes criminal justice by altering the experience of civilians who are recorded. Certain suspects are excited by the camera's attention, and many do sign the releases. However, being video-taped may be an intrusive and humiliating experience for other civilians, whether suspects, witnesses, or victims, and whether or not they give consent to air the footage. Nor does the blurring always effectively conceal their identities. In one incident, the identity of a fourteen-year-old alleged statutory rape victim was revealed on "Cops" without her permission or that of her family (Harris 1991).

"Cops" also reshapes criminal justice by influencing police and would-be police who are viewers. There has been little research on how crime in the media affects the particular audience of criminal justice personnel. Mary Beth Oliver, who has studied "Cops" extensively, said that police academy instructors indicate that these shows have inspired many of their students to enter law enforcement. The students' "whole idea of what it means to be a police officer is based on these very shows," Oliver said (Perigard 1995). Similarly, one would-be police officer interviewed for this research saw regular viewing of "Cops" as part of his training: each episode taught him how to deal with particular situations.

These examples demonstrate that the various influences of "Cops" on the justice system are much more pervasive than is first apparent. "Cops" has televised over nine hundred vignettes of police activity. This means that the program has recorded five thousand to ten thousand hours of policing since 1989. "Cops" has thus affected numerous instances of police activity and touched the lives of many individuals in this way. However, "Cops" has effects far beyond this. It has spawned many imitators such as "American Detective," "LAPD: Life on the Beat," "To Serve and Protect," and Britain's "Blues and Twos" (Corner 1996:184). In fact, in St. Petersburg, Florida, the increasing media consciousness of police has pushed this influence to the next step. Local police now bypass the media and produce their own "Cops"-style reality program, "Police Report," on cable television. These police sometimes take videocameras along as they work and film their own activities for the show (Getz 1995).

Videocameras are increasingly omnipresent in criminal justice, and "Cops" has tried to reach out to all of them. The official "Cops" website has advertised an appeal to "officers, deputies, corrections officers, troopers" and others: "The producers of 'Cops' are looking for amazing, unusual, exciting or weird videotape. Crazy arrests, angry suspects, hot pursuits, bloopers from in car cameras, camcorders, surveillance cameras." The footage was sought for a new video, "Caught on Camera." First prize for the best footage was a trip to Hawaii.

Thus, the media logic of "Cops" had penetrated throughout the justice system. Any footage from any videocamera in the system at any time might potentially appear on "Cops." Increasingly, every criminal justice moment might become a media event.

CONCLUSIONS

There has been vast research on how individual media products affect the views of audiences. This chapter has shown that, while important, this is too narrow a conception to fully capture the profound ways in which media shape our social world. Certainly, "Cops" influences many viewers' attitudes. It demonstrates strongly how the storytelling of mass media can be ideological. Its techniques shape "raw reality" into made-for-TV stories that reinforce existing inclinations among many audience members toward law and order ideology. Yet this is only one way of thinking about its influences. We have also explored how, as reality TV, "Cops" plays a unique role in a broader media package about crime. It affects how we make meanings of other media accounts of crime in news, entertainment, and advertising, even as they, in turn, influence how we understand "Cops." Third, the chapter has shown how "Cops" not only portrays events and practices in the criminal justice system, but it actually helps reshape them. For example, it not only records arrests; it helps shape how they are conducted and experienced by the participants, and even how some future police officers may conduct their arrests.

To conclude, we will consider a fourth, broader way of thinking about media influence. Some theorists have stressed the central role of the mass media in profound long-term processes of social and cultural change. "Cops" is implicated in one such tendency. Some of the aspects of "Cops" discussed above make it increasingly difficult to distinguish what is fact and what is fiction, what is television and what is "real." This brings us finally to consider the notion of "hyperreality" (Baudrillard 1988):

> Hyperreality is a postmodern sense of the real that accounts for our loss of certainty in being able to distinguish clearly and hierarchically between reality

and its representation and in being able to distinguish clearly and hierarchically between the modes of its representation. (Fiske 1994:62)

The expanding penetration of media into all aspects of social life and the mutation of media products into new and hybrid forms are profoundly implicated in the tendency toward hyperreality. Despite its claim to be "raw reality," "Cops" exemplifies this trend toward the blurring of different modes of reality.

Baudrillard (1988) has described the emergence of the "more real than real," hyperreal realms of experience more intense and involving than banal everyday life. "Cops" has a formal property described earlier as "real time," which steps outside the pace and flow of conventional time and places the viewer in a new uncertain "time zone." "Real time" is not simply fictional time: sensory input indicates continuity. Yet things unfold at a strangely rapid pace, and not at a fixed point on the calendar, but in a kind of eternal present. "Real time" fits with Baudrillard's description of the "more real than real."

Reality TV also crosses boundaries between factual and fictional storytelling, and unsettles our hierarchy of the real this way. While there has always been interplay between crime fact and crime fiction, a more recent trend is hybridization. A key example is "America's Most Wanted" with its mix of artifice that suggests journalism with fictional techniques such as actors recreating situations (Cavender and Bond-Maupin 1993). Such programs are part of a broader cultural trend toward blurring of different modes of the real in storytelling (Bondjeberg 1996).

Some of the more baroque reality TV efforts have mixed forms in more outlandish ways. They disturb our sense of what is real by moving "real crime" toward the surreal. For example, the recent program "America's Dumbest Criminals" attempts reality-based crime comedy, featuring both interviews and reenactments. A local police show in Houston, Texas, named "2 Catch a Crook," even introduced a game show element. The program featured a "Catch of the Day." A police host—who became a local celebrity—spun a "Wheel of Misfortune" featuring mug shots, in order to choose a "Bonus Suspect" (Rust 1992).

"Cops" also moves us toward hyperreality by blurring news and entertainment. As industry research suggests, "Cops" is like another form of news for many viewers; however, structurally, its storytelling closely resembles crime fiction. Some "Cops" imitators have taken the blurring of factual and fictional even further. One short-lived program, "DEA," adopted a "Cops"-style *cinema verité* form, but used actors and was apparently a work of dramatic fiction with no claim to being reality-based. One television critic somewhat tentatively listed "DEA" among new reality programs, while noting, "it's difficult to decipher that it isn't real" (Froelich 1991).

As we have discussed, "Cops" does not simply depict the reality of criminal justice. It actually helps constitute that reality, by shaping events in the criminal justice system itself. Thus, "Cops" is also hyperreal in blurring the worlds of television and "real life." For example, the possibility police officers may one day appear on "Cops" suggests a continuity between their working worlds and the world of crime on TV. Consider the blurring realities of one California police officer, who was being recorded in action for "Cops." He and his wife were also big fans of the show: "I watch it all the time. . . . I like the action . . . which is also what I like about being out here [on the beat]. It's an adrenalin rush. It's what a lot of us like about police work—the excitement" (Bernstein 1992). How did viewing many previous episodes of "Cops" shape his behavior when "Cops" actually began recording him on the job? For police officers being recorded, "Cops" may represent a fantasy come true in that they have become cops after being raised on the fictional heroics of police crime dramas. Now they have their chance to be a "television hero."

The expression "reality television" encapsulates the notion of hyperreality by collapsing the real and the represented into one. This chapter has shown how sometimes police carry videocameras during their operations, simultaneously making arrests and producing their own television shows; at other times television crews wear badges and carry guns, chasing down suspects even as they film them. With the advent of reality TV, the blurring of the two institutions reaches a dreamlike extreme. In its contribution to the mixing of factual and fictional realms and to the increasing penetration of television into all aspects of social life, "Cops" pushes us toward the hyperreal.

Yet hyperreality itself is ideological: its shifting kaleidoscope of real and represented can be a spellbinding distraction. "Cops" is about hyperreality but, more importantly, it is about a brute reality: the punitive politics of law and order.

REFERENCES

Altheide, David. 1995. *An Ecology of Communication: Cultural Formats of Control.* Hawthorne, NY: Aldine de Gruyter.

Altheide, David and Robert Snow. 1979. *Media Logic.* Beverly Hills, CA: Sage.

Andersen, Robin. 1996. *Consumer Culture and TV Programming.* Boulder, CO: Westview.

Anderson, Carolyn and Thomas Benson. 1991. *Documentary Dilemmas.* Carbondale: Southern Illinois University Press.

Baudrillard, Jean. 1988. *Selected Writings.* Cambridge, England: Polity.

Bernstein, Sharon. 1992. "The Force Is with Her." *Los Angeles Times,* October 6, p. F1.

Bondjeberg, Ib. 1996. "Public Discourse/Private Fascination: Hybridization in 'True-Life-Story' Genres." *Media, Culture and Society* 18:27–45.

Cavender, Gray and Lisa Bond-Maupin. 1993. "Fear and Loathing on Reality Television: An Analysis of America's Most Wanted and Unsolved Mysteries." *Sociological Inquiry* 63(3):305–17.

Coe, Steve. 1996. "The Reality of Realities: Lower Numbers." *Broadcasting and Cable,* January 15.

Corner, John. 1996. *The Art of Record: A Critical Introduction to Documentary.* Manchester, England, and New York: Manchester University Press.

Curran, James. 1996. "Rethinking Mass Communications." Pp. 119–65 in *Cultural Studies and Communications,* edited by J. Curran, D. Morley, and V. Walkerdine. London: Arnold.

Doyle, Aaron and Richard Ericson. 1996. "Breaking Into Prison: News Sources and Correctional Institutions." *Canadian Journal of Criminology* 38(2):155–90.

Ericson, Richard. 1991. "Mass Media, Crime, Law and Justice: An Institutional Approach." *British Journal of Criminology* 31(3):219–49.

Ericson, Richard, Patricia Baranek, and Janet Chan. 1987. *Visualizing Deviance: A Study of News Organization.* Toronto, Ontario: University of Toronto Press; Milton Keynes, England: Open University Press.

———. 1989. *Negotiating Control: A Study of News Sources.* Toronto, Ontario: University of Toronto Press; Milton Keynes, England: Open University Press.

Fishman, Mark. 1980. *Manufacturing the News.* Austin: University of Texas Press.

Fiske, John. 1987. *Television Culture.* London: Methuen.

———. 1994. *Media Matters: Everyday Culture and Political Change.* Minneapolis: University of Minnesota Press.

Flanagan, Timothy and Dennis Longmire (eds.). 1996. *Americans View Crime and Justice: A National Public Opinion Survey.* Thousand Oaks, CA: Sage.

Freeman, Mike. 1993. "Ratings Are Reality for Off-Net." *Broadcasting and Cable,* April 12, p. 30.

Froelich, Janis. 1991. "Drama in Real Life." *St. Petersburg Times,* June 5, p. D1.

Getz, Ronald. 1995. "A Cops Show of Your Own." *Law and Order,* February, p. 43.

Gunter, Barrie. 1987. *Television and the Fear of Crime.* London: John Libbey.

Haghighi, Bahram and Jon Sorensen. 1996. "America's Fear of Crime." In *Americans View Crime and Justice: A National Public Opinion Survey,* edited by T. Flanagan and D. Longmire. Thousand Oaks, CA: Sage.

Haney, Craig and John Manzolati. 1988. "Television Criminology: Network Illusions of Criminal Justice Realities." Pp. 120–31 in *Readings about the Social Animal,* 5th ed., edited by E. Aronson. New York: W.H. Freeman.

Harris, Scott. 1991. "Rape Case Raises Privacy Issue." *Los Angeles Times,* April 20, p. B3.

Katz, Jon. 1993. "Covering the Cops: A TV Show Moves In Where Journalists Fear to Tread." *Columbia Journalism Review* (January/February):25–30.

Livingstone, Sonia. 1990. *Making Sense of Television: The Psychology of Audience Interpretation.* Oxford: Pergamon.

———. 1996. "On the Continuing Problem of Media Effects." Pp. 305–24 in *Mass*

Media and Society, 2nd ed., edited by J. Curran and M. Gurevitch. London: Arnold.

McLuhan, Marshall. 1964. *Understanding Media*. New York: McGraw-Hill.

Meyrowitz, Joshua. 1985. *No Sense of Place: The Impact of Electronic Media on Social Behaviour*. New York: Oxford University Press.

Oliver, Mary Beth. 1994. "Portrayals of Crime, Race and Aggression in 'Reality-Based' Police Shows: A Content Analysis." *Journal of Broadcasting and Electronic Media* 38(2):179–92.

Oliver, Mary Beth and G. Blake Armstrong. 1995. "Predictors of Viewing and Enjoyment of Reality-Based and Fictional Crime Shows." *Journalism and Mass Communication Quarterly* 72(3):559–70.

Perigard, Mark. 1995. "The Reality Is, Cop Shows Fuel Bias and Fear of Crime." *Boston Herald,* April 25, p. 41.

Poster, Mark. 1990. *The Mode of Information: Post-Structuralism and Social Context.* Cambridge: Polity.

Reiner, Robert. 1992. *The Politics of the Police*, 2nd ed. Toronto, Ontario: University of Toronto Press.

Rust, Carol. 1992. "Officer Ken's Neighbourhood." *Texas Magazine,* August 9, p. 8.

Scattarella, Christy. 1992. "Wrong Raid Captured for Cops Show." *Seattle Times,* May 24, p. A1.

Scheingold, Stuart. 1995. "Politics, Public Policy and Street Crime." *Annals, AAPSS* 539:155–68.

Schlesinger, Philip and Howard Tumber. 1994. *Reporting Crime: The Media Politics of Criminal Justice*. Oxford: Clarendon.

Seagal, Debra. 1993. "Tales from the Cutting Room Floor: The Reality of 'Reality-Based' Television." *Harper's,* November, p. 50.

Smith, Steven Cole. 1993. "Cops File Bulges with Rules Broken, Viewers Captured." *Chicago Tribune,* February 18.

Sparks, Richard. 1992. *Television and the Drama of Crime: Moral Tales and the Place of Crime in Public Life*. Buckingham, England, and Philadelphia, PA: Open University Press.

Thompson, John B. 1990. *Ideology and Modern Culture: Critical Social Theory in the Era of Mass Communication*. Stanford, CA: Stanford University Press.

Zoglin, Richard. 1992. "The Cops and the Cameras." *Time,* April 6, p. 62.

7

Armed With the Power of Television:
Reality Crime Programming and the Reconstruction of Law and Order in the United States

PAMELA DONOVAN

Admittedly there may not be much more to do at 3:00 A.M. in Shirley, Long Island, New York. In 1994, local police staged a raid on a home in that town, suspected of housing a group of drug dealers. A crowd had gathered, some with video capability. As the cops led the suspects out in handcuffs, the crowd began to sing. "Bad boys, bad boys—what'chu gonna do? What'chu gonna do—when they come for you?!"—the theme song from a show called "Cops" that made it onto the pop charts in the summer of 1993. The viewer in the New York City market can watch it every evening of the week and at least twice on the weekend. The Shirley chorus was itself the topic of evening news broadcasts in New York City.

"Cops" is the most popular of a relatively new genre of television dubbed "reality crime programming" in the industry. This includes several different shows that have come and gone: "American Detective," "Missing: Reward," "Secret Service," "Top Cops," and two mainstays: "Cops" and "America's Most Wanted." Segments similar in format to those on reality programming shows began to appear on tabloid television magazines such as "A Current Affair" and "Hard Copy." Crime segments also take up much of the time on the popular "Unsolved Mysteries," and have occasionally appeared on what we would usually call "conventional" news broadcasts.[1]

This chapter is a thematic analysis of reality crime programming as an expanding genre. It asks, What can the viewer learn about crime, punishment, and law and order in the United States by taking the genre's claim to be depicting reality at face value? What are the "realities" of crime as this genre depicts them? It emerges out of a five-year study of random episodes between 1989 and 1994, reflecting the years during which the genre grew and developed to the point of being an expected part of the television lineup. While the chapter will discuss the considerable variability among the shows in terms of format, subject matter, and narration, it will also take the genre to be unique as a whole. Its emergence marks a wedding of new frontiers both for surveillance and spectacle, which is offered as a means of public address toward crime.

FEEDING A CONTINUOUS LOOP

Long before the boundaries between law enforcement and entertainment were as blurred as reality programming tries to make them, such a wedding was prefigured in dystopic literature. *The Running Man (1975)* by Stephen King (writing as Richard Bachman) featured a future in which capture and sentencing took place on a televised game show. In Ray Bradbury's *Fahrenheit 451* (1950), books were outlawed and routinely destroyed by fire, while interactive television became the locus of all communication. In the following excerpt, the protagonist, Montag, is wanted by the state on charges of murder and insubordination. He is hiding in a cottage, watching television. The announcer begins:

> "Mechanical Hound never fails. . . . Tonight this network is proud to have the opportunity to follow the Hound by camera helicopter as it starts on the way to the target . . . nose so sensitive the Mechanical Hound can remember and identify ten thousand odor indexes on ten thousand men without resetting!". . . . He watched the scene, fascinated, not wanting to move. It seemed so remote and no part of him; it was a play apart and separate, wondrous to watch, not without its strange pleasure. That's all for me, you thought, that's all taking place just for me. (Bradbury 1950:119–20)

Forty plus years later, the use of visual technology in tracking criminals is routine. In 1992, one of Britain's most shocking crimes, the kidnap and murder of a two-year-old by a pair of ten-year-olds in Liverpool, was solved when it was discovered that constantly running video cameras, both inside and outside a shopping mall, picked up the abductors on tape. Digital image enhancers allowed technicians to flush out a clear picture of the abductors from the grainy video feed. Nearly as disturbing as the discovery that the murderers were children themselves, was the footage of bystanders encountered by the trio as they walked through town, unfazed by the toddler's cries. Only *the cameras,* omniscient but silent, pieced it together, unfortunately too late for the victim. As in Bradbury's nightmare, such technical capabilities and deployments *actively* transformed and replaced, rather than enhanced, the social capacity for producing public safety and consciousness of physical space itself.

The technology used to bring this mystery to a quick end is the same that gives almost infinite life to tabloid television and reality crime programming. In situ video, presented in a simulated "uncut" fashion, is seeping into the rest of television programming. Even a visually lackluster event as the LAPD's forty-miles-per-hour pursuit of O. J. Simpson wiped out all other programming in most parts of the nation—the availability of the medium itself quickly becoming the story. Such events suggest a regearing of news routines that leaves print (or even traditional formatted television and radio news) media far behind, and always in a dilemma as to whether to report the "media event" itself as news.

It would be a mistake to examine the development of visual surveillance completely divorced from its relationship to spectacle. Portable, inexpensive, and instantly available, video feed now provides the raw materials for reality programming. Video, together with the increasingly thick information infrastructure linking law enforcement agencies, provides the technical impetus for the growth of crimestopper and real-life crime shows.

However, this description explains little about the particular use to which this technology is put. Why the allure of *entertainment*-based aids to law enforcement over other criminological uses of the same technology? The rise, or perhaps the reemergence, of the spectacular in law and order politics parallels, as well, the rapid expansion and sophistication of surveillance capabilities. Michel Foucault argues in *Discipline and Punish* ([1974] 1977) that the importance of spectacle in punishment regimes declines historically with the waning of regal power, or absolutism, and becomes somewhat unimportant and marginal with the ascendancy of rationalized systems of surveillance and control. The needs sated by the spectacle of punishment have waned as rationalized systems of both knowledge and punishment have expanded. This point is well-taken in terms of what is needed for *rulers* to successfully rule and maintain control over subjects. The question remains, however, how the needs of juridically interpellated *subjects* evolve in relationship to both the grand, regime-order changes Foucault describes and to the recent history of political and technological shifts around the issue of crime. The relationship between surveillance and spectacle, twenty years after Foucault's book, seems no longer one of competing images or supersession, but rather might be understood as mutual dependence. Specifically, the surveillance and spectacle aspects of reality programming share a technological, ideological, and emotional foundation. "Witnessing" by the viewer, is a central ingredient in the genre's niche appeal. Spectacle, it seems, is back:

> Because they must be made to be afraid; but also because they must be the witnesses, the guarantors, of the punishment, and because they must to a certain extent take part in it. (Foucault [1974] 1977:58)

Even if a definitive explanation for crime entertainment could be offered, still the particular structure, narrative, and appeal of the programs would remain undetermined.

Reality crime programming is defined in the industry and for the purposes of this chapter as shows that either recreate or intervene in traumatic events that involve illegality, often involving the viewing audience in some aspect of a resolution.

One of the longest running reality crime programs, "America's Most Wanted," features profiles of fugitives wanted by the FBI. Their crimes are often reenacted and identifying details given to the viewers, along with a hotline number. The show also has an interactive World Wide Web site. The hour-long program features several vignettes and updates from previous shows. The segments usually end when we "see" the criminal's escape and/or the victim's rescue. Then, immediately, the chaos of the crime scene, reenacted, is mitigated by the introduction of the actual FBI agents and local officers involved in the actual case, presumably pursuing the actual subject. This part may involve a psychological profile from an FBI forensic.

Most important are the interstices that contextualize what you have just seen. John Walsh, the program host, thanks you, the viewer, who decided to make a difference for providing leads that law enforcement officials have been able to use. A testimonial to the audience's prowess is best exemplified in a segment from "America's Most Wanted" aired in April 1989, on the occasion of the capture of the one-hundredth fugitive. Walsh tells us that there were one and a half million violent crimes the previous year, but "we're working together to fight back, armed with the power of television." A prisoner who was caught after he appeared on "America's Most Wanted" tells us, "I got spotted, and here I am." Then we see ourselves, that is, clips of audiences watching the show in living rooms, station houses, prison recreation rooms. Walsh reiterates that there are sixteen million viewers and "they've formed a partnership with law enforcement officials to capture over one hundred criminals." That is, viewers become partners by doing what they are already doing: sitting there. A beleaguered cop says, "We can't be everywhere. . . . [W]e have to depend on the citizens . . . the last line of offense in capturing the criminal." Reenter the convicted felon who says flatly, "It works." Walsh thanks us again for making a difference.

"Cops," another mainstay in the reality crime programming genre, conforms much more to the documentary tradition. Modeled after Geraldo Rivera's in situ crime documentaries of the late 1970s (which, in turn, added formal prime time sensibility to the less visually engaging police documentaries of the early seventies), "Cops" is one of the most lampooned, yet market-share powerful, of the genre.

None of the programs enjoy a particularly high rating, but the genre has grown from just "America's Most Wanted" and "Cops" to include a variety of specialty shows ("Secret Service," "Real Stories of the Highway Patrol"). It is also clear that a certain "tabloid sensibility" aided not just by reality crime shows, but also by TV magazines such as "A Current Affair" and "Inside Edition," has taken hold in conventional news and informational programs.

These traditional news programs are often quick to condemn the more baroque or extreme incarnations of reality "tabloid" sensibility as a harbinger of professional journalism's decline. However, this and similar criticisms that center around "sensationalism" really produce an analytical stumbling block. It is a criticism that evokes much indignant outrage but explains little about a *substantive* shift in crime's mass presentation. The sensationalistic aspects of the genre do not really distinguish it from much of the rest of television or even mass media in general. Nor is the history of mass journalism one that could be described as a downward trajectory from responsible, sober crime reporting to a frantic and somewhat pornographic set of practices today (Schudson 1978).[2]

Producers and promoters of the genre describe the shows as "reality based," meaning that some aspect of life is being depicted "realistically." It is my purpose here to explore the "realities" of crime and law enforcement as understood by reality crime shows. These shows form a coherent genre, this chapter will argue, through their consensus about what constitutes reality. The genre will be dealt with as a whole, while acknowledging and assessing the implications of certain key differences between shows. The shows have certain common thematic features that draw upon deeper reflexes within American political culture. These reflexes better predict the show's content than actual trends within crime, policing, and justice in the United States.

POLITICAL CONTEXTS

During the 1992 U.S. presidential election, public polls consistently identified "the economy" as the major domestic problem that the country faced, and that designation was widely identified in the press and in popular political cal literature as the decisive factor in the election of Bill Clinton to the presidency. In the late 1980s these same polls consistently reported that Americans identified drugs as the primary domestic scourge. At almost precisely the same time that crime rates started on their first declines in about twenty-five years, the polls unequivocally showed that crime had replaced drugs and the economy as a primary preoccupation among voters. A kind of panic about crime and punishment emerged in the early nineties that engaged the attention of politicians and the mass media, despite stable rates and recent declines.

There is little evidence, by any conventional indicator, that the transition from one recent scourge to another has been fostered by a lessening of the social disorder associated with the previous scourge. Drug use levels had remained relatively constant, the economy had continued to create jobs mainly at poverty level wages and the casualization of the labor force had continued to escalate. The United States is uniquely high in its level of violence and crime compared with other Western, industrialized nations, but this has been the case for years.

Nor is there any discernible and unambiguous rise in the rate of crime—violent or otherwise—in the last twenty-five years. The opposite perception persists, however, and policymakers have enacted more repressive measures, such as tripling the incarcerated population in the same amount of time and removing a degree of autonomy from the judiciary by enacting more mandatory sentencing laws. Many locales, including New York, are embarking on campaigns to reinforce "public order" laws, which essentially criminalize beggars and the homeless who, in creating a public nuisance, symbolize urban disorder and anomie.

In many cases, politicians are fully aware of this gap between perception and the actual crime rate gap. If the election of Bill Clinton to the White House was primarily due to his campaign's focus on the nation's economic troubles, then the victory of Rudolph Giuliani in the 1993 New York City mayoral race could in many ways be said to reflect the increasing fear of crime (Dao 1993). Giuliani, in classic neoconservative fashion, appealed to a cross-class, cross-constituency consensus that crime and public disorder were spinning out of control, and that more repressive measures were needed than those offered by Giuliani's incumbent opponent, a Democrat and African-American, David Dinkins. When, only a few weeks after Giuliani's election, a study of federal crime data confirmed that crime in New York City had decreased by 6 percent under the Dinkins administration, Giuliani was unimpressed. He responded simply that the fear and perception of crime in the city necessitated the same policy initiatives that any genuine increase in crime would, and thus introduced "quality of life policing" (Lewis 1993).

Studies on the fear of crime consistently show an increase in the level of fear parallel to a relatively stable rate of both crimes reported to law enforcement entities and self-reported victimization rates. To explain this gap, a number of factors have been considered, including studies on the influence of mass media images and news coverage in creating what could be termed "surplus visibility" for the issue of crime, of which the Simpson trial is only the most extreme example. I will argue that in many ways, crime as a public-problem category concentrates a host of other less coherent and less openly discussed concerns, including the inchoate role of authority in social life and waning support for participation in many aspects of civic and public life. This content analysis of reality crime programming shows suggests that its appeal is precisely its synthetic attention to real-world evil and these less openly articulated ills. Reality programming offers a way for the viewers to meld their skepticism and their necessary trust of public servants in an increasingly privatized world.

REALITY ONE: IS ANYONE IN CHARGE HERE?

The first reality of reality programming is that it offers violators at their most depraved and, at the same time, assigns them a thinly veiled romance. By contrast, it offers sensitive, knowledgeable, competent individual police officers who, by the end of a given segment, produce some type of resolution. They are not careless in handling evidence, nor are they asked to handle more problems than they can manage, nor are they ever corrupt, foul-mouthed, or simply overwhelmed. They reestablish the moral order. Writer Debra Seagal, who worked as a story editor for "American Detective," remarks, "Why the national obsession with this sort of voyeuristic entertainment? Perhaps we want to believe the cops are still in control" (1993:51). Hall, Critcher, Jefferson, Clarke, and Roberts suggest in *Policing the Crisis* (1978) that in the British press the police are the "primary definers" of crime, and, in turn, crime is the primary definer of social breakdown. The time-space-compression of street crime on television, owing to the demands of both newsroom needs and a sensibility fostered by the urban vigilante films of the 1970s such as *Death Wish* (1974). In *Death Wish*, the protagonist manages to be victimized no less than six times within a few weeks while shopping, walking in the park, and riding the subway. This and similar films of the era contribute to the "surplus visibility" of crime and the sense of siege, necessitating eventually perhaps some means of narrative closure. It is little wonder that since the beginning of the reality crime programming genre in the late 1980s the use of the multiple vignette, originally associated with the eclectic "Unsolved Mysteries" to organize the majority of the shows' material, has become more widespread. "Real Stories of the Highway Patrol" and "Cops" use this format too, into which they fold their less spectacular material. In all of these shows, half-hour or hour episodes contain between four and ten cases.

An interesting side concern illustrates the eroding boundaries between the mass media and law enforcement: American law enforcement officials have expressed dismay at the spread of the true-crime genre, fearing that their officers will engage in "hot-dogging," or showy risk-taking, for a shot at fame (Pooley 1992). In an increasingly privatized world, public servants need public relations, and by extension, viewers need "the thin blue line" since the political consensus is that all else has failed.

REALITY TWO: THE CURIOUS NEED TO "PITCH"
LAW ENFORCEMENT

The second reality of reality crime programming is the perceived need to "pitch" law enforcement. The style of presentation of law and policing in these shows suggests a form of address closer to advertising than that of character development, plot, and engagement with broader institutional contexts sought after in crime drama, fiction, or mystery. The distinction between the pitch for law enforcement and the pitch for these particular shows only appears sporadically.

The presence of a strong pitch for law enforcement suggests implicitly a sense of challenge even though it never identifies the source of this threat. "America's Most Wanted's" host John Walsh explains:

> The success of "America's Most Wanted" comes from one simple premise: citizens are tired of crime, and they got involved by calling this hotline. ("America's Most Wanted," 30 October 1992) Let's face it: the streets of this country just aren't safe anymore, and it's up to us to change that. We can start with John Warda [prison escapee].("America's Most Wanted," 8 October 1994)

Recently, the show has been subtitled, "America Fights Back." Ironically, at present, crime *drama* on U.S. television, attracting many more viewers, evokes a much more circumspect and nuanced picture of crime, law enforcement, and policing compared to reality crime shows. Shows like "Homicide," "New York Undercover," and "NYPD Blue" derive their popularity from this complexity. By contrast, reality crime shows pitch law enforcement by reiterating that "law and order" are back, having vacationed at some time in the recent past. To fight crime, it follows, a united front of viewer-citizens is needed to support police in their embattled project. These same viewer-citizens, by contrast, are nearly completely absent in crime drama. This "pitch" approach, then, is somewhat unique to this genre. It is a political project aimed at harnessing "the power of television."

REALITY THREE: MAKING A DIFFERENCE
BY REMOTE CONTROL

The third reality of reality programming that reaches toward the audience's more general complaints is involvement beyond the instrumental aspects of citizen aid to law enforcement. "America's Most Wanted," for instance, differs from its mugshots in the U.S. Post Office not just in media form but in substance and aims. It desires *categorical* involvement from viewers, not just those who might recognize the fugitive or circumstance presented. In the show's debut year, 1988, it received five hundred calls per show. In 1994, it got three thousand calls per show. But very few of these calls actually led anywhere, indicating that the desire to "get involved" in this way is considerably more widespread than those who may have come in contact with the criminal in question. "America's Most Wanted" often uses guilt appeals to viewers aimed at their complicity-by-way-of-passivity. Of a child molester who kidnaped an eight-year-old and was later picked up on surveillance tape at a convenience store in another locale, host John Walsh says, "Please let's answer this little girl's plea for help. Do the right thing and call us" ("America's Most Wanted," 8 October 1994). Citizens get involved by calling this hotline because they are *tired* of crime; in the virtual world of reality programming, addressing crime involves identifying a specified number of fugitives and "walking those perps" across the national psyche. Maybe you saw him, or not; maybe you just want to know more. "You've made the world a smaller place for fugitives to hide," said Walsh, on the occasion of the capture of two hundred fugitives (May 9, 1992), which conveniently coincided with sweeps week.

This is a genre in many ways about itself and its own possibilities. It implicates itself in the prowess and dedication of law enforcement, in its recent successes, and consistently reminds the viewer that it is *really* involved in catching criminals. This is the greatest similarity between "America's Most Wanted" and "Cops" type formats.

REALITY FOUR: STAY THE COURSE

Reality crime programming emphasizes the apprehension and punishment of criminals, ex post facto, as the primary solution to crime. There are no causes, either structural or proximate. On the one hand, this parallels the American institutional response to crime. The most successful policy initiatives in the United States to combat crime are ex post facto ones: the expansion of the prison system, and mandatory and increased sentencing legislation—neither of which has been shown to have any clear deterrent effect, and both of which sometimes even suggest the opposite (Bowker 1981; Biles 1979, 1983). While all of these trends have a disproportionate negative impact upon poor and minority citizens, the political support for them and other repressive measures relies upon populist, cross-constituency appeal. The initiatives often have a socially cathartic effect, especially in a political and economic context lacking perceived alternatives to address real social devastation and fears.

If incapacitation as a response to crime is at best an ambiguous predictor in criminological research (Gottfredson and Gottfredson 1994; Currie 1985:77, 86–90), it is an article of faith in reality crime programming. The parents of two Texas girls killed at work respond to news that the suspects in the case are due to be sentenced in Mexico for another violent crime:

> It's a blessing, in a way. Because so often, many people who go to prison don't stay in prison in the United States and especially in Texas. ("America's Most Wanted," 30 October 1992)[3]

Walsh notes that the parents believe "Mexican justice could be far more severe than any court in Texas" and that the criminals "could face up to six years in prison in Mexico." The assumption is that had they been extradited to the United States for either attack the sentences would be less and that Mexican imprisonment offered hope that their daughters hadn't "died in vain." It was a very tidy ending. What "America's Most Wanted" particularly shares with the more documentary-style shows like "Cops" is an equation of pursuit, apprehension, and imprisonment with a general impact on crime.

"America's Most Wanted" and "Real Stories of the Highway Patrol" are more overtly ideological than "Cops." The genre as a whole is experiment-ing with balance—"Cops" being quite open-ended, the more highly format-ted shows rather closed or unspontaneous. While this difference partly reflects the different community reference depicted, local urban versus na-tional, even "Cops" undermines localism by making all cities look like one another, from the birds-eye view behind a flak jacket and camera, or from the comfort of a police cruiser.

REALITY FIVE: PERSONALISM AND COLLECTIVE RESPONSIBILITY

Removing all local features—context as much as anything else—reinforces an emphasis on individualism, and is part of reality program-ming's high premium upon personalism compared with the impersonality of "statistics." The host of "America's Most Wanted," John Walsh, got involved via a group he started, the National Center for Missing and Exploited Chil-dren, after his five-year-old son, Adam, was abducted and murdered. Infor-mal discussions with "America's Most Wanted" viewers reveal that poking fun at his stiff posture or the show's almost giddy glorification of authority is not taken well. It is taken as insensitive to this man's tragic loss. This makes him the perfect host—a paramount example of the genre's personalized framing of crime. This personalized frame is often explicitly counterposed to generalizations, as in "just another statistic."

Such a discursive counterposition, however, was already in informal cir-culation before reality programming and tabloid television. In "Death Wish," the protagonist's son-in-law comments on the protagonist's murdered wife and badly beaten daughter, "They're statistics on a police blotter, along with thousands of other people. There's nothing we can do to stop it." Here, both the sense of injustice and, interestingly, *inefficacy* comes directly out of the decentering of personalism in the criminal justice process. This already existing need to repersonalize crime in order to effectively fight it gives rise in turn to "pitches" for particular victims depicted on reality crime programming shows.

Each segment on "America's Most Wanted" and the crime segments on "Unsolved Mysteries" are accompanied by pitches for the victims, usually by relatives or friends, with descriptions like beautiful, innocent, talented, friendly, hard-working. For instance, the mother of Jennifer Mroz, a twelve-year-old killed by stray gunfire, tells us, "She was a good kid, not a trouble maker" ("America's Most Wanted," 6 November 1992). The eight-year-old survivor of the child predator, "daddy's little girl . . . made great strides toward her recovery. . . . [S]he still seems to be the quintessential eight-year-old girl" ("America's Most Wanted," 8 October 1994). Murder victim Denise Huber was "the California girl with the head-turning smile" ("America's Most Wanted," 8 October 1994). While contextual details are of importance only in some very particular instances discussed below, personal ones are essential to depicting both victim and criminal in the typical vignette.

On "America's Most Wanted," victim or local police testimonials are interspersed with reenactments. Actors reenact various scenes, based on witness testimony or conjecture, of the setting and the events leading up to the crime. In recent years, more attention has been paid to atmosphere, culture, and subculture in the reenactments. A segment on a thieving "gypsy" family ("America's Most Wanted," 6 November 1992) is described sarcastically as "this band of gypsies who spent quality time passing down their traditional family values": that is, stealing. The reenactment involved folktales passed from uncle to nephew about why it was alright for him to steal, set to a soundtrack of Romani folk music, with the disclaimer that "most are peaceful law-abiding citizens." The men were shown playing cards in a parking lot while "the women went inside to do the dirty work," which not only emphasizes supposed cultural differences, but returns us to our romantic outlaw—suggesting that they were not men enough to do it themselves.

The same is true of criminal acts perpetrated by individuals in unusual ethnic or class categories—the criminality seems to emerge *from* those milieux, whereas those of "ordinary" races/ethnicities (white, black, Latino) or class strata (working, middle, upper-middle) are simply depraved individuals—either wanton or crazy. A Los Angeles television reporter, Sharon Friendly, was held hostage and raped by a homeless man who she encountered while doing a documentary on Genesis One, a self-governed, self-built housing project where he lived. "America's Most Wanted" (28 May 1994) says that "for the once gregarious Friendly who had so much trust in the less fortunate, there is bitterness and anger," although in the ensuing testimonial she mentions only anger and a desire for revenge against her attacker (and his wife who looked on and did nothing) and nothing about "the less fortunate" in general. Ted Hughes, director of Genesis One, corroborates this rare collective-responsibility theme by telling "America's Most Wanted" that attacker Bill Matthews "pimped the homeless" by drawing negative attention to the community, and by hiding his identity as a felon who had already served sixteen years for rape and murder.

Meanwhile, reality programming carefully cultivates a picture of multicultural America united to fight crime through this new medium. This genre is testimony to the capacity of traditional law-and-order campaigns to reinvent themselves in response to a post-1960s cultural style. The genre is neither ignorant of multiculturalism, nor immune from or ignorant of other social movements such as feminism or consumer rights. For example, none of these shows would dream of blaming women for their victimization. By 1996 "America's Most Wanted" had covered several high-profile hate crimes, including the beating death of a gay man in Queens, New York. "America's Most Wanted" in particular regards victims as heroes. Victims, we are shown, come from all walks of life. The shows are fairly comfortable with social liberalism in general, accommodating a cultural looseness (for example, the use of popular music as backdrop) that markedly differentiates it from pre-1970s incarnations, which often explicitly wove a seamless web between deviancies of various sorts: lifestyle, class, gender obedience, sexuality, ethnicity, criminality, and politics. Reality crime programming, carefully avoids playing those cards that might alienate potential viewers with a general interest in the shows' main narrative flow: victim testimonial, identification, pursuit, capture. This genre is confident enough in its populist aims to cleanse away overt sexism and racism from traditional law and order politics; viewer-citizens are collectively, universally, and uniformly hailed as "tired of crime."

Yet, in another way, reality crime programming's focus on ex post facto aspects of individual crimes also reflects the pace, contours, and conventions of regular television. Seagal (1993) observes that the story must be told in the "same dramatic arc" as a conventional television narrative, with its pacing compliant to the needs of advertising like any other commercially viable show. Thus "reality" seems to look a lot like . . . television.

REALITY SIX: JOIN THE WORLD
OF THE OMNISCIENT

The world envisioned by reality programming is a world that is not just smaller—it is also more transparent. Reenactments interpret and present unknowable things. In "America's Most Wanted's" two hundred fugitives episode, the unclosed case of a murdered hitchhiker is reviewed and the murder is reenacted. Similarly, "America's Most Wanted's" coverage of fugitive FBI agent Brad Bishop's apparent murder of his entire family in Maryland in the 1970s ("America's Most Wanted," 28 May 1994) included a "reenactment" of the murders: Bishop arising from his chair, attacking his wife first, then the children as they lie sleeping, and then his mother as she returns home from walking the dog, having discovered each and every one of the bodies first before Brad catches up with her. Given that Bishop then apparently transported the bodies to North Carolina and set them aflame, the actual sequence of events will probably remain unknown. The camera appears to know things that only the victim and murderer know, heightening the sense of omniscience and efficacy to the medium itself.

REALITY SEVEN: WE HAVE MET THE ENEMY . . .

If in many cases only the perpetrator and the victim know what happened, the omniscient assumptions in the visual texture of the program often slide easily into visual identification with the perpetrator. One example of how this transformation operates is the use of stalking perpetrator–view camera angles. In the fall of 1993, "America's Most Wanted" used an opening credit sequence in which the imputed viewer is the object of cops in riot gear, a zooming patrol car, a descending helicopter, and finally a blinding camera flash taking "your" mugshot ("America's Most Wanted," 13 September 1993). However, in general, these devices tend to be used where some degree of psychopathy is implied and not used where the subject is street crime. In the case of a "serial child predator," we are visually in the shoes of the pervert, leering at cheerleaders practicing their routines—who are filmed from the waist down in slow motion and then from above through a chainlink fence ("America's Most Wanted," 8 October 1994). In the aforementioned Bishop murders, the viewer is visually with Brad the whole way, to witness the look of terror as the shadow of "our own" arm and fist— grasping a heavy hammer—crosses the face of each victim. We even hear, interiorized, heavy and rhythmic breathing. But in a reenactment of a young hood who tries to shoot a cop after emerging from a pickup truck, we are either visually in the third person or in the cop's shoes ("America's Most Wanted," 8 October 1994). The ordinary criminality of the young hood, drug dealer, or heat-of-the-moment attack does not seem to elicit the same sort of symbolic complexity as the predatory kind.

Of course, America has always had an open-secret romance with the outlaw, or the lone criminal figure. This is perhaps not quite the same in Britain, where law and order politics are much less ambivalent. In the British press, crime's fascination/repulsion draw centers around transgression of a corporal sort—"the lower depths"—and its momentary release from respectability (Hall et al. 1978:141). Respectability in U.S. culture is a less compelling demand. Independence and rugged individualism stand in its place.

U.S. crime coverage, while continuing some of the same patterns, has developed different themes. Its fascination with criminality pits the family man who accepts the "burdens" of socialization and collectivity against the lone wolf, finally cut loose of social bonds, headed for a prairie sunset or the heat, danger, and anonymity of the highway. The imaginary figure draws heavily on the imagery of the violent Wild West frontier idea, intensifying the romance that Martha Grace Duncan (1996) finds within English literature for at least several centuries. Jesse James is the preferred image, conjured more than Jack-the-Ripper, even where, as in the Simpson case, the crime bears more resemblance to the latter.

The romance with criminality partially explains the desire not to speak of violent crime in social terms that would suggest a loss of independent will or especially of personal control. There is something satisfying, then, about dealing with the problem in terms of individual willfulness, individual violation, and individual apprehension. This is mimicked not only in reality crime programming's growth as a genre but also in the popularity of courtroom dramas, which carry social problems and controversies in terms of their *legal* incarnation, which by definition must deal with individuals as legal entities and not with social processes.

REALITY EIGHT: SEE HOW THE OTHER HALF LIVE

"Cops" conforms much more, visually, to the documentary tradition, using "original" footage in a highly stylized manner. "Cops" was originally produced in the Broward County, Florida, Sheriff's Office. A great deal of time in this and similar documentary-type shows is devoted to chronicling disorderliness and dysfunctionality, making it much different from "America's Most Wanted's" crimestoppers model. This has an ambiguous effect on the representation of crime. In an episode of "Cops" (8 October 1994) from Los Angeles, one cop, Corey, does a "boardwalk sights" tour. He tells a guy showing off his snake to onlookers that he has to take it away; he complies. Then "we" happen upon Crazy Mary, a small, older woman who has already been detained by three cops; we never learn why—she is possibly rowdy and drunk. Crazy Mary thinks Corey is her husband. She is singing "Please release me/let me go/I don't love you anymore . . . " to every cop on the scene. Corey takes Mary aside and after reaffirming their matrimonial relationship, tells her she is going "to the penalty box." Mary knows about this; she wails, "No! You're gonna attach me to the bench and I've already got diarrhea!" There is no attempt to hide Mary's face.

Similarly, an episode of "Cops" (2 November 1992) was set in Harris County, Texas. A two-minute segment, long for television, depicted a detainee named Mildred, a known prostitute and drug user, handcuffed to a wooden bench and clearly agitated by her situation. She shows the questioning officer her whole-body tattoos and infected track marks, lifting her shirt, meanwhile trying to account for the previous seventy-two hours before her arrest. "Bad dope?" he asks. "Bad junk," she explains, "bad [deleted]. Nobody [deleted] deserves this!" She tries to writhe out of the handcuffs. There is no attempt to disguise her face. Her breasts, of course, are blocked out.

These displays of abjection relate little to the instrumentality of police work, and serve as cautionary tales in their gratuitousness. They are a display of the law's power over bodies in an old-regime way—stray from the straight and narrow and you will be displayed in public, on national television, that is. Mildred's exposure is also a legitimized display of bondage, which suggests even more strongly the repulsion/fascination conflict discussed earlier, and raises the whole question of how much simple voyeurism, or televisual slumming, plays in the growth of the genre.

The other effect of chronicling routine disorder is that it does place crime, to a much greater extent than the crimestoppers model, within the context of ordinary brutality and hopelessness that characterizes the bulk of violent offenses. Unlike "America's Most Wanted," "Cops" does not focus on the spectacular, ironic, or bizarre violation but on an ordinary array of drug dealing, drunk driving, pistol waving, and bar brawling. There is also a fair amount of attention to domestic violence. Cops are often seen defusing volatile situations. All of this is less glamorous than the cops in crime dramas or on "America's Most Wanted." "Cops" visits people and places normally outside the interest of the commercial media, raising the question, Is reality crime programming the accidental Steinbeck of the 1990s? While the viewer moves through city streets with "Cops," much attention is directed to endemic social problems that the patrol officers, speaking on video, do not pretend to be able to solve. Police are shown having a stressful job, but they are rarely depicted as superheroic or even in control of the streets; rather, they keep putting out brushfires. "American Detective," now canceled, used the superheroic motif with the material of ordinary street busts, such as marijuana arrests, and it seems the juxtaposition was less than convincing.

What the "Cops" model provides for the viewer is a safe environment to take all this in. The experience is not only made safe by the distance involved in television viewing, but also by being accompanied by two or more cops in a police cruiser. This offers the viewer a modicum of control that does not exist in real life, as well as an instrumental reason to peer in on things rarely seen close up.

REALITY NINE: A NEW KIND OF CITIZEN

Since violent crimes present a recurrent challenge to the outer limits of social consensus (no one, including criminals, advocates them), they are of natural interest to the polity. How much social engagement and risk of discord does it really take to be against crime as compared any other social issue? Crimes are thus consistently newsworthy. One may stand up and be counted, uncontroversially and without much effort, by watching reality crime programming.

Real life crime shows acclaim us—all of us—as citizens. They attempt to evoke an active polity so much that at times they even allow for internal crises of representation that can be worked through. For instance, in an update on "America's Most Wanted" (April 1989), the murderers of Cesar Cardenas, a Latino boxer from Los Angeles, are shown surrendering themselves. Noted the victim's sister, Lourdes, upon seeing the surrender on television (which *we* got to watch her *watching*), "We were sitting around the TV set and when those guys came on we felt so relieved." Lourdes and Cesar's former coach had sent in a petition with 370 signatures requesting that "America's Most Wanted" air a segment on his murder. Normally, the FBI supplies "America's Most Wanted" with their cases. But it was a prime opportunity to transubstantiate earlier criticism that the show had focused too much on white victims and at the same time fold the petition drive and success into the participatory pitch of the program.

The ninth reality in reality programming is that it construes the reconstruction of citizenship and the public sphere through the categories of law and order. The extent to which this is the case is best exemplified by the relative lack of editing of police brutality in the documentary-style shows. Robin Andersen's review of 1994 "Cops" episodes finds little attempt to put law enforcement's "best foot forward," at least in traditional public relations terms (Andersen 1994). Similarly, Seagal's description of the highly-edited-yet-promoted-as-real-time "American Detectives" has only the worst, untelevisable examples of brutality edited out, such as kicks to the head of a suspect or the use of ethnic slurs. Enough rough handling is left in to raise the suspicion that producers are not worried about offending audience members with such material; on the contrary, the calculation is that such imperfections—errors on the side of repression rather than leniency—only serve to add more personalism and hypercompetence of the cops in action.

In the same vein, reality programming works with a keen awareness of its political context. Reality programming easily fits in with American ambivalence about civic life. At a time when antigovernment and antimedia sentiment are the *lingua franca* of what passes for civic speech, policing as entertainment works well. Law is the *minimalist* function of the state. Consider also the interest in courtroom dramas and real courtroom programming. Action moves forward, the scenes of modern (postmodern?) life are depicted, and characters' humanity and complexity emerge through repetitious engagement with and defense of the "last vestige" of social organization—law. Less definitive and more complex aspects of the constitution of polity, community, or identity seem less important than having the law be on one's side. On television and to some extent in real life, law symbolizes the only remaining vestige of a public sphere in which the moral imperatives are clear and unequivocal.

CULTURAL AND POLITICAL CONTEXTS

"America's Most Wanted" is coproduced by the FBI's Public Affairs Office and a regular production team, an arrangement with similarities to previous programming, such as "FBI" and "Dragnet" in the 1960s. Intimate connections between law enforcement and media sources in American popular culture have long roots. When the FBI took down John Dillinger in the 1930s, the press was invited to the cinema where the ambush was planned; it was a staged event. Dillinger himself was known to take extra risks by seeking out media coverage of his own exploits. The involvement of J. Edgar Hoover in the film industry is also a precedent. Eventually in the 1960s the semifictionalized "FBI" show would run with a very high viewership—at its peak, forty million viewers. Hoover reviewed all of the scripts in order to protect the FBI's image, and picked actors from an approved list. The main difference now is the pitch of realness: live footage, "unfictionalized" cases, the use of real law enforcement agencies, and—not to be underestimated—the appeal of civic involvement. The tone is now populist, rather than technocratic or absolutist. It also addresses a considerably more fragmented and niche-bound viewing audience.

Hall et al. comment in *Policing the Crisis* on the popular appeal of crime stories in the news:

> Crime allows all "good men and true" to stand up and be counted—at least metaphorically—in the defense of normality, stability, and "our way of life." (1978:150)

While the undertones may be slightly different in the United States, there is a general similarity in the popular appeal of crime stories. British sociologists Schlesinger, Tumber, and Murdock (1991:402–3) linked the rise of a similar television genre there that emerged in the 1980s (beginning with "Crime-watch UK") to the rising law-and-order mood under Thatcher and the prefer-ence for increased punitive measures—clearly, the parallel to the United States holds. "America's Most Wanted" was intentionally modeled after "Crimewatch UK" (Younger 1993).

In both countries, law enforcement agencies made decisions to pursue what they called "openness policies" with the public and the press, expand-ing public affairs offices and pursuing a "proactive" relationship with media sources. This made an increasing number of professionals comfortable with the links between media and policing. Contextually, the United States was pursuing a War on Drugs. Polls showed that an increasing number of Ameri-cans wanted to suspend certain constitutional rights to pursue this end (Mor-in 1989). Britain and the United States were also fumbling for a response to terrorism. All of these background factors added up to a new and vague feeling of embattlement, a generalized shift in public sentiment. "People believe in authority again," said the FBI's chief public affairs officer in 1987 about this new television genre. "People want to stand up and be counted. Especially in the fight against crime" (Friedman 1989:35).

CONCLUSION

Reality programming, in two ways, provides closure through spectacle. It addresses viewers in both roles, the warned and the witness, and it also provides narrative or iconic finalities to crime scenarios where there are often none. A great deal of visual or iconic attention in these shows is devoted to arrest: handcuffs, closing prison gates, and so forth, particularly in the self-promotional segments and opening and closing credits. The pri-vate, uncelebrated scaffold or stockade provides retribution as easily as does the public. The revived interest in collective watching, or "witness-ing," likely owes more to a fascination with social decline in a culture lacking a language of the social. This lack itself is implicated in a deepen-ing sense of chaos and fear, combined with the multifaceted trend toward privatism, privatization, and a contempt for "public" anything. Yet, curi-ously, by watching reality crime programming one would never know that prisons, and especially policing, are increasingly themselves privatized affairs.

In a perverse way, reality crime programming tries to revive the public sphere, consistent with John Dewey's observation that "our political com-mon sense philosophy imputes a public only to support and substantiate the behavior of officials" ([1927] 1954:117). By decomposing the matter of crime and society into specific vignettes with individual, nice, competent cops and extremely depraved or delusional criminals, it mends a bridge between the desire for more authoritarian responses to crime and our culture's endemic suspicion of government. What other government function is the object of very earnest, documentary-style, and public-participatory entertainment on television? Crime shows are not an isolated instance of viewership sold as civic activity, but unlike fiction, they demand your attention because you are a participant already. There is real policing happening, whether you choose to watch or not.

The disinterest of the nonviewer, in fact, adds contour to the genre's self-definition: this is reality, on the ground and gritty, for those of you who choose to recognize it and be a part of it. Highbrow criticism of the genre centered around "sensationalism" misfires in two ways. First, it ignores the degree to which such criticism is necessary to the genre's securing of its own niche: it is precisely being more "sensate" about crime and policing than conventional news and documentary that attracts attention. Second, it overestimates the degree to which conventional crime news sources treat the subject matter in a detached, reasoned, and duly perspectival fashion.

The sensational evocation of crime in reality crime programming is also familiar, formally, from the genre's casual use of traditional *film noir* motifs in both popular cinema and television drama. All of these shows avoid the stodginess of earlier crime documentary and traditional crime drama before "Miami Vice." Everything is set to music: up-tempo rock for chase scenes, piano/synthesizer sentimental pieces for the victim testimonial and reflective segments. The visual conventions of *film noir* play a role in both kinds of shows: layered and textured backgrounds, natural lighting and broad compositional use of shadow effects. The visual references to *noir* lift those conventions out of their original evocation of a mix of ennui, cynicism, desire, and mystery and into a new and much more earnest view of crime, order, and law enforcement.

In the Bradbury excerpt, the odd sensation of being the object not just of surveillance but of spectacle stopped Montag cold in his tracks. It was the confluence of two highly visual categories of power that are also, as Bradbury put it, not without their strange pleasure. For Bradbury in the 1950s, such a nexus was dystopic; in the 1990s it is a casual element of the entertainment pantheon. Little is learned from the distinction to be made between Bradbury's protagonist, Montag, a political fugitive who challenged a totalitarian state, and the framework of pursuit in reality programming, which involves primarily violent crimes of opportunity or passion and law enforcement branches in a putatively liberal democratic state. This distinction answers only the question *why law enforcement* and does not answer the question *why reality crime programming.* The populist appeal of the genre lie in the various "identifications" that the viewer can make. For this thought to be explored it is necessary to focus on the strange pleasures, grown in an increasingly circumscribed, remaindered public sphere and attempting, like the country as a whole, to address and harmonize a myriad of contradictory national themes through the specific tool of law enforcement.

NOTES

1. "Unsolved Mysteries," which covers not only crime but supernatural events and missing persons, has the highest rating (ranked 29th out of 118 shows on network prime time) of these shows; "Cops" and "America's Most Wanted" are close to the bottom (86 and 104, respectively) ("The Best and Worst According to Nielsen" *TV Guide*, June 11, 1994, pp. 14-15).

2. In fact, it would be much easier to make the opposite argument. See Michael Schudson (1978), in particular, for the role of sensationalistic accounts of street crime in boosting sales of burgeoning populist, penny press newspapers.

3. This vignette was very cleverly crafted, focusing on what the parents *believe*, rather than consulting the shows' usual source of sentencing authority, the law enforcement agencies and the district attorney's offices involved. Besides reinforcing the myth of American leniency, the strategy was also self-serving in the sense that a crime formerly featured on the show would not have the desired or expected denouement now that the suspects would instead be serving "up to" six years in Mexico.

REFERENCES

Andersen, R. 1994. "That's Entertainment: How 'Reality'-Based Crime Shows Market Police Brutality." *Extra! The Magazine of Fairness and Accuracy in Reporting,* May/June, p. 15.

Bachman, Richard. 1975. *The Running Man.* New York: Penguin.

Biles, D. 1979. "Crime and the Use of Prisons." *Federal Probation* 43:2.

———. 1983. "Crime and Imprisonment: A Two-Decade Comparison Between England, Wales, and Australia." *British Journal of Criminology* 23(April):2.

Bowker, L. H. 1981. "Crime and the Use of Prisons in the U.S.: A Time-Series Analysis." *Crime and Delinquency* (April).

Bradbury, R. 1950. *Fahrenheit 451.* New York: World.

Currie, E. 1985. *Confronting Crime: An American Challenge.* New York: Pantheon.

Dao, J. 1993. "Dinkins and Giuliani Split on Public Safety Issues." *New York Times* (National Edition), October 11, p. A1.

Dewey, J. [1927] 1954. *The Public and Its Problems.* Chicago: Swallow.

Duncan, M. G. 1996. *Romantic Outlaws, Beloved Prisons: The Unconscious Meanings of Crime and Punishment.* New York: New York University Press.

Foucault, M. [1974] 1977. *Discipline and Punish: The Birth of the Prison.* New York: Pantheon.

Friedman, D. 1989. "Wanted: Lowlifes and High Ratings." *Rolling Stone,* January 12, p. 35.

Gottfredson, S. D. and Gottfredson, D. M. 1994. "Behavioral Prediction and the Problem of Incapacitation." *Criminology* 32(August):3.

Hall, S., C. Critcher, I. Jefferson, J. Clarke, and B. Roberts. 1978. *Policing the Crisis: Mugging, the State, and Law and Order.* London: Macmillan.

Lewis, N. A. 1993. "Crime Rates Decline; Outrage Hasn't." *New York Times* (National Edition), December 8, p. B6.

Morin, R. 1989. "Many in Poll Say Bush Plan Is Not Stringent Enough." *Washington Post,* September 8. [ACLU Reprint.]

Pooley, E. 1992. "Cop Stars: How Police and Gangsters are Cashing in on Today's Mania for True-Crime Entertainment." *New York,* March 16, p. 47.

Schlesinger, P., H. Tumber, and G. Murdock. 1991. "The Media Politics of Crime and Criminal Justice." *British Journal of Sociology* 42(3):407–8.

Schudson, M. 1978. *Discovering the News: A Social History of American Newspapers.* New York: Basic Books.

Seagal, D. 1993. "Tales from the Cutting Room Floor: The Reality of 'Reality-Based' Television." *Harper's,* November, p. 51.

Younger, J. 1993. "What John Walsh Really Wants." *Amtrak Express,* May/June.

IV

Crime, Criminals, and Victims

8

The World of Crime According to "Cops"

PAUL G. KOOISTRA, JOHN S. MAHONEY,
and SAUNDRA D. WESTERVELT

INTRODUCTION

Television in this country has long presented racist images of minorities. In recent years, racial and ethnic images have become more positive, particularly in the area of television fiction. However, in the nonfiction world of television, subtle forms of racism are still prevalent. The presentation of African-Americans in television news, for example, systematically promotes antiblack sentiment through its emphasis and portrayal of crime stories (Entman 1990).

In the past decade a new form of television "news" has developed: reality-based police shows such as "Cops," "American Detective," "America's Most Wanted," "Top Cops," and "True Stories of the Highway Patrol." These programs employ actual or dramatized accounts of crimes. They have become "television's hottest genre" for their profitability and popularity (Sauter 1992; Fennell 1992). Arguably, these shows have a greater impact on audiences' concern over crime and attitudes toward minorities since they are presenting presumably factual accounts of the social world and in a more intense dramatized form than found in television news. Yet few studies have systematically examined the content of such shows. Instead, broad general impressions are offered that vary from author to author. Friedman argues that programs like "Cops" are good because they demystify police work and also perform "something of a public service: never has crime looked so real. Or so shabby. Or so pointless" (1989:26). Katz (1993) claims that shows such as "Cops" show how dangerous and complex a policeman's job might be and criticizes the press for focusing only on issues of police brutality and racism. Zoglin (1992) notes that supporters of these shows say they humanize police and can help prosecutors fight crime.

In contrast, Rapping claims that tabloid crime shows "are sleazy, crude, and quite often openly racist. They are meant for an audience for whom niceties of taste and gradations of moral nuance and subtlety are not important" (1994:36). And Waters (1989) suggests that these shows exploit suffering for their own profit and contribute to the belief that everyone arrested of crime is guilty, even before a trial has occurred. Rapping even suggests that these shows "present a world view that . . . flirts dangerously with certain aspects of fascist ideology" (1992:35). Crimes, these programs seem to suggest, are acts of irrational (and often drug-induced) evil committed by dark-skinned males and promiscuous females. These lawbreakers are a breed of humans different from us who reject many of "our" cherished social values.

This chapter examines the images of crime and race presented in one such program, "Cops." This show was chosen because it is one of the most popular of its genre according to Nielsen ratings, is frequently aired (in some communities several times a week), and is one of the oldest and probably best known of the reality-based crime shows on television. We scrutinize the types and social dynamics of crimes portrayed. Such dynamics include the race of offenders, victims, and police. We hypothesize that nonwhites will be disproportionately portrayed as criminal offenders. Furthermore, although nonwhites are frequently the victims of serious street crimes, we hypothesize that nonwhites will seldom be underrepresented as the victims of serious crime in these shows, in comparison to official crime data.

RACE ON TELEVISION

There has long been concern over the presentation of minorities in mass media. For much of television's history, as MacDonald notes, broadcasters had been "comfortable with racial stereotyping, whether it was the abrasive representations so abundant in the 1950s or the subtler stylizations of the 1970s" (1990:248). In the early days of television, the series "Amos 'n' Andy" portrayed black men as clowns or con men hectored by bossy black women. The problems they confronted in their daily lives were many, though primarily the result of their own ineptitude and unrelated to race (Ely 1991; MacDonald 1983). Images of blacks as overly emotional and servile dominated television shows in the 1950s and early 1960s. The few attempts to show blacks in more positive roles were met with resistance by southern television affiliates, which refused to air them. Since the networks needed to have their shows carried in as many cities as possible, stereotypical images of minorities acceptable to white southern audiences dominated (Montgomery 1989:15). In the 1970s, the image of minorities on television changed dramatically. One reason was the rise of black activism, as the NAACP and the Congress of Racial Equality (CORE) helped bring about congressional hearings that criticized the television industry for its inattention to minorities both on the screen and in its hiring practices (Montgomery 1989:22; MacDonald 1983). Another reason was court rulings that a local television station failing to meet the needs of its community by acting in a discriminatory manner could have its license renewal denied. The result was that southern affiliates could no longer refuse to carry television shows on the basis of the racial characters they contained (Montgomery 1989:23–24). But the primary reason for the rise of positive African-American characters in television fiction was the discovery that blacks were heavy users of the medium. "The TV networks . . . turned to black viewers to bolster sagging primetime ratings" (MacDonald 1990:248). Beginning with daytime soap operas in the mid-1960s and continuing through urban dramas such as "I Spy," "Rockford Files," "Hill Street Blues," "Miami Vice," and "L. A. Law," blacks began appearing as strong and successful characters—doctors, lawyers, detectives—on television. "The Cosby Show" in 1984 epitomized the positive representation of African-Americans.[1]

A transformation also began to take place on television news sets throughout the 1970s and 1980s as well. Local news operations in the vast majority of American communities have hired black reporters and anchors, in part to attract black audiences (Entman 1990).

CRIME AND RACE ON TELEVISION

Crime is an extremely popular topic in television fiction. About 30 percent of prime time television entertainment programming is crime shows, with crime being the largest subject matter for television fiction (Gerbner and Gross 1980; Surette 1992). Previous content analyses of crime shows reveal an overrepresentation of violent crime. Murder and robbery are the most common forms, with murder accounting for about 25 percent of all television crime.

While images of blacks in television fiction have rarely been positive, stereotypes of minorities as criminals have been uncommon. Studies show that white criminals from higher socioeconomic backgrounds are overrepresented (Dominick 1973; Estep and MacDonald 1984; Garofalo 1981; Potter and Ware 1987). This is partly because of formula demands; that is, in order to have powerful heroic crime fighters, it becomes necessary for them to have formidable foes such as organized crime figures or business cartels. However, the underrepresentation of minorities as criminals is also because of concern about negative stereotyping of minorities and the potential organized protests that might result. Todd Gitlin (1983:286–324) notes that standards policies deliberately limited the portrayal of nonwhites as criminals in television shows. Programs such as "Hill Street Blues" that featured black and Hispanic lawbreakers in an attempt to be "realistic" about crime often had to struggle with network executives and even minority actors on the show to do so.

The nonfiction world of television presents a somewhat more complicated picture of the relationship between race and crime. The amount of attention paid to crime on television news parallels that of fiction television. About 10–15 percent of national news involves crime (Cirino 1972; Graber 1980), while about 20 percent of local news is crime stories (Graber 1980). The image of crime on nonfiction television is similar. Sheley and Ashkins (1981) note that murder and robbery comprised about 80 percent of reported crimes on New Orleans's television news, although police data showed them to be far less common.

But the picture of crime painted by news reports is somewhat unclear. According to Graber (1980:57–58), criminals in the news tend to be either violent street criminals or higher class property offenders. According to Surette (1992:63–64), criminals shown on the news tend to be slightly older than that reflected in official arrest statistics. Although there is some attention given to white collar crime, researchers argue that there is an underrepresentation of elite crime (Evans and Lundman 1983; Molotch and Lester 1981; Quinney 1970). Regardless, although the public may be indignant about corporate crime, it may be safe to assume that it is more concerned about street crime. And street crime, as it is seen in nonfiction television, is primarily an activity of young minority males. Sheley and Ashkins (1981) found that blacks accounted for over 80 percent of robbery suspects on New Orleans television. Entman's study of television news in Chicago showed that violent crime committed by blacks accounted for about 41 percent of all local news stories, and that stories would suggest that blacks are more dangerous than whites:

> [T]he accused black criminals were usually illustrated by glowering mug shots or by footage of them being led around in handcuffs, their arms held by uniformed white policemen. None of the accused white criminals during the week studied were shown in mug shots or in physical custody. (1990:337)

Furthermore, white victimization by blacks appeared to have high priority as new stories.

In the past decade a new form of "nonfiction" television has emerged: tabloid-style shows that blur even further the distinction between fact and fiction, a trend noted by numerous media scholars (Altheide 1976; Fishman 1980; Manoff and Schudson 1986; Postman and Powers 1992). As we noted earlier, these shows have proliferated because they are inexpensive and yield relatively high returns in viewership. Most analyses of these shows have been mixed and anecdotal. Oliver (1994) has done one of the few systematic content analyses of reality-based police shows: "America's Most Wanted," "Cops," "Top Cops," "FBI, The Untold Story," and "American Detective." She found that violent crime was overrepresented as was the proportion of crimes solved. The shows also presented a world where white characters were more likely to be police officers, and nonwhites were more likely criminal suspects. These depictions were only slight exaggerations from those found in official data. However, Oliver concludes that these programs are more likely to portray "a cast of characters in which nonwhites are typically the 'bad guys,' and a plot which most often features the 'restoration of justice' though often through aggressive behaviors" (1994:189) of heroic white police officers.

TELEVISED VIOLENCE AND FEAR OF CRIME

At the root of these analyses of race and crime on television is a concern for the impact that these images have on viewing audiences: do they contribute to concern about crime and foster racist attitudes? Studies of the impact of mass media images on audiences are complex, confusing, and contradictory. A good starting place in examining this issue is the work of George Gerbner and his associates (Gerbner and Gross 1976, 1980; Gerbner, Gross, Jackson-Beeck, Jeffries-Fox, and Signorielli 1978; Gerbner, Gross, Morgan, and Signorielli 1980). Gerbner examined the relationship between watching large amounts of television and the viewers' perception of the world. His assumption was that much of television content contained repeated themes, which he identified through "cultivation analysis." Gerbner and his associates began an annual content analysis of television shows in 1968 to identify what they called "cultural indicators," messages about wealth, violence, beauty, power, and prejudice that are portrayed symbolically and may subconsciously influence viewers. These cultural indicators provided quantified measures of the social world depicted on television and were compared to other measures of the social world, such as those found in government statistics. Finally, survey respondents with varying amounts of television exposure were asked questions about their perceptions of the world. Gerbner and his colleagues found that frequent viewers of television were more likely to have a view of the world that matched the images repeatedly presented through the medium than that reflected by official data (the presumed "real world"). Since violent acts pervaded television, these heavy viewers saw the world as a meaner and more dangerous, crime-ridden place than government statistics suggested.

Other studies have criticized and refined Gerbner's arguments, positing that perceptions of crime are more influenced by the context in which crime and violence are presented. Researchers suggest that when individuals attempt to construct reality, they judge the veracity of media sources (Hawkins and Pingree 1981; O'Keefe 1984). Nonfiction accounts presented by what are considered to be reliable sources have more weight than fictional accounts. Some studies report that if a high proportion of crime news focuses on local crime and portrays it in sensational ways or stresses its random, unpredictable nature, it leads to greater fear of crime among readers or viewers (Heath 1984; Liske and Baccaglini 1990). Surprisingly, news of distant sensational crime reduces fearfulness and anxiety about local crime (Heath 1984). From these studies we may draw three general conclusions. First, nonfictional images have greater impact than fictional ones.[2] Second, the more a message or theme is repeated, the more influential it becomes. Third, the closer the crime is to home, the more it may generate fear among viewers. Shows such as "Cops," which are presented as *factual*, would therefore be more likely than fictional television shows to produce fear of crime. Furthermore, "Cops" is a show that is broadcast *frequently*, allowing for repetition of themes. In some communities, including the one in which our data were gathered, seven episodes are aired weekly. However, for most viewers, the episodes shown on "Cops" describe crimes in distant locales, although the format of the show—traveling each episode to a different community—may make it seem that crime could be happening anywhere. Nonetheless, our position is that "Cops" and similar reality-based programs probably are not significant factors in producing *personal fear* of crime. However, they may be significant in shaping a general view of crime and increasing *social concern* over crime as a serious societal problem (Barrile 1984). As Surette suggests: "The media provide both a foundation for the public's various final images and the mortar with which the public constructs its social reality" (1992:96). These shows influence our perceptions of the nature and extent of crime. Furthermore, Roberts and Doob (1990) have found that tabloid-style coverage of crime in newspapers creates the greatest support for harsh sentences for lawbreakers. We assume that tabloid-style television shows may have similar effects depending on the images of crime, criminals, and victims they present. In short, although shows like "Cops" may not increase fear of safety in one's own familiar community, they may induce greater concern for crime in other locales: distant cities with large minority populations or even *nearby* minority neighborhoods into which most viewers seldom venture.

METHOD

Sample

The television show "Cops" was recorded for analysis for two-week periods in March, June, and September of 1994. Forty-two half-hour programs containing a total of 135 criminal vignettes comprised our sample. These vignettes, usually three or four per show, were our unit of analysis.

The data gleaned from the sample included roles involved in the "dramas" presented in each criminal vignette. These roles were classified as "law enforcement," "suspected criminal," and "victim." The estimated age, gender, race (white; nonwhite, including Hispanic; other; and "don't know") were coded for each type of actor. In cases where there were multiple actors of differing races, these were coded "mixed." Our unit of analysis was not the individual person, but the type of actor. Thus, if there were multiple black female victims of the same age, these were coded as just one unit of victim.

Also examined were the relationship between the victim and offender, whether a weapon was used in the crime, and the type of crime committed. Crimes were categorized as violent, property, drug, other "victimless," domestic, and other. Finally, we noted whether an arrest for a crime was made.

Our hypotheses were: (1) the proportion of violent crime featured on "Cops" would be much greater than that reflected in official data; (2) crimes would be cleared by arrest at much higher rates on "Cops" than official data indicate; (3) the percentage of nonwhite offenders on "Cops" would be greater than found in crime statistics; and (4) the victims of crime on "Cops" would be disproportionately white, compared to official statistics. Lawlessness on "Cops" would be typically violent crime committed by nonwhites, often claiming whites as victims.

Analyses

The first set of analyses compares the world of crime found on "Cops" with that described in the *Uniform Crime Reports* (UCR) for 1994. Here we examine the types of crimes portrayed, the racial composition of the actors involved, and the outcomes (e.g., arrested or not arrested). Our second set of analyses examines the dynamics of crime; that is, what relationships are shown between victims and offenders, and what types of crimes are associated with which types of offenders.

The data in Table 1 indicate that "Cops" overrepresents violent crime. Murder, rape, aggravated assault, and robbery are staples of "Cops," accounting for about 43 percent of all crime shown. Drugs and other victimless crime, typically sex-related (e.g., prostitution), also frequently appear as featured acts of lawlessness. Property offenses, which year after year comprise about 85 percent of the crime tallied by the FBI's Crime Index, account for less than 10 percent of crime on "Cops." Interestingly, domestic violence is also popular, accounting for a little over 12 percent of crime shown on "Cops." (These were classified as violent crimes, aggravated assaults, and are not shown separately in Table 1.)

Table 2 provides a more direct comparison between crimes shown on "Cops" and their prevalence as measured by the *UCR Crime Index*, which

Table 1. Frequency and Percentage of Crimes on "Cops"

Crime Types	Number	Percent
Violent	58	43.0
Property	11	8.1
Drugs	30	22.2
Other victimless	27	20.0
Other	9	6.7
Total	135	100.0

Table 2. Index Crimes on "Cops" and in the UCR (1994)

Type of Crime	"Cops"		UCR	
	Number	%	Number	%
Violent	58	84	1,864,168	13
Property	11	16	12,127,507	87
Total	69	100	13,991,675	100

includes only certain violent (murder, rape, robbery, aggravated assault) and property (larceny, burglary, auto theft, arson) crimes. If we count only index crimes shown on "Cops," violent crime (fifty-eight cases) totals 84 percent and property crime (eleven cases) 16 percent.

We also should observe that, because of the format of the program, corporate crime committed by more affluent and predominantly white males does not enter the picture. Cops on "Cops" pursue crime in the streets rather than crime in the suites.

Table 3 presents information about the racial and ethnic representation of actors—law enforcement, criminal suspects, and victims—involved in crime vignettes on "Cops." While nonwhites are rarely portrayed as criminals in fictional television shows, in "Cops" they account for slightly over half of all criminal suspects. This is a slight exaggeration from arrest data

Table 3. Racial Characteristics of Roles on "Cops"

Race	Suspects		Law		Victims	
	Number	%	Number	%	Number	%
White	64	47.4	84	62.2	39	28.9
Nonwhite	66	48.8	7	5.2	37	27.4
Mixed	0	0	43	31.90	0	0
Unknown	5	3.7	1	0.7	59	43.7
Total	135	100.0	135	100.0	135	100.0

provided by the *Uniform Crime Reports* (U.S. Department of Justice 1995:217), where nonwhites typically account for slightly less than half of all arrests for violent crime and about one-third of all property crime arrests. The image of criminality presented by "Cops" suggests that crime is more likely to be committed by nonwhites than whites.

Table 3 also provides data about the race of law enforcement personnel. In about two-thirds of crime vignettes, law officers are white, and in about 30 percent of cases there are white and nonwhite police presented. Very rarely are just nonwhite law enforcement figures shown. Typically, "Cops" presents crime as a drama in which white police officers do battle against nonwhite criminals.

Finally, Table 3 describes the racial characteristics of victims of crime presented on "Cops." It shows that 28.9 percent of victims shown are white, and 27.4 percent are nonwhite. The largest category of victims is "unknown," accounting for 43.7 percent of victims. In cases where a victim is clearly indicated, *over half are white* (51.3 percent)!

Our data (Table 4) also show that only about 41 percent of the crimes involve exclusively male victims; women alone are victims in 23 percent of the cases. In thirty vignettes (22.2 percent), the sex of the victim is not known. The most common age for victimization is estimated as being between twenty-one and forty, with victimization rates for younger or older age groups being relatively rare (Table 5).

Some comments are in order regarding the high percentage of "unknown" victims. This ambiguity plays well into the market demands of the medium because it allows for easy audience identification with the victim role regardless of race, age, or gender of the viewer. In many cases where "unknown" victims are specified, the crime is sale of illegal drugs. The "victim" of these crimes presumably is "society."

It is the image of the victim where "Cops" most radically departs from the image of crime presented in official government statistics, which indicate that nonwhites, and especially young black males, have the highest rates of victimization for the types of crime commonly pictured on tabloid crime shows.[3] By underplaying nonwhites as victims of crime, shows like "Cops" foster an attitude toward crime control that calls for increased severity for the

Table 4.   Gender of Known Victim on "Cops"[a]

Gender	Number	%
Male	43	41.0
Female	24	23.0
Both	38	36.0
Total	105	100.0

[a]In thirty cases the gender was unknown.

Table 5. Estimated Age of the Victim on
          "Cops"

Age	Number	%
>13	4	3.0
13–20	12	8.9
21–40	42	31.1
41–65	13	9.6
65+	0	0.0
Unknown	64	47.4
Total	135	100.0

"other" who commits crime rather than one that suggests modifying the social environment where crime occurs—creating jobs, improving education and other social services—so that victimization of poor and nonwhite citizens might be reduced.

Table 6 compares the percentage of crimes cleared by arrest on "Cops" with that presented in the UCR. According to the UCR about 21 percent of Index offenses are cleared annually, with much variation for different offenses. Typically, only about 18 percent of property crimes are cleared in a given year; clearance rates for violent crime are much higher (44.6 percent), with murder having the highest clearance rate. The war on crime presented on "Cops" is being fought much more effectively. Almost 75 percent of all crimes are cleared by arrest. Almost two-thirds of violent crimes end with the arrest of the criminal suspect, and for virtually every other type of crime covered the arrest rates are even higher. The sole exception is for domestic disturbances, where only 29.4 percent culminate in the arrest of the assailant.

We also examined whether there were differences in the types of crimes committed on "Cops" by differing race. Table 7 reveals some striking differ-

Table 6. Crimes Cleared by Arrest in the UCR and "Cops"[a]

Type of Crime	UCR		"Cops"				
	%	Number	%	Yes	No	DK	Total
Violent crime	44.6	778,730	65.8	25	09	04	38
Property crime	17.7	2,131,700	88.8	08	01		09
Drug offenses			95.5	21	01		22
Other victimless			96.6	26	01		27
Domestic			29.4	05	12		17
Other			72.7	16	05	01	22
Total	21.4	2,910,430	74.8	101	19	05	135

[a]UCR data from U.S. Department of Justice (1995:Table 29, "Total Estimated Arrests, U.S., 1994").

Table 7.   Race of Offender by Type of Crime on "Cops"[a]

| Type of Crime | White | | Nonwhite | | |
	Number	%	Number	%	Total
Violent	8	12.7	26	40.0	34
Property	2	3.2	7	10.8	9
Drugs	13	20.6	8	12.3	21
Other victimless	16	25.4	10	15.4	26
Domestic	10	15.9	7	10.8	17
Other	14	22.2	7	10.8	21
Total	63	100.0	65	100.0	128

[a]Excluded are seven cases where the race of the offender was unknown (N = 5) or where both white and nonwhite offenders were presented (N = 2).

ences. Although the number of offenders who are white is quite similar to the number of nonwhite lawbreakers, nonwhite criminal suspects are disproportionately associated with violent crimes. About 40 percent of all crimes committed by nonwhites are violent ones, while this is the case for only 12.7 percent of white suspects. White offenders are most commonly associated with crimes such as prostitution or those categorized as "other." These include such offenses as leaving the scene of an auto accident, attempting to purchase prescription drugs through false pretenses, and reckless driving. In all, twenty-six of the thirty-four violent crimes (76 percent) and seven of nine property offenses (78 percent) coded were allegedly committed by nonwhites.

Official data such as the Uniform Crime Reports (U.S. Department of Justice 1995) suggest that minority group members are involved in a disproportionate share of criminal activity. Although blacks comprise 12 percent of the population, they account for about 47 percent of violent crime arrests and 34 percent of property arrests. These data have been suspect, however. A number of studies claim that racial discrimination in the arrest process may account for why violent crime seems disproportionately a black phenomenon (Dennifer and Schutt 1982; Huizinga and Elliott 1987). But the image of crime presented by "Cops" further exaggerates these figures and suggests that the vast majority of serious crimes are committed by nonwhites.

Finally, we examined the extent to which crime on "Cops" was portrayed as an interracial phenomenon. The data presented in Table 8 show that crime on television is typically intraracial, consistent with that of official data. When the race of both the victim and offender are known, we find that all crimes featuring white offenders were directed against white victims, and about 75 percent of crimes with nonwhite criminal suspects involved nonwhite victims. However, in about 25 percent of the crimes shown, nonwhite suspects claimed whites as victims. There were no portrayals of white sus-

Table 8. Race of Offender by Race of Victim on "Cops"[a]

Race of Offender	White	Victim	Nonwhite	Victim	Unknown	Victim	Total	
White	26 (54.2)	(66.7)	0 (0.0)	(0.0)	22 (45.8)	(57.9)	48 (100.0)	(42.1)
Nonwhite	11 (18.6)	(28.2)	34 (57.6)	(91.9)	14 (23.7)	(36.8)	59 (100.0)	(51.8)
Mix	0 (0.0)	(0.0)	0 (0.0)	(0.0)	2 (100.0)	(5.2)	2 (100.0)	(1.8)
Unknown	2 (40.0)	(05.1)	3 (60.0)	(8.1)	0 (0.0)	(0.0)	5 (100.0)	(4.4)
Total	39 (34.2)	(100.0)	37 (32.5)	(100.0)	38 (33.3)	(100.0)	114 (100.0)	(100.0)

[a]Excluded are twenty-one cases where race of offender or victim is unknown.

pects involved in crimes against nonwhites. In the eleven situations of non-white on white crime shown, over half involved violent crimes.

DISCUSSION

Tabloid television shows could be informational and provide a useful service for viewers. In following law enforcement officers into some of the unfortunate neighborhoods where crime sometimes occurs, they could help place crime into a broader social context. These programs could provide a forum where those whose voices are rarely heard in the media might express their opinions. They could show just how mundane and ordinary most crime and most criminals are; that crime is not typically the well-planned violent act of the sexual psychopath, but rather is the bumbling larceny of the boy next door. Sometimes they do. Occasionally a thoughtful cop will describe the living conditions of victims and offenders and suggest that the lack of jobs, the declining schools, and the decay of housing and social services may explain more about crime than simply the mental state of those captured in the war on crime. And every so often the ambivalence and anguish of the victims of domestic crime slips through.

But generally the world of crime shown on "Cops" is one where violent crime is far more common than property offenses, and where crimes by organizations and the affluent are not portrayed. Crime is a battle between white police officers and nonwhite violent offenders, and the war on crime ends in arrest almost 75 percent of the time. Most crime is intraracial, but in the few cases where crime crosses racial boundaries, it is always nonwhite criminals claiming whites as victims; in more than half of these cases, the crime is a violent one. In situations where victims of crime are clearly identified, over half the time they are white. In almost half of the cases, the victim is ambiguous or unknown. Often these consist of drug crimes, where "society" is the victim. Such ambiguity allows for an interpretation that any and all of us may become victims of crime.

It could be claimed that "Cops" is simply a mirror image of crime in our society, or at least no more of a distortion of the "crime problem" than politicians and official data suggest. Our findings suggest otherwise. Crime on "Cops" clearly differs from the picture of crime painted by official government statistics. It makes more sense to conclude that crime on this show, like other versions of tabloid television, is a caricature of crime that is shaped more by the organizational demands of television than by carefully documented representations of reality. The bizarre and sensational take precedence over the typical and ordinary. The accessibility of information is a critical factor; there are no lengthy investigations into lawlessness of the powerful. Instead, reporters simply follow police officers about as they search for juicy bits of street crime that might play well for the camera. Even the crimes uncovered using this approach are polished and sanitized for mass consumption. Debra Seagal describes her experience as editor for another "reality-based" television show, "American Detective":

> By the time our 9 million viewers flip on their tubes, we've reduced fifty or sixty hours of mundane and compromising video into short, action-packed segments of tantalizing crack-filled, dope-dealing, junkie-busting cop culture. How easily we downplay the pathos of the suspect; how cleverly we breeze past the complexities that cast doubt on the very system that has produced the criminal activity in the first place. How effortlessly we smooth out the indiscretions of the lumpen detectives and casually make them appear as pistol-flailing heroes rushing across the screen. (1993:51)

Footage from various crime episodes is seamlessly edited together to enhance the story being told, and in some cases the actual violence filmed has to be cut from the show because it is too violent. Facts are selected, shaped, and twisted to fit the crime formulas being used.

There are two important ways that this study could be extended. First, more data need to be gathered on the images of crime and criminality presented on "Cops" and other tabloid crime shows. Although forty-two shows comprised our sample, these do not yield enough data for a detailed analysis on subsets of crime vignettes. For example, it would be useful to know more about just what types of crimes involve nonwhite offenders and white victims. Our data yielded eleven cases, but these were too few to attempt any significant statistical analysis. Second, more research needs to be done on the characteristics of heavy viewers of tabloid television. Who are they, and what do they make of these shows? It is our assumption that shows like "Cops" reinforce the view that the world is a dangerous place, especially large American cities with substantial minority populations, but we have no data on viewers to support this.

Despite these limitations, this study has two important implications. First, since nonwhites are heavily represented in "Cops" as lawbreakers, negative racial stereotypes are perpetuated. Whereas the media are extremely sensitive about presenting caricatures of minorities in fiction formats, here in reality-based television where there might be greater influence on audiences' perceptions, the oversimplified and uncritical image of crime as predominantly the activity of black males is common.

Second, since whites are disproportionately shown as victims of serious crime, this may have the effect of making whites more concerned about crime as a social problem. As Karmen observes, a person is more than twice as likely to be injured in an automobile accident than to be physically harmed by an assailant:

Yet campaigns to improve highway safety, remove drunken drivers from the road, and add crash protection devices like air bags to vehicles attract much less attention and arouse much less passion than campaigns to make the streets safer by cracking down on criminals. (1984:50)

Increased concern for crime is evident by the dramatic rise in the home security business. In 1988 about 10 percent of households used security systems. By 1997 that figure is expected to reach 20 percent (Rodger 1995). Currently, home security has become a five billion dollar industry, with sales in certain areas expected to grow as much as 50 percent in the next few years (Fitzgerald 1994; Abdeddaim 1995).

But while concern for crime is growing, less sympathy is extended to nonwhite populations, who are more likely to be the victims of serious crime. As Rapping notes:

The language, the brutality, the tackiness of the social scene, the bad hair, the untidy lawns, dirty sidewalks are a turnoff. We would not wish to have any of the participants—criminals, cops, or victims—over for dinner. These are not our neighbors; they are the people we see on subways and sidewalks, begging or dozing. (1994:37–38)

Shows like "Cops" reinforce the idea that criminals are not like us. It is not the sixteen-year-old neighbor, the college student we date, or the corporate executive that we need to worry about. It is the black male in the ghetto, the illegal alien from Mexico, the working-class girl from a broken home who are criminals. They are a strange and dangerous breed driven to crime not because of poverty or injustice, but because they suffer from biological or psychological flaws. Consequently, politicians have no difficulty selling the idea of an increasingly punitive criminal justice system with fewer constitutional restraints to keep our neighborhoods safe from the demonic "other" we have constructed as criminal.

NOTES

1.   Parenti points out, however, that while the "Cosby Show" is an advancement in black imagery, it is a sitcom that "still has Black people playing for laughs" (1992:141). The National Commission for Working Women of Wider Opportunities for Women (WOW) criticized TV for presenting an inaccurate view of racial matters in America, noting that only 10 percent of minorities on TV were working class or poor and claiming that the medium painted a misleading view of a racially harmonious world where injustice resulted from character flaws rather than social structures (in MacDonald 1990:250).

2.   Parenti (1992:3) would disagree and argue that fictional media poses a great-

er influence on values and beliefs because the audience is less aware of the ideological messages embedded in the texts than is the case for nonfictional media presentations.

3. This is deceptive because we are comparing percentages with rates of victimization. It is true that the percentage of crimes where whites are victimized is high, since whites comprise about 88 percent of the U.S. population. However, in looking at crime from the viewer's perspective, rates seem a valid figure to use since they reveal the chances of personal victimization more than percentages would.

REFERENCES

Abdeddaim, M. 1995. "Safety in Numbers: Retailers Jump into Home Security." *HFN* 69/4(October, 23):1.

Altheide, David. 1976. *Creating Reality: How TV News Distorts Events.* Beverly Hills, CA: Sage.

Barrile, Leo. 1984. "Television and Attitudes about Crime. Do Heavy Viewers Distort Criminality and Support Retributive Justice?" Pp. 141–158 in *Justice and the Media,* edited by R. Surette. Springfield, IL: Charles C. Thomas.

Cirino, R. 1972. *Don't Blame the People.* New York: Vintage.

Dennifer, D. and R. Schutt. 1982. "Race and Juvenile Justice Processing in Court and Police Agencies." *American Journal of Sociology* 87:1113–32.

Dominick, J. 1973. "Crime and Law Enforcement on Primetime Television." *Public Opinion Quarterly* 37:241–50.

Ely, Melvin. 1991. *The Adventures of Amos' N' Andy.* New York: Free Press.

Entman, R. M. 1990. "Modern Racism and the Images of Blacks in Local Television News." *Critical Studies in Mass Communication* 7(4):332–45.

Estep, R. and P. McDonald. 1984. "How Prime-Time Crime Evolved on TV, 1976–1983." Pp. 110–23 in *Justice and the Media,* edited by R. Surette. Springfield, IL: Charles C. Thomas.

Evans, S. and R. Lundman. 1983. "Newspaper Coverage of Corporate Price-Fixing." *Criminology* 21:521–41.

Fennell, Tom. 1992. "True-to-Life TV." *Maclean's* 105(December 7):48.

Fishman, Mark. 1980. *Manufacturing the News.* Austin: University of Texas Press.

Fitzgerald, Kate. 1994. "Gizmos Turn Home Protection into a Boom: Rising Fear of Crime Moves Consumers to Make Fortress out of Home." *Advertising Age,* January 10, p. 1.

Friedman, David. 1989. "True Grit." *Rolling Stone,* April 6, p. 26.

Garofalo, J. 1981. "Crime and the Mass Media: A Selective Review of Research." *Journal of Research in Crime and Delinquency* 18:319–50.

Gerbner, G. and L. Gross. 1976. "Living with Television: The Violence Profile." *Journal of Communication* 26:173–99.

———. 1980. "The Violent Face of Television and Its Lessons." Pp. 149–62 in *Children and the Faces of Television,* edited by E. Palmer and A. Dorr. New York: Academic Press.

Gerbner, G., L. Gross, M. Jackson-Beeck, S. Jeffries-Fox, and N. Signorielli. 1978.

"Cultural Indicators: Violence Profile No. 9." *Journal of Communication* 29:177–96.

Gerbner, G., L. Gross, M. Morgan, and N. Signorielli. 1980. "The Mainstreaming of America: Violence Profile No. 11." *Journal of Communication* 30:10–29.

Gitlin, Todd. 1983. *Inside Prime Time.* New York: Pantheon.

Graber, Doris. 1980. *Crime News and the Public.* New York: Praeger.

Hawkins, R. and S. Pingree. 1981. "Some Processes in the Cultivation Effect." *Communication Research* 7:193–226.

Heath, L. 1984. "Impact of Newspaper Crime Reports on Fear of Crime: Multimethodological Investigation." *Journal of Personality and Social Psychology* 47:263–76.

Huizinga, D. and D. Elliott. 1987. "Juvenile Offenders: Prevalence, Offender Incidence, and Arrest Rates by Race." *Crime and Delinquency* 33:206–23.

Karmen, Andrew. 1984. *Crime Victims.* Monterey, CA: Brooks/Cole.

Katz, Jon. 1993. "Covering the Cops: A TV Show Moves In Where Journalists Fear to Tread." *Columbia Journalism Review* (January/February):25–30.

Liske, A. and W. Baccaglini. 1990. "Feeling Safe by Comparison: Crime in the Newspapers." *Social Problems* 37(3):360–74.

MacDonald, J. Fred. 1983. *Blacks and White TV.* Chicago: Nelson-Hall.

———. 1990. *One Nation Under Television.* New York: Pantheon.

Manoff, K. and M. Schudson. 1986. *Reading the News.* New York: Pantheon.

Molotch, H., and M. Lester. 1981. "News as Purposive Behavior: On the Strategic Use of Routine Events, Accidents and Scandals." Pp. 118–37 in *Manufacture of News,* edited by S. Cohen and J. Young. Newbury Park, CA: Sage.

Montgomery, Kathryn. 1989. *Target: Prime Time.* New York: Oxford.

O'Keefe, G. 1984. "Public Views on Crime: Television Exposure and Media Credibility." Pp. 514–37 in *Communication Yearbook* 8, edited by R. N. Bostrum. Thousand Oaks, CA: Sage.

Oliver, M. 1994. "Portrayals of Crime, Race, and Aggression in Reality-based Police Shows." *Journal of Broadcasting & Electronic Media* 38(2):179–92.

Parenti, Michael. 1992. *Make-Believe Media: The Politics of Entertainment.* New York: St. Martin's.

Postman, Neil and Steve Powers. 1992. *How to Watch TV News.* New York: Penguin.

Potter, W. J. and W. Ware. 1987. "An Analysis of the Contexts of Antisocial Acts on Primetime Television." *Communication Research* 14:664–86.

Quinney, R. 1970. *The Social Reality of Crime.* Boston: Little, Brown.

Rapping, Elayne. 1992. "Tabloid TV and Social Reality." *Progressive* 56(August):35–37.

———. 1994. "Cops, Crime, and TV." *Progressive* 58(4, April):36–39.

Roberts, J., and A. Doob. 1990. "News Media Influences on Public Views on Sentencing." *Law and Human Behavior* 14(5):451–68.

Rodger, W. 1995. "Home Security: Demand, Better Tech Fuel Sales." *Washington Business Journal* 14(19, September 22):18.

Sauter, Van Gordon. 1992. "Rating the Reality Shows—And Keeping Tabs on the Tabloids." *TV Guide,* May 2–8, p. 18.

Seagal, Debra. 1993. "Tales from the Cutting Room Floor: The Reality of 'Reality-Based' Television." *Harper's,* November, p. 50.
Sheley, J. and C. Ashkins. 1981. "Crime, Crime News, and Crime Views." *Public Opinion Quarterly* 45:492–506.
Surette, Ray. 1992. *Media, Crime and Criminal Justice: Images and Realities.* Pacific Grove, CA: Brooks/Cole.
U.S. Department of Justice; 1995. *Crime in the United States, 1994: Uniform Crime Reports.* Washington, DC: USGPO.
Waters, Harry F. 1989. "TV's Crime Wave Gets Real." *Newsweek,* May 15, p. 72.
Zoglin, Richard. 1988. "Realism in Television." *Time,* May 16, p. 97.
———. 1992. "The Cops and the Cameras." *Time,* April 6, p. 62.

9

Mixed Messages:
Images of Domestic Violence on "Reality" Television

DIANNE CYR CARMODY

For decades, researchers have argued that television provides us with half-ltruths by only reflecting crime that is interesting, exciting, or sensational (Cavender and Bond-Maupin 1993; Pandiani 1978). Several studies have supported this assertion and demonstrated that the "typical criminal" and the "typical crime" on television news and police dramas bear little resemblance to reality (Oliver 1994; Sheley and Ashkins 1981). Repeatedly, researchers have noted that the media tend to overrepresent violent crimes and underrepresent nonviolent offenses or property crimes (Graber 1980; Oliver 1994).

This misrepresentation of crime may be found on news programs, crime dramas, and the relatively new "reality" television programs (Bortner 1984; Surette 1992). While news programs claim to be objective and accurate, their coverage of crime focuses instead on crimes that are unusual and violent. In a recent analysis of crime news, Surette (1992) notes that newsworthy items are defined as those which are uncommon. Surette argues that the news media's lack of attention to more typical kinds of crime presents viewers with a distorted view of the crime problem in America.

Historically, police dramas have also presented unrealistic portrayals of criminal offenders and their victims. Some scholars have suggested that fictional police programs reinforce images of a "mean and dangerous" world and support positive perceptions of police. Surette notes that police dramas tend to emphasize a "war" metaphor, in which criminals are seen as predators and strong social control measures are presented as necessary and appropriate. Most police dramas also depict police officers in a positive light, successfully solving crimes and dispensing justice before the next commercial break.

The most recent addition to crime programming, reality-based police shows, has attracted large audiences in recent years (Fennel 1992). These programs, many of which utilize actual video footage of police officers at work, differ in important ways from the police dramas of the past. Unlike police dramas, reality-based programs feature live action shots taken with hand-held cameras or reenactments of spectacular cases. They provide short crime stories without examining the context of events. The viewer rarely knows what events preceded or followed the crime. Often, the viewer is forced to rely on the official interpretation of the event offered by the officer on the scene (Andersen 1994).

The impact these "infotainment" programs may have on public perceptions of crime remains unclear. Like police dramas, they tend to overrepresent violent crimes and present successful portrayals of police officers as "crime fighters" (Estep and Macdonald 1983; Alpert and Dunham 1992). While a positive image of police may not harm viewers, it is important to explore the images of the "typical criminal" and the "typical crime," as presented by reality television programs. Such images may serve to heighten viewers' fear of crime, and reinforce stereotypes of criminal offenders and their victims.

While some may argue that the media fascination with violent crime is harmless, others note that it may result in inaccurate perceptions of victimization risk and increased fear of crime among viewers. Gerbner and Gross note, "We have found that people who watch a lot of TV see the real world as more dangerous and frightening than those who watch very little. Heavy viewers are less trustful of their fellow citizens and more fearful of the real world" (1976:41).

This connection between media images of crime and viewers' fears may be especially important for women. One of the most consistent findings in the research on the fear of crime is that women tend to fear criminal victimization more than men (Crawford, Jones, Woodhouse, and Young 1990; Gordon and Riger 1989). This is an interesting pattern, since crime surveys show that young men suffer the greatest risk of violent victimization (with the exception of sexual assault). In spite of this, women's fear of crime is three times higher than that of men (Stanko 1992). This inconsistency has led some to assume that women's higher levels of fear are linked to the horrors of rape, which may be combined with other crimes. Thus, women may be more fearful of *any* victimization, since a sexual assault may accompany it (Warr 1984). In this way, Ferraro (1995) claims that sexual assault may "shadow" other types of victimization among women, increasing women's fear of all types of crime.

Feminist theorists, however, argue that women's fear of violent crime results in part from being physically abused by a husband, boyfriend, or other intimate, an experience largely untouched by crime surveys (Smith 1988). Thus, higher fear levels among some women may be based in their own experiences as victims of domestic violence.

IMAGES OF DOMESTIC VIOLENCE

Media images of violence against women may also increase feelings of fear and powerlessness among female viewers (Reid and Finchilescu 1995). Since the media depiction of women most typically focuses on their role as victims, these images may serve to perpetuate and reinforce fear among women (Gerbner and Gross 1976). Additionally, media depictions of crimes against women may also perpetuate negative attitudes and stereotypes about women. In an analysis of media accounts of sex crimes, Benedict notes that two central narratives emerge: victims are depicted as either "virgins" or "vamps." This dichotomy shapes the media coverage of the cases, and supports "rape myths," such as "women provoke rape," "only promiscuous women are victimized," and "women cry rape for revenge" (1992:14–18). Cultural support for rape myths has been linked to victims' self-blame and reluctance to report rapes to the police (1992:14–18).

Domestic violence researchers have also identified negative stereotypes or myths associated with female victims of spouse assault (Bart and Moran 1993). These include "the masochism thesis" (Caputi 1992) and "the drunken bum theory" (Kantor and Straus 1990). Additionally, some consider domestic assaults to be "minor lovers' quarrels," rarely resulting in serious injuries. Others support the view of domestic assaults as "mutual combat" between opponents of equal size and strength. Finally, some consider the victim of domestic violence to be uncooperative, refusing to assist in the prosecution of the offender. All of these stereotypes assign some responsibility to the victim of domestic violence, and may serve to discourage women from reporting assaults to the police. Additionally, such images may reinforce women's fear of crime. Because these stereotypes of victims of domestic violence are central to the current analysis of reality police programs, each is examined in more detail below.

The Masochism Thesis

As its name implies, the masochism thesis suggests that victims of spouse assault obtain some gratification or pleasure from their victimization. This approach clearly removes responsibility from the perpetrator and blames the victim. While few publicly support the masochism thesis directly, many do question why battered women hesitate to leave abusive mates. In fact, "Why doesn't she just leave?" is one of the most frequently asked questions concerning battered women. Unfortunately, the barriers faced by many battered women are overwhelming, and may include economic or emotional dependence on the abuser, fear of retaliation, lack of community resources, and the need to support and protect dependent children (Barnett, Miller-Perrin, and Perrin 1997). In spite of a lack of empirical support, the masochism thesis clearly remains a part of our popular culture.

The Drunken Bum Theory

The drunken bum theory also relieves the batterer of responsibility, since it asserts that spouse abuse is caused by alcohol or other drugs. If a perpetrator is drunk at the time of the attack, he may use that to explain or excuse his abusive behavior. Research suggests that alcohol does play a role in about one out of four instances of wife assault (Kantor and Straus 1990). This connection is not as clear as it may seem, however. Although alcohol use is a factor in some cases of domestic violence, it is not the root cause of the assaults (Zubretsky and Digirolamo 1994). Browne (1987) notes that abusive individuals are typically abusive whether sober or drunk, and Kantor and Straus (1990) remind us that the majority of men who drink do not hit their wives. Thus, a direct or causal relationship between alcohol abuse and domestic violence is not supported by the research.

The Lovers' Quarrel

Other myths perpetuate the image of domestic assault as a minor lovers' quarrel or a situation involving "only minor injuries." In this sense, domestic assaults are considered unimportant, and certainly not "real" crimes. This image of domestic violence lacks empirical support. In a recent study, Bachman and Carmody (1994) utilized national data to compare injuries sustained by female victims of assaults perpetrated by intimates and strangers. Women who were assaulted by an intimate were significantly more likely to sustain an injury than those assaulted by a stranger. Additional research shows that domestic violence is a leading cause of injury among women, hospitalizing more victims than rapes, muggings, and car accidents combined (Stark, Flitcraft, Zuckerman, Gray, Robinson, and Frazier 1981). Clearly, the image of domestic assaults as minor lovers' quarrels is not supported by empirical research.

Mutual Combat

Some also believe that domestic violence situations typically involve mutual combat, rather than the abuse of one person by another. In this sense, the event may considered a "fight among equals," where both participants sustain injuries. Proponents of this view often note that in a national study of American families, Straus, Gelles, and Steinmetz (1980) found that almost half of the couples who reported violence said that both partners had used force. However, Straus and his colleagues were quick to point out that men had a higher rate of using the most injurious forms of violence, and were more likely to engage in repeated acts of violence. Additionally, Straus et al. failed to determine if the violent acts reported by respondents were taken in self-defense. The myth of mutual combat is also challenged by findings from other national studies. The 1994 National Crime Victimization Survey found that women are more likely than men to be victims of intimate assault. In fact, women experience over ten times as many violent victimizations by intimates. So, while men are more likely to be assaulted by strangers, women are at much greater risk of assault by intimates (U.S. Department of Justice 1994).

The Uncooperative Victim

Finally, one of the most popular stereotypes of battered women is that they will not follow through with prosecution (Ferraro 1989). This image of the uncooperative victim may be linked to the "masochism thesis" described above, or the victim may be considered too timid, uneducated, or belligerent to cooperate with police. According to this view, police response to domestic violence calls might be considered a waste of valuable resources, which would be better served by having police respond to "real crimes." This image of the uncooperative victim is challenged by research that suggests that victims of domestic assault may suffer from "battered woman syndrome" or "learned helplessness" (Walker 1979). In response to repeated, long-term victimization and intimidation, victims may appear unwilling to cooperate with police. Frequently, this response is linked to the psychological aspects of battering: extreme fear, diminished self-esteem, and lack of perceived options. In this situation, the victim may appear to be uncooperative, when in fact, she fears for her life. This response may actually be quite rational, given the circumstances. A victim or her children may have been threatened with further injury if she does cooperate with the police. Thus, a lack of victim cooperation does not necessarily mean that victims of domestic violence are stubborn, irrational, or overly emotional. Instead, refusing to cooperate with police on the scene may be a rational victim response.

These myths surrounding domestic violence, its perpetrators, and its victims tend to shift the responsibility for domestic violence away from the perpetrator, and frequently assign blame to the victim. If these myths are supported by the media, viewers may be distracted from the real issues related to domestic violence: the systematic, repeated abuse of power and control. On a more practical level, these myths may also discourage victims from utilizing police services. Since research suggests that domestic assaults tend to escalate in frequency and severity over time (Straus and Gelles 1990), discouraging victims from seeking help may result in more severe injuries or deaths.

Police in the United States respond to domestic violence calls up to eight million times a year, making domestic assault the single most frequent form of violence police encounter (Sherman 1992). Accordingly, police response to domestic violence has received considerable attention in the research community (Sherman and Berk 1984; Carmody and Williams 1987; Sherman 1992). Unlike most other crimes of violence, domestic assaults have historically been seen as "private family matters," and police have been accused of minimizing or ignoring these crimes. More recently, research attention has focused on deterring batterers and protecting victims (Sherman 1992; Carlson and Nidey 1995), as well as the relative risk of officer injury at domestic violence calls (Hirschel, Dean, and Lumb 1994). Mandatory arrest and proarrest policies have influenced police response to domestic assaults and many departments now have implemented specialized training for officers. However, few studies have examined police attitudes towards departmental domestic violence policies. Feminist theorists argue that police departments as organizations continue to promote traditional sex roles and encourage police officers to avoid intervention in "private family matters." Others note the persistence of the public image of "domestics" as less serious than other assaults. The police role at a domestic disturbance may be seen as "social work" rather than "fighting crime," and the ability of the police to deter future assaults and protect the victim is often called into question (Schmidt and Sherman 1996; Breci 1986).

This chapter examines the image of crime, criminals, victims, and police on reality-based crime shows. The analysis is divided into two parts. First, the types of crimes portrayed, as well as their typical resolution, are briefly examined. Demographic characteristics of suspects, victims, and police officers are also summarized. The second portion of the analysis compares the depiction of domestic and nondomestic assaults on these programs. Specifically, the analysis examines the presentation of domestic violence cases in light of the myths and stereotypes described above. Is the masochism thesis supported? Is the perpetrator presented as a drunken bum? Are domestic assaults depicted as minor lovers' quarrels or mutual combat between equals? And finally, is the victim of domestic violence described as uncooperative, refusing to participate in the prosecution of the offender?

METHOD

Two programs were recorded for analysis in this study: "Cops" and "Real Stories of the Highway Patrol." Both are marketed as "reality-based" police shows. While "Cops" is filmed live via a hand-held camera, "Real Stories of the Highway Patrol" involves reenactments of sensational cases, combined with some live footage. Both programs emphasize the dangerous and exciting aspects of police work and frequently include high-speed chases, the use of weapons, and heroic officers. Programs aired between December 1994 and May 1995 were included in the analysis. The 33.17 hours of programming (excluding commercials) included 388 crime vignettes or cases (178 "Cops," 210 "Real Stories of the Highway Patrol"). The vignette served as the unit of analysis.

Characteristics of the incident (type of crime, location, resolution, etc.), suspects, victims, and police officers (gender, race, approximate age, etc.) were coded for each vignette. In some vignettes, several different crimes were depicted. For example, one "Cops" vignette involved a murder, a high-speed chase, and a drunken suspect. In these vignettes, the "primary" offense was identified by coders as the crime that received the most attention by police. In the case described above, the primary offense was the murder. In cases where multiple victims or offenders were involved, only the primary victim or offender was coded. Once again, the primary victim/offender was the individual receiving the most attention in the vignette. Demographic information (approximate age, gender, race) for victims, offenders, and up to two police officers was also included in the coding of each vignette. Coding of these variables was based on the coder's visual examination of the vignette.

The coders were five undergraduate students (four females and one male, all Caucasian). Reliability of the coding scheme was assessed by having each vignette coded by two coders. There was 96 percent agreement among the coders concerning the race, gender, and age of the characters, and the resolution or outcome of the case.

Because the second part of the analysis involves a comparison of domestic and nondomestic assaults, all vignettes involving an assault were further examined to determine the relationship between the victim and offender. Assaults between spouses, cohabitants, and intimates (including boyfriends and girlfriends) were coded as domestic assaults. Others were coded as nondomestic assaults. Frequently, the designation of these cases as "domestics" was also made by the police officer en route to the scene. Assaults were defined as unlawful physical attacks upon a person. They included assaults with or without a weapon, but excluded sexual assaults or attacks involving theft (robbery).

FINDINGS

The first part of the analysis focuses on the depiction of crime, suspects, victims, and police on "Cops" and "Real Stories of the Highway Patrol." Table 1 shows the distribution of crimes depicted in the programs. For purposes of comparison, rates of crimes included in the FBI Crime Index

Table 1. Frequency (%) of Crimes in "Reality" Police TV Shows[a] and the FBI Crime Index[b]

Index Crimes	TV[c]	FBI
Murder	5.2	0.2
Rape/sexual assault	2.1	0.7
Robbery	9.8	4.7
Assault (domestic and nondomestic)	48.0	8.0
Burglary	7.7	20.0
Larceny theft	7.2	55.3
Motor vehicle theft	20.0	11.0

[a]"Cops," "Real Stories of the Highway Patrol," aired December 1994–May 1995.
[b]U.S. Department of Justice (1994).
[c]Percentages based on the 194 vignettes involving FBI index crimes.

(U.S. Department of Justice 1995) are provided. Among these Index crimes, it is clear that the violent crimes of murder and assault are overemphasized on reality police programs, while larceny, theft, and burglary received relatively little attention. This pattern is consistent with previous research, which demonstrates that violent crimes are overrepresented on "reality" programs (Cavender and Bond-Maupin 1993; Oliver 1994).

The gender, race (white, nonwhite), and approximate age of the primary officer, suspect, and victim are summarized in Table 2. Also included was a measure of apparent income level of the suspect and victim. Utilizing information based on the individual's clothing, automobile, and/or housing, coders categorized suspects and victims as high, middle, or low income. Clearly, officers tended to be white males and most suspects were male. Forty-three percent of the suspects were nonwhite, and the majority were depicted as poor. Both suspects and victims tended to be in their early thirties, while FBI statistics suggest that most offenders are younger.

Table 2. Characteristics of Police Officers, Suspects, and Victims on "Reality" Television Police Shows[a] (*n* = 388)

Primary police officer	Age (mean)	35.6
	Sex (male)	93.3%
	Race (nonwhite)	13.7%
Primary suspect	Age (mean)	32.2
	Sex (male)	87.3%
	Race (nonwhite)	43.3%
	Income (low)	65.9%
Primary victim	Age (mean)	31.1
	Sex (male)	55.0%
	Race (nonwhite)	33.8%
	Income (low)	49.6%

[a]"Cops," "Real Stories of the Highway Patrol" aired December 1994–May 1995.

Domestic and Nondomestic Assaults

Next, the analysis focused exclusively on vignettes involving assaults (forty-two domestic, fifty-one nondomestic). Domestic assaults represented 14.6 percent of all crimes on "Cops" and 7.1 percent of all crimes on "Real Stories of the Highway Patrol." Table 3 summarizes the comparison of domestic and nondomestic assaults, as they were depicted in these programs. The first section compares the depiction of suspects. Suspects were more likely to be identified as repeat offenders in domestic assaults, although this difference was not statistically significant. On several occasions, police officers, as they were narrating and/or explaining the situation to the camera, emphasized that "domestics" tend to involve repeat offenders. Many stated that they were frustrated with their apparent lack of impact on offenders, and

Table 3. Characteristics of Suspects, Victims, and Police in Domestic and Nondomestic Assaults on "Reality" Television Police Programs[a] (n =93)

	Nondomestic		Domestic	
Characteristic	Assaults %	(n = 51) n	Assaults %	(n = 42) n
Suspect				
Repeat offender	19.6	(10)	31.0	(13)
Two or more suspects	40.0	(20)	7.1	(3)**
Suspect had a weapon	58.8	(30)	38.1	(16)*
Suspect used a weapon	49.0	(25)	26.2	(11)*
Suspect arrested	73.1	(38)	70.0	(28)
Victim				
Two or more victims	32.4	(12)	10.5	(4)*
Nonwhite victim	48.6	(17)	27.8	(10)
Male victim	78.4	(29)	27.8	(10)***
Victim injured[b]	53.8	(28)	29.3	(12)*
Police				
Weapon used against police	22.0	(11)	11.9	(5)
Police officer injured	9.6	(5)	2.4	(1)
Police drew weapon	33.3	(17)	31.0	(13)
Police discharged weapon	15.7	(8)	9.5	(4)
Female police officer	21.6	(11)	7.1	(3)
Situation				
Race to the scene	62.7	(32)	29.3	(12)**
Mutual combat	24.0	(12)	30.0	(12)
Alcohol use involved	26.0	(13)	47.6	(20)*

[a]"Cops," "Real Stories of the Highway Patrol" aired December 1994–May 1995.
[b]Injury required medical attention.
*p < .05. **p < .01. ***p < .001.

their perceived inability to deter future assaults. Clearly, this depiction of domestic violence calls may support the masochism thesis, as well as the image of the uncooperative victim. For example, one case on "Cops" involved a female victim who had been assaulted by her live-in boyfriend. The police officers noted that they had been called to the residence on several previous occasions, and they were annoyed with the victim's apparent resistance to their efforts to help. The victim stated that if she left her boyfriend, she would likely be homeless, but the police officers continued to describe her as uncooperative, noting that "[s]he keeps going back to him, no matter how badly he beats her" ("Cops," February 1995). Further analysis of the domestic assault vignettes, not included in Table 3, revealed that in about one-third of vignettes (32.4 percent), police officers expressed frustration with the chronic nature of the crime. Additionally, in 26.5 percent of the cases, they specifically discussed their frustration with what they perceived as a lack of victim cooperation.

Nondomestic assaults were significantly more likely to feature multiple suspects and the use of weapons. While about half of the nondomestic assault vignettes involved weapons, data from the National Crime Victimization Survey (Maguire and Pastore 1995) suggest that approximately 32 percent of all assaults involve a weapon. Thus, it appears that the reality police program depictions of nondomestic assaults slightly exaggerate the role of weapons in these crimes.

Finally, it is interesting to note that suspects were arrested at nearly the same rate in both types of assault. In both domestic and nondomestic assault vignettes, approximately 70 percent of offenders were arrested. This differs from the *Uniform Crime Reports* (U.S. Department of Justice 1994) statistics, which indicate that approximately 55 percent of all assaults known to the police are cleared by arrest. Thus, cases included on "Cops" and "Real Stories of the Highway Patrol" appear to overemphasize police use of arrest in assault cases.

Next, victim depictions were compared. Victims of domestic assaults clearly tended to be female, while victims of nondomestic assaults were overwhelmingly male. This pattern is consistent with FBI statistics. However, nondomestic assault vignettes more frequently depicted victims who were injured and required medical attention. This image supports the myth that domestic violence assaults rarely result in severe injuries, and are instead simply minor lovers' quarrels and not real crimes.

The next section of Table 3 summarizes depictions of police officers on reality police programs. While none of the findings were statistically significant, nondomestic assault vignettes were more likely to depict police officers in aggressive behaviors (drawing and discharging weapons), suggesting that these situations represented more serious crimes. Interestingly, officer injury appeared more frequently in the nondomestic assault vignettes. This is inconsistent with research that shows that domestic violence calls result in a larger proportion of injuries to officers than other calls (Hirschel et al. 1994).

Finally, female police officers were more frequently included in vignettes depicting nondomestic assaults. In fact, female officers appeared in only three domestic assault vignettes, and they were never featured as the primary officer on the scene. Since women currently represent approximately 16 percent of sworn police officers and detectives nationwide, their virtual absence in domestic violence vignettes is intriguing. In one notable vignette ("Cops," May 1995), a female officer assisted a male officer on a domestic violence call. She was instructed to "talk some sense" into the female victim, and proceeded to provide information about the local shelter for battered women. Her presence seemed to calm the victim, and they engaged in a brief discussion of the situation. Meanwhile, the male officers were focused on arresting the offender and forcing him out the door to the waiting patrol car. In this case, the female officer was portrayed in a social work or counseling role, while the male officers focused on the "real" police work.

The last section of Table 3 offers some final comparisons of domestic and nondomestic assault vignettes. Nondomestic assaults were significantly more likely to feature a "race to the scene." Once again, this suggests that nondomestic assaults were depicted as more serious or urgent than domestic assaults. This depiction also offers some support for the myth of the lovers' quarrel, and the assumption that domestic assaults usually result in minor injuries.

It is also interesting to note that 24 percent of the nondomestic assaults and 30 percent of the domestic assaults involved a mutual combat situation, where both the victim and offender sustained injuries. In these cases, police interpretation of the event was utilized to identify the roles of victim and perpetrator. Since most vignettes lack information concerning the context of the assaults, viewers must rely on these police interpretations exclusively. It is intriguing that nearly the same proportion of domestic and nondomestic assault vignettes involved mutual combat.

On "Cops" and "Real Stories of the Highway Patrol," domestic assaults were significantly more likely to involve the use of alcohol. This clearly supports the "drunken bum" myth of domestic violence. In fact, this interpretation was frequently offered by the officer on the scene. In many cases, the primary officer focused on the abuse of alcohol as an explanation of, or excuse for, the violence. One vignette from "Cops" involved an obviously intoxicated offender. The police officer focused his attention on the batterer, recommending that he attend Alcoholics Anonymous meetings, virtually ignoring the needs of the victim, who was clearly in need of medical attention ("Cops," March 1995).

CONCLUSION

This chapter offers an exploratory analysis of two reality-based police shows: "Cops" and "Real Stories of the Highway Patrol." While "Cops" utilizes clips of live film footage as viewers are invited to ride along with officers, "Real Stories of the Highway Patrol" combines reenactments of dramatic cases with eyewitness interviews and some live footage. Both programs have been immensely popular, depicting high-speed chases, drug raids, stakeouts, and highway accidents.

"Cops" and "Real Stories of the Highway Patrol" are representative of a new genre of police program, a modification of the crime show (Cavender and Bond-Maupin 1993; Surette 1992). By mixing informational and entertainment formats, the distinction between the two may be blurred. The "video realism" of the programs encourages viewers to interpret the images of criminals, victims, and police officers as accurate and real (Cavender and Bond-Maupin 1993). By locating the camera in the back seat of the patrol car, viewers are invited to ride along and witness firsthand the fight against crime.

This content analysis of two reality-based police programs reveals several interesting patterns. First, these programs overrepresent violent crimes, suggesting that the majority of police work involves dangerous violent offenders. The programs also underrepresent women police officers, especially in supervisory roles.

Perhaps the most interesting findings appeared when domestic and nondomestic assault vignettes were compared, revealing important differences in the images of suspects and victims, as well as the role of the police. Specifically, depictions of nondomestic assaults more easily conform to the stereotypical assault image: armed attacker, serious victim injury, and threat to police officers. Domestic assault vignettes, in contrast, contain several patterns that do not match current research in the field, and may support harmful myths concerning victims of domestic violence.

The masochism thesis, which asserts that victims of domestic violence obtain some gratification from the abuse, and the stereotype of the uncooperative victim, received some support on these programs. People seem willing to blame battered women, and the longer the woman remains after the abuse, the more likely it is that people will find her blameworthy (Barnett et al. 1997). Clearly, a victim's refusal to leave a violent relationship may be explained by many factors other than masochistic tendencies, but the format of these programs does not permit the careful examination of these issues. Since the average vignette lasts less than five minutes, little time is available to explore the complex emotional and psychological trauma experienced by a victim of intimate violence. Research suggests that battered women remain in abusive relationships for a wide range of reasons: economic dependency (Strube and Barbour 1983), fear of retaliation (Browne 1987), fear of loneliness (Varvaro 1991), and lack of perceived social support (Shepherd 1990; Tan, Basta, Sullivan, and Davidson 1995). Additionally, victims of domestic violence may face powerful psychological barriers to escape (Walker 1979). Unfortunately, the complexity of these situations was not reflected in the vignettes under study. Instead, viewers are left with the image of the victim as uncooperative or even to blame for her own victimization.

Nearly a third of the domestic violence vignettes involved a mutual combat situation, where both parties were violent. In addition, domestic violence vignettes emphasized victims with relatively minor, non-life-threatening injuries. These depictions perpetuate the stereotype of domestic assaults as minor lovers' quarrels and minimize the potential lethality of these assaults. This minimization of victim injuries is challenged by studies of emergency room admissions, which show that 20 to 50 percent of female patients are victims of domestic abuse (Campbell and Sheridan 1989). Additionally, we know that nearly a third of female homicide victims are killed by an intimate (U.S. Department of Justice 1994). Clearly, many domestic assaults are not simply lovers' quarrels.

Finally, domestic assault vignettes emphasize the role of alcohol abuse, with use of alcohol evident in nearly half of the domestic violence vignettes. In several cases, police officers specifically highlighted the role of alcohol in domestic violence. While it is important to consider the connection between alcohol and violence, reality crime shows seem to draw our attention to alcohol as the primary explanation. Most domestic assaults do not involve the use of alcohol. To focus on alcohol as an explanation or excuse for domestic violence distracts attention from other, more plausible explanations (Kantor and Straus 1990) and also shifts responsibility away from the offender.

In summary, the image of crime, criminals, and victims on reality police programs appears to bear little resemblance to reality. The current study supports earlier research that notes that media depictions of crime focus on events that are sensational and unusual. Like other television programs, reality police programs reinforce a variety of myths about domestic violence, its victims, and offenders.

These myths are potentially harmful to the victims of domestic violence in several ways. First, we know that women report higher levels of fear of crime (Stanko 1992). Programs that emphasize the role of women as victims of violent crime, and fail to offer accurate depictions of these events, may perpetuate this fear among viewers. Additionally, images of domestic violence that shift the blame away from the offender and onto the victim may discourage women from seeking police assistance. Since early intervention in domestic violence is crucial (Straus and Gelles 1990), media images that discourage victims' efforts to obtain assistance are potentially dangerous. Research tells us that without intervention, domestic violence tends to increase in frequency and severity over time (Straus and Gelles 1990). Anything that discourages a victim from seeking help may therefore increase her risk of severe injury or death.

Reality police programs did not create these myths about domestic violence, and they alone will not change the public view of this problem. However, it is important to examine the impact of the media on viewers' attitudes toward domestic violence, its perpetrators, and victims. Clearly, perpetuation of these myths may serve to impede effective public policies regarding domestic violence.

REFERENCES

Alpert, G. P. and R. G. Dunham. 1992. *Policing Urban America.* Prospect Heights, IL: Waveland Press.

Andersen, R. 1994. "'Reality' TV and Criminal Injustice." *Humanist,* September/October, p. 8.

Bachman, R. and D. C. Carmody. 1994. "Fighting Fire with Fire: The Effects of Victim Resistance in Intimate Versus Stranger Perpetrated Assaults Against Females." *Journal of Family Violence* 9(4):319–31.

Barnett, O. W., C. L. Miller-Perrin, and R. D. Perrin. 1997. *Family Violence Across the Lifespan.* Thousand Oaks, CA: Sage.

Bart, P. B. and E. G. Moran (eds.). 1993. *Violence Against Women: The Bloody Footprints.* Newbury Park: Sage.

Benedict, H. 1992. *Virgin or Vamp: How the Press Covers Sex Crimes.* New York: Oxford University Press.

Bortner, M. A. 1984. "Media Images and Public Attitudes toward Crime and Justice." Pp. 15–30 in *Justice and the Media,* edited by R. Surrette. Springfield, IL: Charles C. Thomas.

Breci, M. G. 1986. *Police Response to Domestic Disturbances.* Ph.D. dissertation, Department of Sociology, Iowa State University, Ames.

Browne, A. 1987. *When Battered Women Kill.* New York: Free Press.

Campbell, J. C. and D. J. Sheridan. 1989. "Emergency Nursing Interventions with Battered Women." *Journal of Emergency Nursing* 15:12–17.

Caputi, J. 1992. "The Sexual Politics of Murder." In *Violence Against Women: The Bloody Footprints,* edited by P. Bart and E. Moran. Newbury Park: Sage.

Carlson, C. and F. J. Nidey. 1995. "Mandatory Penalties, Victim Cooperation, and the Judicial Processing of Domestic Assault Cases." *Crime and Delinquency* 41(1):132–49.

Carmody, D. C. and K. R. Williams. 1987. "Wife Assault and Perceptions of Sanctions." *Violence and Victims* 2(1):25–38.

Cavender, G. and L. Bond-Maupin. 1993. "Fear and Loathing on Reality Television:

An Analysis of 'America's Most Wanted' and 'Unsolved Mysteries.'" *Sociological Inquiry* 63(3, Summer):305–17.

Crawford, A., T. Jones, T. Woodhouse, and J. Young. 1990. *The Second Islington Crime Survey.* Middlesex: Middlesex Polytechnic.

Estep, R. And P. T. Macdonald. 1983. "How Prime Time Crime Evolved on TV, 1976–1981." *Journalism Quarterly* 60:293–300.

Fennel, T. 1992. "True-to-life TV: Realistic Shows Earn Top Ratings." *Maclean's,* December, p. 48.

Ferraro, Kenneth J. 1995. *Fear of Crime: Interpreting Victimization Risk.* Albany: State University of New York Press.

Gerbner, G. and L. Gross. 1976. "Living with Television: The Violence Profile." *Journal of Communication* 26:173–99.

Gordon, M. and S. Riger. 1989. *The Female Fear.* New York: Free Press.

Graber, D. 1980. *Crime News and the Public.* New York: Praeger.

Hirschel, J. D., C. W. Dean, and R. C. Lumb. 1994. "The Relative Contribution of Domestic Violence to Assault and Injury of Police Officers." *Justice Quarterly* 11(1):99–117.

Kantor, G. and M. A. Straus. 1990. "The Drunken-Bum Theory of Wife Beating." In *Physical Violence in American Families,* edited by M. A. Straus and R. J. Gelles. New Brunswick, NJ: Transaction.

Maguire, K. and A. L. Pastore (eds.). 1995. *Sourcebook of Criminal Justice Statistics 1994.* Washington, DC: U.S. Department of Justice, Bureau of Justice.

Oliver, M. B. 1994. "Portrayals of Crime, Race, and Aggression in 'Reality-Based' Police Shows: A Content Analysis." *Journal of Broadcasting and Electronic Media* Spring: 179–92.

Pandiani, J. 1978. "Crime Time TV: If All We Knew Is What We Saw." *Contemporary Crises* 2:437–58.

Reid, P. and G. Finchilescu. 1995. "The Disempowering Effects of Media Violence Against Women on College Women." *Psychology of Women Quarterly* 19:397–411.

Schmidt, J. D. and L. Sherman. 1996. "Does Arrest Deter Domestic Violence?" Pp.43–53 in *Do Arrests and Restraining Orders Work?* edited by E. S. Buzawa and C. G. Buzawa. Thousand Oaks, CA: Sage.

Sheley, J. F. and C. D. Ashkins. 1981. "Crime, Crime News, and Crime Views." *Public Opinion Quarterly* 45:492–506.

Shepherd, J. 1990. "Victims of Personal Violence: The Relevance of Symonds' Model of Psychological Response and Loss Theory." *British Journal of Social Work* 20:309–32.

Sherman, L. W. 1992. *Policing Domestic Violence.* New York: Free Press.

Sherman, L. W. and R. A. Berk. 1984. "The Specific Deterrent Effects of Arrest for Domestic Assault." *American Sociological Review* 49(2):261–72.

Signorielli, N. and N. Morgan. 1988. *Cultivation Analysis.* Newbury Park, CA: Sage.

Smith, M. D. 1988. "Women's Fear of Violent Crime: An Exploratory Test of a Feminist Hypothesis." *Journal of Family Violence* (March):29–38.

Stanko, E. A. 1992. "The Case of Fearful Women: Gender, Personal Safety and Fear of Crime." *Women and Criminal Justice* 4(1):117–35.

Stark, E., A. Flitcraft, D. Zuckerman, A. Gray, J. Robinson, and W. Frazier. 1981. *Wife Assault in the Medical Setting: An Introduction for Health Personnel.* Monograph Series No. 7. Washington DC: Department of Health and Human Services, National Clearinghouse on Domestic Violence.

Straus, M. A. and R. Gelles. 1990. *Physical Violence in American Families.* New Brunswick, NJ: Transaction.

Straus, M. A., R. Gelles, and S. Steinmetz. 1980. *Behind Closed Doors: Violence in the American Family.* New York: Doubleday.

Strube, M. J. and L. S. Barbour. 1983. "The Decision to Leave an Abusive Relationship: Economic Dependence and Psychological Commitment." *Journal of Marriage and the Family* 45:785–93.

Surette, R. 1992. *Media, Crime and Criminal Justice: Images and Realities.* Pacific Grove, CA: Brooks/Cole.

Tan, C., J. Basta, C. M. Sullivan, and W. S. Davidson. 1995. "The Role of Social Support in the Lives of Women Exiting Domestic Violence Shelters." *Journal of Interpersonal Violence* 10:437–51.

U.S. Department of Justice. 1994. *Violence Between Intimates: Domestic Violence.* NCJ Publication #149259. Washington, DC: Government Printing Office.

———. 1995. *Crime in the United States, 1994.* Washington, DC: Government Printing Office.

Varvaro, F. F. 1991. "Using a Grief Response Assessment Questionnaire in a Support Group to Assist Battered Women in their Recovery." *Response* 13(4):17–20.

Walker, L. E. 1979. *The Battered Woman.* New York: Harper and Row.

Warr, M. 1984. "Fear of Victimization: Why Are Women and the Elderly More Afraid?" *Social Science Quarterly* 65:681–702.

Zubretsky, T. M. and Digirolamo, K. M. 1994. "Adult Domestic Violence: The Alcohol Connection." *Violence Update* 4(7, March):1–2, 4,8.

10

Crime Fighting by Television in the Netherlands

CHRIS BRANTS

INTRODUCTION

This chapter examines the origins and subsequent development of a long-running crime program on Dutch television named "Opsporing Verzocht" (O.V.).[1] The manifest aim of the program is no different from its foreign counterparts such as "Crimewatch UK" in Great Britain, "Aktenzeichen XY . . . Ungelöst" ("Case XY . . . Unsolved") in Germany, or "America's Most Wanted" in the United States: to help the police solve crime and catch criminals by engaging the help of television viewers. And like these programs, it is put together by journalists working for a broadcasting company with the help of the police. But there the similarity ends.

Unlike any other crimewatch program, O.V. is based on a government decree that shapes both format and content, determines the responsibilities of broadcasters and police, and requires special watchdog committees to oversee the selection of cases and guard against unwanted side effects. It is a very low key, even dull program, which is reluctant to show anything more exciting in the way of reconstructions than a rolled-up tarpaulin to represent a body dragged from a canal, or a car pulling away fast round the corner. It consists mainly of talking heads: middle-aged journalists and camera-shy policemen. And yet it has been popular from the very start in 1984 and has claimed a reasonable clearance rate (varying from 25 to 50 percent), while the police remain convinced that it is more than worth their while to continue the cooperation.

In order to understand the success of O.V., and to assess the changes it may have to make in the future, we need to look at its history in the light of two notable features of Dutch culture, both at present under increasing pressure: the mild penal climate that has always been a main characteristic of Dutch criminal justice, and a broadcasting structure with built-in notions of social responsibility and legal restrictions on programming. Together, these features ensure a low-key approach to crime and criminals by the media that is very different from most other European countries and certainly from the United States.

In the coming pages I shall briefly describe the criminal justice system and the broadcasting structure in the Netherlands, to form a framework against which to examine O.V. and some of its rather surprising idiosyncrasies. Hopefully this should provide some clue as to why, in these days of satellite and cable, international programming, and reality television, people should want to watch a program that is (intentionally) old-fashioned and anything but dynamic.

JOURNALISM AND CRIMINAL JUSTICE IN THE NETHERLANDS

Traditionally, the Dutch have always had a tolerant attitude toward crime and criminals, abolishing the death penalty and corporal punishment in the nineteenth century and maintaining a very low incarceration rate during the twentieth. At present twelve out of every thousand persons over eleven years of age in the Netherlands are punished for a felony. Of these twelve, nine are fined, two are sentenced to prison (but not necessarily incarcerated), and one does community service (Berghuis 1994). There is also a qualitative side to this quantitatively low level of punitivity in Dutch society and there is a good deal of evidence that in that sense, too, the criminal justice climate in the Netherlands is indeed milder than elsewhere (Downes 1988; Blankenburg and Bruinsma 1991; "Foreign Views on Dutch Penal Policy" 1992; Hulsman and Nijboer 1993).

There is a tendency to decriminalize private morality (prostitution, underage sex, adult pornography, soft drugs, homosexuality) and there is at least serious doubt at all levels as to the wisdom of continued criminalization of hard drugs. Criminal policy is geared toward developing deterrents (other than the threat of prison) and alternative sanctions, especially where juveniles are concerned. The effectiveness of prison as a corrective is regularly debated (and doubted) in public, not least by the prosecution service and judiciary (and recently by the minister of justice). Harshness in prison is not part of the punishment and prison regimes are definitely soft in comparison with most other countries (one prisoner to a cell, proper sanitation, procedurally guaranteed prisoners' rights and legal remedies, boards of prison visitors with the power to overturn unlawful or arbitrary decisions by the governor). An ongoing concern for the effects of the criminal justice system on the criminals it processes and an understanding of the criminal as a human being with the right to be treated as such are shared by the judiciary, the criminal justice authorities, and even to a certain extent the general public.[2] As well as a public debate on fundamental rights and due process in criminal procedure, there is, therefore, also an awareness of the potentially damaging effects of stigmatization and a certain degree of consensus that criminals and their families have a right to privacy and to protection, not only from trial by media, but also from unnecessary exposure of their private lives.

At this point, and not to give the impression that Holland is some sort of penal paradise, bear in mind that all things are relative, that the Dutch criminal justice system is an instrument of repression and social control like any other and as such tends to serve vested interests and preserve the status quo, and that times are changing. Recent changes in policy and practice, which include a lot of no-nonsense rhetoric, harsher sentencing for some crimes (notably dealing in hard drugs and the violence associated with organized drug running), and increasing police autonomy and the use of secret proactive policing methods, do not however necessarily reflect changes in public attitudes toward "ordinary criminals," although eventually they will perhaps inevitably influence public opinion. Rather, they should be taken as indicators of wider developments, such as international pressure (the "war on drugs" waged by other countries, the "federalization" of Europe and its police forces) and a changing balance of power within the Dutch criminal justice system itself. I shall return to these issues and their possible effect on the media representation of crime and crime control later. Suffice it to say here that, until well into the 1990s trust in the ability of the criminal justice authorities both to control crime and to uphold the rule of law (an unshakable conviction that the system worked and worked fairly) formed the fundamental basis of the public attitude to crime and crime control.

The media in the Netherlands both reflect and influence public and political attitudes on crime. Crime reporting, mainly the work of newspapers, is subdued and subject to a self-imposed and government-approved code of ethics that includes concern for the privacy of both suspects and victims of crime. Television journalists are reasonably circumspect in dealing with crime and only very recently have such phenomena as talk shows and "sob TV" made their appearance and come to include crime (and criminals). The broadcasting system in Holland, however, cannot be understood without reference to a principle that is sometimes known in English as "pillarization" (a direct translation from the Dutch *verzuiling*) but is more often referred to as "the politics of accommodation" (Lijphart 1975; Brants 1993). It is to this that we must turn first.

This principle was so central for so long to all aspects of Dutch society that its remnants linger on in a fundamental outlook on life in general that is still reflected in politics, media, law, culture, and criminal justice,[3] even after the "revolution" of the 1960's and what came to be known as *de*pillarization. Pillarization implies that social stratification according to class is intersected by "vertical stratification" according to fundamental religious or political beliefs: not free-floating, but organized (in churches, political parties, social movements) and dominating almost all aspects of life. Thus, Catholic workers were organized in Catholic unions, Protestant children attended Protestant schools, socialists tuned into their own socialist broadcasting station, liberals read their own liberal newspapers and joined liberal—or more likely "nonaligned"—football clubs.

The most important feature of the politics of accommodation in the Netherlands was that of bargaining and compromise between the elites at the top of the four main "pillars" of Dutch society: Catholics, Calvinists, secular conservatives, and social democrats. The "price" that society paid for the relative peacefulness of this arrangement, in which the elite possessed an equal stake in continuation of the system, is an inherent secrecy at the top and pacification of the "lower levels" of society; the politics of accommodation were also the politics of acquiescence and paternalism, resulting not only in a relative absence of class conflict, but also a relative immunity of the elite from criticism.

One of the most easily discernible aspects of the latter was the way in which the media were organized and functioned. Broadcasting organizations belonged to the different pillars, and one of their most important roles was to pass on (uncritically) the message from the pillarized elites to their several constituencies (Brants 1989). As a general system of social control, the criminal justice system was not part of any pillar, but was nevertheless most definitely part of the establishment in which the pillarized elites had an ongoing interest, and therefore of the politics of accommodation, allowing its functionaries their fair share of immunity from criticism by the media. Journalists were not expected to be, and neither were they, much more than purveyors of the moral message contained in criminal law.

Among other things, pillarization gave rise to the peculiar Dutch system of public broadcasting that is regulated by law and has remained intact until very recently. Broadcasting laws concerned both organization and content, requiring that programs reflect a reasonable ratio (later worked out in percentages) of information, education, culture, and entertainment. As to the organizational structure of broadcasting, time on the air was divided between the different pillars according to the size of the organization, with membership and number of subscribers to each broadcasting company's own television magazine as determinants of size. The journalistic climate that this system engendered has ensured that broadcasting companies and the journalists they employ have always taken their social responsibility as purveyors of invasive messages very seriously and have regarded it as their duty to bring not only entertainment, but also information, education, and culture to the masses.

This is not only the result of pillarization, but is also the inevitable product of its combination with the welfare state that the Netherlands has become since the end of World War II: a social and political arrangement in which citizens look to the state and its satellite organizations to provide for their every need, "from cradle to grave." The peculiar contribution of pillarization has been to ensure that a subtly directed consensus, not conflict, has been the outstanding feature of that arrangement—a consensus that includes, in general, approval of the way in which the criminal justice system operates and how crime, criminals, and crime control should be represented in the media.

Given the scope of this chapter, this outline of the main aspects of two such broad social institutions as the media and criminal justice has only touched very briefly on their most patently obvious characteristics. I have done no more than try to give the reader some idea of how different the criminal justice and broadcasting situations in the Netherlands are, compared to a country like the United States or, for that matter, Great Britain. For although British and Dutch public broadcasters may share ideas on social responsibility and television journalism that should not need to depend on audience ratings and advertising revenue, the flavor of public discourse with regard to crime is very different.

As a result of the pillarized structure of the media, the dependency upon the criminal justice authorities as primary definers of newsworthy crime has probably always been greater in the Netherlands than elsewhere, with public discourse on crime more likely to be openly shaped by the authorities than by the media. Although the criminal justice system did come in for its fair share of criticism at the end of the 1960s, notably for being too far removed from the changes in values and morals that were the hallmark of those turbulent years, it managed to accommodate that criticism by introducing reforms that allowed the press easy access to figures of authority and by providing extensive information on policy to journalists. Both the police and the Public Prosecution Service maintain good relations with the media and assign the task of coping with the press to special officers. Press conferences on policy and on current cases are routine. Journalists depend on them and on personal contacts with the police and prosecution service for most of their information (investigative journalism is a relatively new phenomenon in the Netherlands), while the criminal justice authorities rely on the media not to publish information that would damage an ongoing case, unduly stigmatize suspects, or present policy in an unfavorable light. That this leaves the press wide open to manipulation by PR-conscious police and prosecutors is obvious, although journalists are not inclined to see it that way and regard cooperation with the authorities on matters of crime control as part of responsible journalism (Brants 1993).

Television producers too have seen it as their task to bring the official message to their audience (a message, as we have seen, that was informed from 1950s onwards by an increasing concern for human rights and humane justice). This may explain the tendency, until recently, to leave crime reporting very much to the newspapers and to avoid real-life *Dutch* crime as part of the everyday package of TV entertainment (as opposed to foreign programs, which appear widely on Dutch television), because of the greater stigmatizing and stereotyping effect of television (Brants and Brants 1994). Although this is changing, the combination of the typically Dutch remnants of pillarized broadcasting and the type of considerations that, until now, have dominated public discourse on media and criminal justice still provides broadcasters with a frame of reference for dealing with crime and criminals in which programs such as O.V. were conceived and have to fit.

"OPSPORING VERZOCHT": A SHORT HISTORY

Ideas for a program that would elicit the help of the public in solving crime first came up in 1969, when the Dutch broadcasting company AVRO (best described in pillarization terms as nonaligned, if slightly conservative) was approached by the German program "Aktenzeichen XY . . . Ungelöst" and asked to help in a German case with Dutch implications. Language problems prevented permanent cooperation. However, in late 1969, the minister of justice appointed a working group to study the desirability of developing "crime detection by television." The report that this group produced in 1971 enumerates the possible negative side effects: stigmatization and violation of suspects' privacy, an incitement to witch hunts and vigilantism, reinforcement of existing stereotypes and prejudice, heightening the fear of crime and spawning imitation. These however could be counteracted by "due care in presentation," by avoiding sensationalism and by installing watchdog committees to control the selection of cases and to evaluate the program on an ongoing basis.

Four years later, two experimental installments (broadcast live from the police station in the Hague) took place in October 1975 and March 1976. There was a great deal of criticism from social and welfare services, probation officers, criminologists, and legal scholars, all of it reflecting the same points already made by the working group in 1971. Nor were the results of the programs themselves very encouraging: there were enough appreciative viewers, but these had not helped solve any of the cases. It was too much trouble for too little result and the idea was shelved. Six years later and, after somewhat complicated infighting among broadcasting companies, AVRO once again became the producer of a crime-detecting program called "Opsporing Verzocht."

In 1982, the minister of justice issued a governmental decree stating that, "the police feel the need for greater opportunities of communicating with the public." The decree (which closely follows the recommendations of the 1971 report) still provides the legal framework and restrictions for O.V.

today, determining to a large extent both format and content. It spells out the type of cases that may be handled by the program: very serious crimes such as murder, manslaughter, robbery with violence, violent sexual crimes; theft, if the aim is to trace goods or rightful owners; missing persons if crime or children under twelve are involved; escaped prisoners if there is a risk that they will commit serious crimes or are dangerous. The decree also requires that each program feature an item on crime prevention (examples are how to recognize a stolen car, how to make one's house burglar-proof or what to do about con men). Finally, the Ministry of Justice required that O.V. offer a quiet, unobtrusive presentation that avoids all sensationalism.

As well as setting out what the program should look like, the minister also provided for monitoring. The decree established two watchdog committees. One was called the *Begeleidings—en Evaluatiecommissie Periodieke Opsporingsberichtgeving per Televisie* (BEPOT) and charged with evaluating the program, including possible side effects (reporting to the minister after every series of programs on the desirability of continuation). Its chairperson was to be a judge or magistrate, with four members from the Ministry of Justice, one from the police, one from the criminal intelligence service, one from the crime prevention department, and one from AVRO. BEPOT was quietly dissolved in 1989 and its tasks taken over by the head of the police department of the Ministry of Justice.

The other committee is the *Selectiecommissie Periodieke Opsporingsberichtgeving per Televisie* (SPOT), which deals with selecting cases and making sure that O.V. conforms to both police standards of detection and to principles of privacy protection, all of this in the light of whether the case is suitable for visualization. The chair is one of the heads of the district prosecution service. The other members are from the Ministry of Justice, the criminal intelligence service, the crime prevention department, and five police districts. AVRO attends meetings in an advisory capacity only. As a watchdog committee, SPOT clearly represents the interests of the criminal justice authorities. It still exists and it determines which cases will be featured on the program and what information is given or withheld. It is then up to AVRO to present the case in a visual format, but always within the limits of the decree.

DULL, DECENT, DEPENDABLE

The Actual Program

There are two ways cases are considered for inclusion in O.V.: the district chief of police may consult the public prosecutor and then nominate the case to SPOT, or SPOT may take the initiative and approach the police, offering the services of O.V. Selection of cases must of course take account of the criteria set out in the decree, but is also based on the chance of solving the crime through viewer participation and on maintaining the balance of the program as a whole (not too much of the same and a geographical spread over the country). The second phase of selection takes place after consultation with police and prosecutors in the districts concerned. The final selection is made after consultation with AVRO on the possibilities of visualization. Ninety percent of all cases concern homicide, robbery with violence, and violent sexual crime.[4] All costs (with the exception of the committees) are borne by AVRO, some 150,000 guilders (80,000 dollars) per program.[5]

After the cases have been selected, the SPOT secretary, who is also the program's "police producer," and the AVRO editor, who is also the main presenter, visit the police for information, discuss what to show and what not to show, and decide on text and images. The AVRO journalist writes the script, fixing the complete text of the program. Police representatives and journalists are bound by this script and adhere strictly to it. After filming and cutting, the police officers who will appear on screen view the material. Police suggest which items to show during the invariable part of the program that attempts to trace the owners of stolen goods. Interviews are practiced first in order to make sure that everyone knows what to say.

Partly because of the set script, the program itself is decidedly dull and somewhat amateurish in presentation and consists of five selected cases, one item requesting viewers to phone in if they recognize stolen property, and one item on prevention. There is nothing flashy about either background or presenters (previously a middle-aged respectable-looking man, nowadays male and female, but equally presentable and equally middle-aged). The studio is quiet, very like an old-fashioned newsdesk and quite unlike the American style newsdesk setting that "Crimewatch UK" favors. The old-fashioned effect is heightened by the presenter reading the script— no newfangled tricks of the trade such as computers here. The police, in complete contrast to the actual situation, appear on the program as guests. The presenter asks the police officer questions and receives answers according to the set text. Nevertheless, and despite their practice run, the police officers are visibly nervous and ill at ease: they need prompting, mumble at the desk or stare fixedly at the camera, stumble over words, and generally look and sound as if they are giving evidence in court straight out of their notebooks. Items may start or end with film fragments at the scene of the crime and cautious reconstructions, and may be interspersed with police sketches, clues, and exhibits such as clothing.

Restrictions and Self-Censorship

For reasons of privacy, and in order to maintain the presumption of innocence and avoid trial by media, photographs of suspects are rarely shown on Dutch television. This also applies to O.V., with exceptions made for dangerous escaped prisoners and for security videos of robberies actually taking place. Each new technological development in this field (police sketches and videotape) requires special permission from the minister before it can be used. Permission is given in decrees, which set out the requirements that a case must meet before images of suspects may be shown. The general requirement boils down to an assessment of whether the interests of society in having the image shown are greater than the privacy interests of the suspect.[6]

Reconstructions rarely include actors, there is never any blood, and there are very few special effects. Looking back on the first five years of the program in a behind-the-scenes book, one of the presenters declared that selected cases would not include underworld murders, organized crime, etc., there being no direct public interest in solving the murder of one underworld boss by another (Simon 1989:34). He also stated categorically that the program would not offer rewards (although in normal investigations it is not unusual for the public prosecutor to offer a reward for information): "[I]n our opinion, it is logical to ask citizens to help solve crime, for no greater reward than the knowledge that they have contributed to their own safety and have acted for the good of society" (Simon 1989:47).

The latter is possibly a projection of AVRO's own declared motivation. From the very beginning the broadcasting company insisted its motives were based exclusively on considerations of social responsibility. The program enhanced AVRO's identity as a nonaligned public broadcaster serving the common good in its informative programs and appealing to "the decent man in the street." Indeed, "common sense" underlies text and content of the program. Presenters regularly use qualifications such as "beastly crime," "cowardly robbery," and "we must catch this man," and on screen there seems to be little scope for finer shades of distinction with regard to criminality. However, despite the "law and order" flavor of the script and the fact that program producers have (repeatedly) said that the "end justifies the means" (see, e.g., Kloosterman and Jägers 1989:45), this should not be taken literally. Not only are the means legally restricted, there also seems to be a real awareness among program producers that the sensitivity of the subject requires more than normal journalistic care.

As well as stressing social responsibility and public welfare, AVRO has always insisted that in no way should O.V. be seen as entertainment. At the same time, it set up its own system of monitoring the effect of the program. Regular audience research of all television by broadcasting companies is normal in Holland, but AVRO commissioned separate and more extensive research into O.V. and published annual reports on the findings. Questions on fear of crime, views on the police, general notions about crime, as well as viewers' ideas about the program are always included in order to monitor possible changes in attitudes to and fears about certain types of crime or crime in general that may have resulted from viewing the program. This fits well with government strictures on avoiding stigmatization of suspects and sensationalism (which might compound public fears).

Clashing and Coinciding Interests

In many ways, the interests of AVRO and the criminal justice authorities coincide. And in probably just as many ways, these interests clash when wider considerations are involved. In the Dutch system of broadcasting, broadcasters depend on membership and (interdependent) audience shares and ratings of programs, and base decisions on (dis)continuation of programs on these figures. Although the program producers deny that such figures influence decisions about O.V. (it being allegedly public interest alone that prompts their broadcasting of it), the very nature of the program requires a large and appreciative audience. If help by the public in solving crime is the decisive element, then the more potential helpers the better. Indeed, one of AVRO's conditions for cooperating originally was that the selection of cases would focus on recent crimes, allowing the police at the same time to use O.V. not as a last resort but as a legitimate part of police investigation. This of course enhances the percentage of cases solved, while viewers are likely to be more appreciative of a program involving recent crime, in which case they are more likely to watch again next time. The police have the same interest here, and their condition for continuation is a large enough audience to make crime solving feasible.

Inevitably then, clearance rates have always been presented as an important reason for continuing the program and have provided one of the main arguments against criticism. What the clearance rate is, however, is in itself anything but clear. In any event, it has never been more than 50 percent (but that was highly unusual). The average is somewhere between 25 and 30 percent (not counting the stolen property), but one may well ask what the definition of "clearance rate" is. There seems to be some confusion here, as different writers make different claims. A long-standing presenter of the program always put it at 50 percent (Simon 1989:15) and defined clearance rate as "perpetrator apprehended." The first secretary of the BEPOT, who wrote the reports recommending continuation, was unsure what clearance rate meant, but thought it meant "perpetrator known as a result of the broadcast," but not necessarily apprehended, let alone convicted.[7] Groups who opposed the program as likely to lead to public anxiety, stereotyping, and stigmatization put their own interpretation on the figures and came up with rates under 10 percent (Godfroy and Van der Velden 1984). According to the police, absolute figures for 1993 (*APB* 1994) are as follows: 77 cases in 13 broadcasts; 31 solved, with 61 suspects apprehended: These include 1 out of 5 rape cases, 15 out of 29 cases of mugging, 9 out of 16 violent robberies, and 3 out of 22 homicides. But again, it is difficult to know what "solved" means.

The average audience that watches O.V. has gradually dwindled to half its size when the program first started: from 25 percent of the audience share in 1982 via an all-time low of 8.9 percent in 1992 to 11.6 percent in the 1993–1994 season, with by far the largest segment of the audience consisting of elderly people with a fairly low level of education.[8] In itself this is not unusual: as program choice (via cable and satellite) increases, especially for young people, dwindling audiences have become a feature of the old pillarized broadcasters in Holland.[9] But there is a special problem here for O.V., considering the link between a large audience and the program's crime-solving capacity, which also provides its special legitimization. Importantly, however, it is a great favorite with those incarcerated in prison and other penal institutions[10] and the police say that these viewers provide a large number of significant tips. In general, police still insist that the program is worth their while in terms of crimes solved. This is difficult to judge. Although O.V.'s clearance rate is not particularly good it is no worse than other programs of its sort, and we should bear in mind that the crime rate in the Netherlands (particularly the sort of crime shown on O.V.) is very much lower than in the United States or Great Britain, so that in absolute figures the crimes solved through O.V. make a greater impact.

However, the criminal justice authorities have manifest interests in O.V. that transcend its crime-solving capacity. When asked by a member of parliament whether the clearance rate of the cases shown on O.V. actually justified prolongation, the minister of justice answered that the program had other functions too, one of which was to provide a means of promoting a favorable image of the police among the general public (July 31st 1984, Hand. TK 1983–1984:1037). Although this was taken to mean showing the public that the police actually do something about crime, the figures show that the audience appreciates O.V. for a number of other reasons related to favorable images and goodwill toward the police.

From the very beginning, viewer appreciation and audience ratings of O.V. have been exceptional. Routine audience research gives an almost invariable figure of around 7.5 and has shown no change as the audience share went down. (A fixed panel of viewers is asked to score the show on a scale of 10; an average of 7.5 is very high and approaches the sort of scores given to important soccer matches.) When the panel is asked to name the aspects of the program it appreciates most, 97 percent say it is useful (although only 68 percent see its usefulness in crime solving, 96 percent say that the fact that they could help to solve a crime is an aspect they appreciate). Importantly, the panel regards the program as trustworthy (95 percent), objective (92 percent), and displaying good taste (68 percent). Few people admit to watching it for pure entertainment; rather, the audience is inclined to think it informative and educational.[11] The producers have always regarded O.V. as a means of improving the image of the police in the sense that "we want to show the viewer that the policeman is just an ordinary person doing his job" (van den Heuvel 1986:6). In this they appear to have succeeded: in 1991, 89 percent of viewers thought the police sympathetic and reliable, if not necessarily efficient (only 55 percent thought them capable of solving serious crimes).

The Future

Two developments in the Netherlands seem likely to affect the format of O.V. although it remains to be seen whether they will change its essential nature. Both are sometimes referred to under the wider label of "Americanization." On the one hand there has been, over the past ten years, an increasing attempt on the part of the police to develop an autonomous and adversarial crime-fighting role within an inquisitorial system, in which they are traditionally controlled by the Public Prosecution Service and relegated to a subordinate role in investigating crime. This has been partly the result of the rise of a perceived threat of organized crime and its international, transborder implications. Although the police originally succeeded in breaking away from the Public Prosecution Service, in developing a high degree of expertise in proactive and undercover policing (often learned in the United States), and in presenting organized crime as the greatest threat to society and as warranting extensive freedom of movement and new powers of investigation for the police, they seem to have overplayed their hand and there has been a serious backlash in public opinion. A public and political debate, fueled by scandals about illegal police operations and corruption, raged during 1995 and 1996 about the necessity of regaining control of the police, with their proactive, secret "American" methods, their emphasis on the "war" on organized crime, and expensive crime-fighting equipment. All this was seen as taking resources away from what people really need and want in the way of policing in everyday life, and undermining the rule of law as most people understand it. It has seriously damaged both the image of the police and the inherent trust in the good faith of the criminal justice authorities. Journalists have played no small role in exposing scandals, and investigative journalism has taken off with a vengeance.

A tendency among television journalists and broadcasters to be less mindful of the needs of the criminal justice authorities and to be less circumspect about crime and criminals has, moreover, been encouraged by another form of Americanization: the opening up of broadcasting to cable and satellite television that has fundamentally changed the Dutch broadcasting system. The term "Americanization" in broadcasting was once almost synonymous with "American imperialism": it was thought that, after Coca Cola and blue jeans, American television stations and their programs would conquer the world, taking the place of Dutch products and in that sense breaking through the carefully constructed system of socially responsible broadcasting in the Netherlands. However, although American soaps and talk shows are popular, Dutch programs with the same format are more popular still, and Americanization refers not so much to competition from American programs as to an increasingly rapid change in Dutch broadcasting itself, its financing and very viability.

As long as pillarization remained the dominant feature of society, membership and identity of a broadcasting organization were foreseeable and determined by the pillar to which it belonged (a members' meeting each year called the board of governors to account as a form of direct democratic control and expressed satisfaction or dissatisfaction, as the case may be, with program policy). But as depillarization took hold and the system opened up in the 1960s to incorporate other nonpillarized broadcasters and to allow television advertising, broadcasting organizations were forced to cast their net wider for members and adjust their programming to appeal to the public in general rather than to a pillarized segment of it. Not until the 1990s, however, did competition from satellite and cable television finally result in a completely different type of broadcasting in Holland. For the first time, broadcasting organizations have left the structure of public broadcasting, with its sharing out of time on the air and advertising revenue according to size (public membership), and gone commercial.

This means that they are no longer subject to legal programming restrictions and are therefore in a better position to make popular programs aimed at a large audience. In view of the devastating competition for the old broadcasting companies, they too are pushing for the lifting of all legal restrictions and programming requirements. In the future, all Dutch broadcasting companies will have to depend on their ability to capture and hold large audiences that will attract advertisers. Moreover, local and regional broadcasters have gained increasing access to the cable, and local crime features high on their list of priorities. It remains to be seen whether notions of social responsibility will go entirely by the board and certainly whether the sort of self-censorship that governed broadcasting activities in the field of crime will still be feasible. Both in informative and entertainment programs, with broadcasters no longer seeing themselves as beholden to the authority of the criminal justice system, the more popular broadcasting companies are inclined to want to set their own agenda on crime and criminals anyway and to ignore any journalistic code or ethical considerations that might still govern the original broadcasters from the days of pillarization.

New Crimewatch-type programs have emerged that are much more sensational (and more critical of the police) than O.V. ever was. "Deadline" (originally called "Crime Time") is broadcast by TROS, a public broadcasting corporation—although of commercial origin—with an entertainment orientation. Although the police cooperate, there is not the symbiotic relationship that appears to exist with O.V.. The producers make no secret of the fact that the program offers amusement, action, sensation, and information around crime and related topics, only some of which include inviting viewers to help with solving actual crimes. A newcomer to the Dutch screen is a program called "Peter R. de Vries" after its originator and presenter, an investigative "crime journalist." It, too, is sensational, although it differs from "Deadline" in its highly critical approach to the criminal justice system. It is investigative journalism by television, exposing scandal and possible corruption, and a piquant detail is that Peter de Vries is not averse to committing felonies himself (such as obtaining information under false pretenses) in order to make his point. The program is new and there are as yet no significant data on audience shares and ratings. More recently, "real" reality TV, in which journalists follow police cars to the scenes of crimes and accidents has emerged, especially on local broadcasting stations. Judging by what actually appears on the screen, there seem to be no restrictions on the amount of blood or nastiness here. Some of these stations have also—even more recently—taken to producing their own brand of O.V. in cooperation with local police forces. Given the restricted budgets of most local stations, these programs are no more than a few minutes on the air, with perhaps a police sketch or (very limited) reconstruction. Nevertheless, as phenomena they are the handwriting on the wall insofar as future development is concerned.

It is not surprising that, from the 1990s onwards, there has been a visible shift in attitudes among both program producers and criminal justice authorities with regard to the future of O.V. (see, e.g., Bromet 1992:19). There is a feeling that competition from independent commercial broadcasters and other broadcasting companies, and the rise of local and regional television, will require essential changes to the format and presentation of O.V.. One indicator of future problems is that, following the decline in audience shares, the police at district level seem to be losing interest and now nominate less than half of the cases that appear on the program. The former chairman of SPOT has indicated that the extreme caution with which all parties approached O.V. may have made it too dull. According to one of the new presenters, "[O]ur approach has to be more juicy if we want the public to cooperate. Especially in these days of blood on the ceiling, even in children's hour" (Bromet 1992:9). The new chairman of SPOT, however, insists that entertainment is taboo: "This is television, so it must not be too dull, but it is also police work, so amusement is out" (Strooblad 1993:9). As of yet, changes have been limited: a more exciting introduction, livelier colors in the studio, an offer of rewards every now and then, and slightly more exciting reconstructions.

It might be thought that Americanization would diminish the attractions of a program like O.V., but there are several indications that it may be able to hold its own, even against new and more exciting crime programs. Although, for instance, "Deadline" appeals to a younger audience, audience shares are only slightly higher than for O.V. (an average of around 13 percent) in 1991, while audience ratings are notably lower (on average 6.6). Audience research shows that the public regard this infotainment program as too shallow for the important subjects it deals with: to much "tainment" and not enough "info" (Broekman 1991). Although the relaxing of broadcasting restrictions and increasing competition from national and foreign programs may still prove the undoing of O.V., it should also not be forgotten that in some ways the program seems to have hit on a formula that may be more lasting than would seem feasible at first sight. It is interesting that the variables political affiliation, education, and social class are significant (though not very) as far as the composition of the audience is concerned, but play no part at all in appreciation scores. Variation in scores, moreover, is very small. From this we may conclude that the program itself is very uncontroversial and pleasing to a widely diffuse audience.

It is the very unobtrusiveness of its presentation that impresses viewers and creates an atmosphere of objectivity and dependability, of the police doing their job. According to unpublished audience research by Dutch broadcasters, after each broadcast fear of crime in general goes down slightly and people are less concerned about their personal safety. Only 23 percent of the audience find O.V. frightening and 22 percent (overlapping percentages) think it sensational. In these days of Americanized policing and broadcasting, it is the combination of real crime and being unsensational that is O.V.'s greatest asset. It is also an asset to police, whose reputation has been badly tarnished by recent revelations about their methods and lack of accountability. O.V. is reality television with a difference. In its version of policing, corpses do not bleed and the police are what the police should be: decent, dependable, and accountable, just doing a job that is not so nasty after all, and needing all the public support they can get.

NOTES

1. The name is police jargon and is untranslatable. It means something like "request information on the whereabouts of . . . "

2. Surveys sometimes indicate a more punitive attitude among the general public. However, when the figures are broken down, people still seem willing to maintain reasonably tolerant attitudes. It is not clear whether these attitudes are changing dramatically. A recent survey found increased public support for introducing the death penalty (an option definitely not on the political agenda), but other research has failed to confirm an increase in punitive thinking. See Moerings

(1994:253–69), which are reports from the conference How Punitive are the Netherlands?

3. De Haan (1990:66–70) and Downes (1988:74ff.) both refer to pillarization as part of the explanation for the comparatively mild penal climate of the Netherlands and the seemingly high level of tolerance that obtains there.

4. In one of its unpublished annual reports, BEPOT noted the distortion, put it down to the difficulty of visualizing other cases such as fraud (which is not necessarily true), and then considered that broadcasting a suitable case should take precedence over distortion as a side effect. One could, of course, argue that the possibility of such side effects should be a criterion for deciding on the suitability of the case.

5. This sum, although decidedly meager by American standards, is almost twice the amount that AVRO receives from license fees and advertising revenue per hour and is therefore indicative of what the organization is prepared to invest in O.V.

6. Police sketches are seen as distinct from actual photographs, in that they show a type, not a person. The possible danger of this is not that a person's privacy may be violated, but that innocent persons of the same type may be wrongly identified and accused (not so much a weighing of the interest of the individual against society, but of two social interests). The decree on police sketches, therefore, requires that additional information in individual cases (clothing, make of car, scars, accent), which would serve to individualize the suspect, is also provided so as to minimize the risk of wrongful identification.

7. In an interview with the author.

8. By comparison, in 1990 both "Crimewatch UK" and "Aktenzeichen XY . . . Ungelöst" drew audiences of 20 percent against O.V.'s 14 percent.

9. And compared to other Dutch programs, O.V. does quite well. Among the most watched programs in September 1991, it shared fifth place with a Dutch language soap, "Allo Allo."

10. Most prisoners in Holland have TV in their cells, although the audience research on O.V. (which makes a special point of monitoring prison audiences) shows that it is one of the programs that prisoners prefer to watch during recreation. Some prisons allow recreation time to go on longer until the program is finished.

11. These figures, taken from NOS audience research on O.V. in 1993–1994, do not differ significantly from findings in other years.

REFERENCES

Algemeen Politieblad (APB). 1994. 2:32.

Berghuis, A. C. 1994 "Punitiviteitsfeiten." Pp. 299–313 in *Hoe punitief is Nederland?* edited by M. Moerings. Arnhem: Gouda Quint b.v.

Blankenburg, E. and F. Bruinsma. 1991. *Dutch Legal Culture.* Deventer: Kluwer.

Brants, C. 1993. "Justice Done and Seen to Be Done? The Institutionalized Relationship Between the Press and the Criminal Justice System in the Netherlands." *International Criminal Justice Review* 3:60–77.

Brants, C. H. and K. L. L. Brants. 1994. "Van vermaak tot lering en terug, televisie, punitiviteit en de tijdgeest." Pp. 253–69 in *Hoe punitief is Nederland?* edited by M. Moerings. Arnhem: Gouda Quint b.v.

Brants, K. 1989. "From Pillar to Post, Broadcasting and Politics in the Netherlands." In *Broadcasting and Politics in Western Europe,* edited by R. Kuhn. London: Croom and Helm.

Broekman, S. 1991. "Crime Time. Verpakte misdaad-informatie op de televisie?" Doctoral thesis, University of Amsterdam.

Bromet. J. 1992. "Nelleke van der krogt, Opsporing Verzocht mag best wat smeuiger." *AVRObode* (August 31):18–19.

Downes, D. 1988. *Contrasts in Tolerance.* Oxford: Oxford University Press.

Eijkman, Annoesjka L. 1991. "Een hellend vlak. Een aanzet tot verdieping van het inzicht in Opsporing Verzocht als televisieprogramma." Doctoral thesis, University of Amsterdam.

"Foreign Views on Dutch Penal Policy." 1992 *Tijdschrift voor Criminologie* 34:187–86.

Godfroy F. and R. Van der Velden. 1984. *Opsporing Verzocht. Mensenjacht via de televisie.* Den Bosch: Kri Boek, Vereniging van Reclasseringsinstellingen.

Haan, Willem de. 1990. *The Politics of Redress. Crime, Punishment and Penal Abolition.* London: Unwin Hyman.

Heuvel, J. van den. 1986. "'Opsporing Verzocht' bruikbaar hulpmiddel voor de Nederlandse politie." *Tijdschrift voor de Amsterdamse Politie* (December):4–7.

Hulsman, L. H. C. and J. F. Nijboer. 1993. "The Dutch Criminal Justice System from a Comparative Perspective." Pp. 309–58 in *Introduction to Dutch Law for Foreign Lawyers,* edited by J. Chorus, Th. Gerver E. Hondius and A. Koekoek. 2nd rev. ed. Deventer: Kluwer.

Kloosterman, Y. and Jagers K. 1989. "Interview with Will Simon." *Aktueel* (June 8):45–47.

Lijphart, A. 1975. *The Politics of Accommodation,* 2nd red. ed. Berkeley: University of California Press.

Moerings, M. (ed.). 1994 *Hoe punitief is Nederland?* Arnhem: Gouda Quint b.v.

Simon, Will. 1989. *Opsporing verzocht. Resultaten, feiten en achtergronden.* Naarden: A. J. G. Strengholt's Boeken.

Strooblad, M. 1993. "Tien jaar Opsporing Verzocht: Drie van de vier horloges gaan terug naar de inbreker." *Politiemagazine* 6:8–9.

Werkgroep opsporingsberichtgeving per televisie. 1971. *Verslag van de werkgroep opsporingsberichtgeving per televisie.* Unpublished internal report, The Hague.

11

"Témoin N°. 1":
Crime Shows on French Television

HUGH DAUNCEY

French reality-based television crime shows are a recent phenomenon, having first appeared only in the mid-1990s. In 1990 the details of a new crime show series proposed by one of the major television channels created such consternation among TV regulators and the judiciary that it was canceled even before the first program could be shown. Although during the early 1990s programs showing the problems of missing persons familiarized viewers, police, regulators, and magistrates with the new genre of reality programming (RP), France waited until 1993 for the next appearance of a major crime show, *"Témoin N°. 1"* ("Prime Witness").

The popularity of *"Témoin N°. 1"* and the difficulties that it has encountered with government, judiciary, and industry regulators are, in large part, explained by a crisis in confidence in the police and the legal system of France. In the context of such a crisis and with the increasing loss of faith in values of community and solidarity in society as a whole, the French public has been interested to see television investigating the problems of individual citizens in reality shows. Although not the longest running of the reality shows (it was phased out in December 1996) and not the only show to trespass on the activities of the police and the legal system, the crime show *"Témoin N°. 1"* became the prime target for critics of the role of RP in French society.

"Témoin N°. 1" was made possible by two factors. First, the public dissatisfaction at failures of police investigations was compounded by concern over the independence of the judiciary from political interference. Second, the French television industry was searching for a new form of low-budget, high-audience, prime-time programs. The combination of these two factors overcame the previous reticence of TV channels to fight the case for such shows. First we shall consider the general context of contemporary French policing and justice. Then we will examine developments in France's TV industry that created the "commercial imperative" for RP shows. Finally, the history, content, and style of *"Témoin N°. 1"* will be discussed in detail.

PROBLEMS OF CRIME AND JUSTICE

From 1963 to 1993, recorded crime in France increased significantly. Murders increased by a factor of 2, burglaries by a factor of 8, and thefts involving violence by a factor of 23. The police have been unable to control crime and have been considered, along with the legal system, to be failing to defend France from a rising tide of delinquency.

Since the late 1970s and early 1980s, the vocabulary of policing and justice has adopted the term *sécurité* to describe the objectives of the new laws and sentencing policies. During the center-right presidency of Giscard d'Estaing (1974–1981), governments tightened legislation on delinquency and crime in general, entrusting a major review of policing and sentencing to Justice minister Alain Peyrefitte. Since the "rapport Peyrefitte" of 1977 and the resulting law of February 1981 known as the *loi Sécurité et liberté*, parties of both right and left have agreed over the need to address citizens' feelings of insecurity. Although governments of the Right (from 1986 to 1988, and from 1993 to the present) have tended to adopt slightly tougher attitudes toward crime (especially at the instigation of the hard-line interior minister Charles Pasqua), the Left's decision in 1983 to abrogate no more than a few articles of the *loi Sécurité et liberté* indicated a political consensus identifying the causes of increased criminality in the problems of troubled urban areas and the need for ongoing modernization of the police and reform of the judicial system.

Public perceptions of crime and *insécurité* are closely linked to the problems caused by France's high rate of unemployment and to the social tensions engendered by the presence of large numbers of foreign workers and young second-generation immigrants, often concentrated in the most underprivileged of urban areas.[1] Amplified by the racist policies of the extreme-right *Front National* political party, a distrust of young unemployed immigrants has emerged in the general public. The public suspects this population of high rates of delinquency. Moreover, this population has poor relations with the police because of harassment and occasional police blunders.[2] The persistence of unemployment levels of 12 percent (currently over three million) is deemed to be turning France into a society increasingly divided between the "haves" and the "have-nots," and the effective "exclusion" from normal society that unemployment forces on citizens is seen as an obvious cause of criminality.

Faced with increasing crime, the judiciary finds itself in the difficult position of being underfunded and considered insufficiently independent of government. France is currently undergoing a crisis of faith in its legal system, which is seen to be inefficient in stamping out crime and tainted by its apparently compliant attitude toward government pressure to settle cases involving political corruption. Although France is employing more and more examining magistrates and gradually increasing the budget of the Justice Ministry, greater and greater demands placed on the judicial system mean that its efficiency is still questioned.

Public concern in the 1980s and 1990s over the failings of the police and the legal system provided the audience for reality crime shows in the increasingly commercialized French television industry. Reality shows of all kinds, but especially crime and missing persons programs, provided TV channels embroiled in cutthroat competition for viewers with easy-to-produce, inexpensive material.

FRENCH TELEVISION IN THE 1990S: COMPETITION

Political, ideological, economic, and technological pressures have all driven French broadcasting toward more variety and competition, and increased attention to commercial criteria in programming choices, both in public service TV and in the private channels. The intense competition for ratings resulted from the substantial changes in the French broadcasting system in the 1980s and the early 1990s. These changes were brought about by the breakup of the traditional public service framework of three state-owned channels and the creation of other channels with different financial bases and operating with new goals. In the 1990s, French television has evolved a dual system in which public service channels (*la télévision publique*), which are partly funded by the TV license fee (*la vignette*), compete with commercial channels (*les télévisions privées*) for audience and advertising.

In the early 1980s, when changes were first made to the old, essentially Gaullist TV system, France enjoyed three state television channels of public service broadcasting, and an absence of commercial television. Under the first presidency of François Mitterrand, the early years of socialist government saw initial moves toward the eventual dismantling of the public service monopoly and increasing freedom of communication in television, based on the July 1982 law on *liberté de communication* (freedom of communication).

PRIVATIZATION AND COMMERCIALIZATION

The creation of the pay TV channel Canal Plus in November 1984 shook the broadcasting system, since it represented the first concrete move away from the TV system inherited from the Gaullist and Giscardian ORTF-derived structures of the 1970s. For the first time in French television, viewers could watch something other than public service channels, rather than having to be satisfied, as they had since 1974, by the state's three TV channels (France 1, France 2, and France 3). In 1987, as part of the free-market economic policies of the center-right Chirac cohabitation government, France's leading public service channel TF1 was privatized, introducing more competition into the *paysage audiovisuel français* ("French audiovisual landscape," or PAF for short). Previously, the number of channels had been increased by the granting of fifth and sixth stations, first to France 5 and TV6 (under the socialist government) and then (under cohabitation) to La Cinq and M6 in 1986.

In addition to changes in the ownership and raison d'être of cable channels, reforms were undertaken throughout the 1980s to the long-standing production monopoly of the state-owned *Société française de production* (SFP), from which channels had been obliged to purchase programs. Since 1982, channels have been allowed to diversify their sources of program production, giving more varied programs and stimulating the French production industry, albeit often in cooperation with foreign partners (Hare 1994).

For some analysts of the French audiovisual landscape, 1991–1992 is a turning point in the metamorphosis of French TV from public service monopoly into an advertising-dependent and ratings-driven free market. In this view, saturation TV coverage of the Gulf War, combined with increasing competition between channels, made viewers realize that they could survive watching slightly less television; in turn, competition intensified between channels to attract advertising (Chaniac and Dessault 1994:3–4). Because of its failure to obtain high enough audience figures and sufficient advertising revenues in 1991, the fifth terrestrial channel, La Cinq, was forced to cease broadcasting, and after its final liquidation in April 1992, the channel's frequency was reallocated to the new quality public service channel Arte–La Sept.

Arte and its production company La Sept were created as a corrective to the effects of the commercial imperative during the late 1980s and the early 1990s. At least in the view of Hervé Bourges (former chief executive of TF1 and Director-General of Antenne 2/FR3 and the current president of the regulatory *Conseil supérieur de l'audiovisuel*, CSA), the rapid growth of reality shows in TF1's programming in 1991–1992 marked another element in the slide toward commercialism that had originated in 1987 in the financial difficulties and editorial changes accompanying the channel's privatization (Bourges 1993:85–86).

Bourges's preferences are for a "state commercial television," which would combine the financial and commercial expertise of the private sector with the ethical standards and civic duties of traditional French public service broadcasting. Analysis of the distribution of reality shows among French TV channels indicates that public service stations have been less enthusiastic than their commercial competitors to adopt this new genre of program. Such reluctance to embrace the vogue for these popular and popu- list television programs perhaps results from a disinclination on the part of *télévision publique* to become too openly involved in what is sometimes seen to verge on *la télévision poubelle,* or trash TV.

THE "COMMERCIAL IMPERATIVE" AND CULTURE

The evolution of French television in the 1980s and 1990s has been principally guided by movement toward a system of coexisting public ser- vice and commercial channels, with competition for viewing figures and advertising triggering debate and conflict over issues of quality, cost, culture, and commercialism. French television has also participated in France's per- manent desire to protect her cultural identity in the international system, and was also a feature in the arguments over French "cultural exception" in GATT during the early 1990s. France believes that her culture and language are different (and special) and need (and deserve) to be shielded from the Americanization and globalization of culture by some form of "cultural protectionism." Creating and maintaining quality French television is a way of supporting French culture at home and abroad. This wider political and cultural significance of everyday French television explains at least in part some of the furor created by reality shows such as *"Témoin N°.1,"* whose "low cultural value" is seen by some to undermine France's claims to cultur- al superiority. More so in France than in other European countries such as Britain, television crime shows are judged by more than simply legal criteria.

The seriousness with which the French state considers the protection of French culture in audiovisual matters is illustrated by the directive given to French channels in January 1991 to broadcast 50 percent of films and pro- grams "made in France" and 60 percent of French or European Community origin. Added to such constraints on program choice, the government also obliged national channels to plow back 15 percent of sales revenue into French programs (with the further condition of broadcasting not less than 120 hours per month of French production at prime time), and to encourage independent program producers with 10 percent of sales revenue. In this context of state pressure to screen French productions at prime time and of commercial pressures to attract maximum viewing figures and advertising revenues, the stage was set for the appearance of French RP. The govern- ment's insistence on quality and on national production of programs was not entirely effective, since the commercial need to produce low-cost programs highly attractive to viewers encouraged the use of cheap program formulas. The low-budget, wide-appeal programs would fill the gap left by the outdated genre of French variety entertainment shows and by more costly French or Hollywood films.

CRIME SHOWS ON FRENCH TV: *"LA TRACE"* AND *"TÉMOIN Nº.1"*

Crime shows are but one type of reality programming. The genre of reality shows on French TV encompasses many different kinds of programs. The simplest taxonomy of French RP divides the shows according to their dominant subject matter. In this perspective there are three main types: (1) everyday dramas of courage, (2) talking about feelings, and (3) civic action.

Everyday dramas of courage are shows that deal typically with rescues and the work of emergency services, as in *"Urgences"* ("Emergencies") and *"La nuit des héros"* ("Nights of Heros"). Shows that talk about feelings include the programs whose number and popularity have caused some analysts to suggest that they typify French reality television. These programs are concerned with love, sex, and family relationships (Kilborn 1994:430). "Civic action" is a category of reality shows exemplifying many of the deeper issues concerning French politics and society raised by this new television; crime shows fall within this group. These shows in particular have raised the issue of television's capacity to create parallel "institutions" of policing, justice, and arbitration, which might undermine the role of traditional law and order and professional expertise. Table 1 summarizes the details of the major French reality shows involving crime, the courts, and missing persons.

The *"Témoin Nº.1"* crime show, in fact, has been the most controversial of France's reality programs. Produced by Pascale Breugnot for TF1 and presented monthly from March 1993 by Jacques Pradel (and Patrick Meney), this show represented the resurrection of an earlier planned series of a program called "La Trace." In 1990, *"La Trace"* was shelved because of French fears that the program would give rise to informing and civil unrest.

In 1993, initial reactions to *"Témoin Nº. 1"* were similarly influenced by concern over a possible revival in the French "tradition" of informing, which dated to the period of collaboration. There was also concern about destabilizing the fragile relationship between the French media and the legal system. The media in France are highly critical of the apparent political influences over the legal system, and the judiciary resents the intrusions of the press, radio, and television into its activities. Between 1993 and the withdrawal of the program in late 1996, the ongoing debate about *"Témoin Nº.1,"* crystallized most of the major doubts about reality shows held in France concerning their legality, quality, and effects on French society. As one the longest running of the shows, the very continuity of *"Témoin Nº.1"* helped to anchor French reality programming as well as to provide examples

Table 1. Crime/Court/Missing-Person Shows, 1990–1996

Title and Channel	Start	End	Topic and Presenter
Perdu de vue (TF1)	October 1990	Continuing	Tracing missing persons (Jacques Pradel)
Cas de divorce (La Cinq)	June 1991	April 1992	Adaptation of US show "Divorce Court" using French law
Défendez-vous (A2)	September 1991	July 1992	Simulated courtroom arbitration between individuals in conflict
La Trace (TF1)	April 1990	Canceled	Tracing missing persons (Ladislas de Hoyos)
"Témoin No. 1" (TF1; Pascale Breugnot)	March 1993	(Monthly)	Presented by Jacques Pradel and Patrick Meney. Appeals for assistance from the viewing public to resolve unsolved crimes.
Etat de choc (M6; Philip Plaisance)	January 1993	Monthly until June 1993	Presented by Stéphane Paoli. Reconstitution of crimes, interviews with witnesses, protagonists and magistrates.
Mea Culpa (TF1)	March 1992	May 1993	Attempted conciliation between individuals and groups in conflict (Patrick Meney)

Source: Compiled from Le Monde, Télérama, and Libération.

of its problems. Before we look in detail at *"Témoin No.1,"* however, it is useful to consider the crime/missing-persons program that never was— *"La Trace"*—whose failure to reach the screens in 1990 nevertheless paved the way for another missing-persons show entitled *"Perdu de vue"* ("Lost from Sight") and then for *"Témoin No.1"* itself.

"LA TRACE" (TF1, 1990): ATAVISTIC FEARS OF INFORMING

TF1's *"La Trace"* ("The Trace") was to have been a prime example of the new trend in French television toward more interactivity between studio and the watching public, with a greater emphasis on the everyday problems of ordinary people. This first reality show of the 1990s would have combined all the features of crime RP programs: examining unsolved minor crimes (*fait divers*) through reconstructions, discussions in the studio with various "experts," and appeals to viewers. However, in 1990 the government and the judicial system demonstrated unease at the possible implications of such a program formula, and requested that the regulatory authorities for French television and radio should investigate the pros and cons of the issue. The *Conseil supérieur de l'audiovisuel* (CSA or the High Audiovisual Council) is the body that oversees the content of television and radio programs. Responding to the concerns of the government, the CSA informed TF1 that any such program should not encourage informing and should not intervene in ongoing trials or interfere with personal liberties. The Justice Ministry suggested creating a *comité d'éthique audiovisuel* (Committee of Broadcasting Ethics). Viewers associations and various *syndicats de magistrats* (legal profession trade unions) also had expressed their reservations.

Such official reservations about *"La Trace"* might have proved unimportant had events not then occurred that reinforced concerns about having viewers telephone with information. In May 1990, the Jewish cemetery in the town of Carpentras was desecrated by skinheads. The actions of the right-wing skinheads reminded France of previous problems of anti-Semitism and informing during the Occupation. The incident heightened tension in a political context influenced by the memories of Vichy France and the painful legal proceedings against collaborators such as Paul Touvier and René Bousquet. The assistant CEO of TF1 announced the cancellation of *"La Trace."*[3]

Despite the reservations of the legal profession and government, since 1990 reality shows have taken root in French television, leading to screening of programs more controversial in style, format, and content than the unfortunate *"La Trace"* in 1993. A program that bridged the gap between *"La Trace"* and what was to follow was *"Perdu de vue"* ("Lost from Sight"), which has become the longest running of all the reality shows. *"Perdu de vue"* has been broadcast on TF1 (usually in fortnightly alternation with *"Témoin Nº. 1"*) since 1990. The program, produced by Pascale Breugnot and presented by Jacques Pradel, regularly attracts large audiences through its rituallike investigation of missing persons. The program features family members in studio phone-ins and discussions, and emotional dramatizations (Mamou 1995; Dumay 1995). In September 1996, the program was felt by many to have intruded too publicly into private grief when it involved itself in the traumatic Belgian child abduction scandal. In general, however, *"Perdu de vue"* has been less controversial than *"Témoin Nº. 1,"* which it has now outlasted.

"TÉMOIN Nº. 1": TV JUSTICE OR CHEAP THRILLS?

"Témoin Nº. 1" is the French version of the British program "Crimewatch UK." The French word *témoin* means witness, so the title of the show could be translated as "Prime Witness." The program is directly inspired by its UK forerunner, and Jacques Pradel, the smooth, ever-reasonable presenter seems to have been chosen to emulate the British presenter Nick Ross.[4] In Britain, the concerns raised by programs such as "Crimewatch UK," "Crime Stoppers," and "Crimebusters" have been addressed in the official Grade Report (Working Group on the Fear of Crime 1989) and by other academic studies (Schlesinger and Tumber 1994). In France, however, the debate has been wider and more heartfelt because of traditional French unease at the possibilities of informing.

"Témoin Nº. 1" was created and produced by Pascale Breugnot for TF1, the commercial channel most concerned with viewing ratings and advertising revenues. *"Témoin Nº. 1"* was a key instrument in TF1's ratings strategy, occupying the midevening prime-time slot after the main forty-minute news program, which commences at 8:00 P.M.[5] Lasting for a full two hours, *"Témoin Nº. 1"* filled TF1's evening schedule, frequently competing with popular full-length feature films on all the other channels. The greatest popularity of the show was reached in February 1996, when *"Témoin Nº. 1"* attracted an audience of 8.5 million viewers, representing 16.3 percent of the viewing public.

Pascale Breugnot, the program's producer, is the principal exponent of reality programming in France. Coming from the TF1 reality show production line, this show combines all the features of the genre that lead to the cancellation of *"La Trace"* in 1990. In fact, the threat of *"Témoin Nº. 1"* to moral standards went further than that of *"La Trace"* through its appeal for viewer participation and the possibility of discrediting existing traditional mechanisms of law and order. As with "Crimewatch UK," the principle of *"Témoin N°. 1"* was simple: unsolved crimes were presented to the viewing public in the form of filmed reconstructions, and viewers were encouraged to telephone the studio where the presenter of the program animated a discussion between police, examining magistrates, witnesses, and victims. *"Témoin N°. 1"* is a kind of *"Perdu de vue"* whose appeal is heightened through the inclusion of crime and violence. Both programs worried government, judiciary, and viewers' organizations on their first appearance because of the encouragement to intervene in the lives of others.

From the beginning of its first series in 1993, *"Témoin N°. 1"* purportedly aimed to present its investigations in as sober a style as possible. Even the monthly scheduling of the show represented TF1's desire to distinguish the program from other (weekly) reality shows and game programs. Despite the care expended by its creators to make the program acceptable, *"Témoin N°. 1"* immediately attracted criticism with the very first program, which was screened on March 1, 1993.

This program addressed the problems of the police and investigating magistrates in a number of unresolved child murders. Many critics and analysts of French television deemed this topic unnecessarily emotional for a reality show with claims to seriousness and public service (Psenny 1993). In addition to the choice of topics, there was criticism of the filmed reconstructions of events (which confusingly mixed actors and real witnesses), the extravagant camera work, the use of melodramatic music, and even the studio decor. As with TV crime shows in the United States (Cavender and Bond-Maupin 1993), such effects of filming, *mise-en-scène,* and musical accompaniment were all intended to heighten the "spectacle" of the show.

The various criticisms of *"Témoin N°. 1"* arose notwithstanding the efforts made by its producers to deal only with unsolved cases in which there was no suspect. The producers agreed not to screen identikit photos or to broadcast live phone calls. They promised to obtain approval from the families of the victims and the legal authorities before showing reconstructions. They also promised to transmit any phone leads immediately to the examining magistrates. In some senses, *"Témoin N°. 1"* found itself in the catch-22 situation of undermining its own validity through its concessions to the police and legal authorities: the more TF1 accepted modifications to the original program format, the more *"Témoin N°. 1"* could cause confusion in the minds of viewers. The presence of police and magistrates "live in studio," for example, was seen by some to blur the lines between what remained a reality show (however ostensibly careful and serious) and the traditional, official procedures of policing and justice (Erhel 1993).[6]

"Témoin N°. 1" has now been withdrawn, the last program airing in December 1996. During its four years, arguably it acquired a certain re-

spectability as the flagship of French reality shows. The program's popularity with viewers, however, at no time made it immune to criticism from the legal establishment and television industry regulators. A succession of minor scandals arose as *"Témoin N°. 1"* occasionally overstepped its own limits, or, in trying something new, contravened CSA guidelines for acceptable TV.

As early as October 1993, when the second series of programs was getting under way, the apparent breakdown of safeguards intended to ensure close collaboration between the television journalists and representatives of the examining magistrates occurred. The show's presenters directly called for witnesses to come forward with information, instead of allowing such appeals to be made only by examining magistrates. Another problem arose in late March 1994 when *"Témoin N°. 1"* was deemed to have diverged from its stated intentions of working in partnership with the police and legal system. A murder case was brought to TF1 by the lawyer of the victim's parents and was then broadcast against the advice and without the participation of the examining magistrate.

In fall 1995, the Carpentras affair, which had sabotaged *"La Trace,"* returned to haunt *"Témoin N°. 1"*: the search for the culprits was relaunched because of new allegations that the vandalism of the cemetery had not been perpetrated by right-wing skinheads but by local high school students. By inviting the examining magistrates and witnesses to participate in a program on September 18, *"Témoin N°. 1"* became embroiled in a heated and divisive debate over anti-Semitism and extreme right-wing politics. The realization that declarations made on the program by witnesses were not entirely reliable and the subsequent failure to advance the investigations showed for some commentators that TV justice was fraught with too many problems (Porte 1995; Braudeau 1995). Later, *"Témoin N°. 1"* fueled doubts about its own seriousness by devoting serious consideration to the Roswell aliens/ UFO story. It continued to create consternation among the legal profession in February 1996 by promising air time to an imprisoned suspect (Broussard 1996).

The program's producers and presenters claimed that such slips either were minor errors of organization, or could be justified by the needs of reality programming to respond to issues that interest the audience. But analysts of French RP tend to believe that reality shows, by their very nature, must increasingly sensationalize in order to maintain viewers' interest and audience figures. After three years on the air, the self-styled "TV appeal to the nation" from a suspect planned in early 1996 was seen by many as a publicity stunt for the program. It also seems that this kind of crime show must inherently entertain an ambiguous relationship with the official structures of justice and the police. In 1994, there were claims that only six months after its first program *"Témoin N°. 1"* was already becoming distanced from its "safe" formula of collaboration with examining magistrates; it was pursuing a "freedom of action" intended to maintain its notoriety and its attractiveness to viewers (Chemin 1994).

It is not easy to decide how far the producers of *"Témoin N°. 1"* were driven by the desire either to create a "parallel" system of criminal investigation and justice or to create programs that are simply interesting to viewers. To some it seems that the apparent readiness of TF1 to respect the legal profession was no more than a ploy to perpetuate the programs' official and public acceptance.

The producers of *"Perdu de vue"* and *"Témoin N°. 1"* repeatedly rebut claims that their programs sensationalize human suffering. The fact that they make every effort to work with the police and examining magistrates proves, they say, their good intentions (Meney 1995). Although doubts over the altruism of TF1 persist, the Breugnot-Meney-Pradel team believed that *"Témoin N°. 1"* provided an invaluable service for citizens for whom traditional methods of criminal investigation had failed. They argued that the occasional freedom that the program allowed itself from the conditions and safeguards imposed by the *CSA* regulatory body and the legal system were justified by its good intentions. Such a belief served to condone occasional ethical-legal slips. It also facilitated a split between the program and the judicial system, as *"Témoin N°. 1"* exploited cases where the police and legal investigation had failed but TF1 produced both results and audiences. Much of the French debate over reality shows in general and over *"Témoin N°. 1"* in particular has focused on the fear that, like pornography, they may trap viewers and program providers in a descending vortex of stronger and ever more ethically unacceptable thrills (Girard 1993).

CONCLUSION: *"TÉMOIN N°. 1"* AND THE DECLINE OF FRENCH REALITY TV

During late 1995 and 1996, the vogue for reality shows in French television began to show signs of weakening, as a variety of programs such as *"Témoin N°. 1,"* *"Perdu de vue,"* and *"Bas les masques"* ("Drop the Mask," France 2) reached almost respectable middle-age. In September 1995, France 2 canceled a new documentary series called *"La preuve par l'image"* ("Proof by Pictures"), after the first program's apparent manipulation of material caused an uproar among viewers and television journalists. The program relied on secretly filmed footage. For the leading channel of public television, such an ethical violation was deemed to be unseemly (Kerviel 1995; Darge 1995). TF1 also submitted to pressure from the legal profession and the Justice Ministry by canceling at the eleventh hour a planned reality show, *"Enquête publique"* ("Public Inquiry"). The program intended to examine controversial court cases where doubt over the original ruling had arisen (Humblot 1996).

In April 1996, Etienne Mougeotte, an assistant CEO of TF1, expressed the view that "provocation" no longer had any place in French television. He claimed that the reality shows of his channel had reached maturity. He denied that *"Témoin N⁰. 1"* had encouraged either informing or the establishment of "parallel justice" (Dutheil et al. 1996). In June 1996, France 2 decided to withdraw its prime reality show, the popular *"Bas les masques"* program, famous for the gentle psychological probing of its presenter Mireille Dumas, and representative of a very different kind of RP from that of TF1.

The ending of *"Témoin N⁰. 1"* in December 1996 was a logical step in this process of program review. As analysts of programming debated whether the genre of reality programming had finally exhausted the interest of the viewing public, it became clear that the most famous of reality shows was canceled partly because of the simple need to renew TF1's schedules and partly because it was failing to attract audiences (Arrighi 1996). As TF1 panicked over its falling viewing figures, the inability of *"Témoin N⁰. 1"* to find advertisers made it a natural candidate to be replaced with a newer variant of reality programming such as Pascale Breugnot's *"Le monde de Léa"* ("Léa's World"). There also were new French series or soaps similar to those screened by France 2 in competition with TF1's previously dominant reality shows (Brocard 1997; Lalanne 1997).

The decline of reality programming and the weakening position of *"Témoin N⁰. 1"* within the genre is the result of a number of trends in French broadcasting and French politics and society in general. First, RP has been unsuccessful in defining a role for itself. Its defenders claim that it is "brotherly TV" (*la télé du frère*) replacing "fatherly TV" (*la télé du père*) characteristic of the patriarchal bad old days of state-controlled television in the 1960s and 1970s. But its critics point to its voyeuristic tendencies, its exploitation of individual suffering, and its distortion of the reality it claims to show. In the early 1990s, in a social context of perceived rising crime, of *malaise dans les banlieues* (suburban unease), of *insécurité* (fear of crime), and of a judicial and political system discredited by successive scandals, the desire to try other channels of redress was understandable; as one famous left-wing weekly news magazine put it: "Nanny television is blooming on the ruins of the Welfare State" (*Nouvel Observateur* 1992).[7]

In 1992 Jacques Pradel defended RP against the criticisms of the intelligentsia, defining his *télé du frère* as psychological support for a society ill at ease with itself:

> In *"Perdu de vue"* as in *"L'amour en danger"* ["Love at Risk"] we don't reflect the image of winners in society, we break with everything we've been taught: that emotions are a weakness, that crying and breaking down are not allowed.

> We break taboos, exploring personal areas and the no-man's-land of the inti-
> mate. We make programs that make room for doubt. (Pradel 1992)[8]

This therapeutic role for RP has not really been accepted, as various scandals have shown. A revealing example of *la télé du frère* was provided by
TF1 in May 1993 with its short-lived program about neighbor disputes and
crime, "Mea culpa." "Mea culpa" ended with a furor over its final broadcast,
which (beating its previous viewing record) showed a studio confrontation
between an adolescent rape victim and a "representative sample" of the
inhabitants of her village (*Le Monde* 1993).[9] Some saw this as a collective
trial by TV and as a distortion of the actual events, which had actually
occurred in another village. It soon transpired that aspects of witnesses'
statements had been manipulated by TF1 in the interests of creating "a good
reality show" (Mamou 1993).

   "Témoin N°. 1" has also been guilty of manipulating investigations, topics, and presentational style in order to maximize audience interest. It has
often seemed that the "brotherly TV" claimed by its proponents has not been
properly created by French reality programming. The various mistakes of
"Témoin N°. 1" show how the creation of parallel structures of policing and
justice has not come about. The current furor in France about "exclusion"
and social divisions between citizens, in connection with government plans
for the reform of the judicial system, should undermine reality programming's attractiveness in claiming to provide new forms of social and legal
mediation.

   It is possible that French politics and society are beginning to come to
terms with a nexus of problems that overshadowed the growth of RP in the
early 1990s. These include what historians have dubbed "the Vichy syndrome" and the uncertainties persisting throughout the Fifth Republic concerning the efficiency of the underfunded legal system and its independence
from political interference. Given the general lack of controversy or protest
in Britain at "Crimewatch UK" or in the United States at "America's Most
Wanted," it is interesting to consider that the strong objections in France to
reality crime shows derive from the historical connotations of informing.
Underlying the unease fostered by programs such as *"Perdu de vue"* and
"Témoin N°. 1" was the sociocultural legacy of the Occupation and the
mass-informing suffered by the French under Vichy and during the purges of
the Liberation.

   Comparative studies of reality programs in other countries, specifically in
Britain and Germany, explained the success of programs like "Crimewatch
UK" by the "civic principles" (*sens civique*) of the British and the Germans.
The problem attributed to France was that the *sens civique* of her citizens
was underdeveloped, or otherwise distorted. For example, philosopher and
political scientist Raymond Aron suggested that informing was a French

national sport. Whereas the screening of early reality shows took place in the context of Carpentras, reality shows in the mid-1990s have become less controversial (and less interesting to viewers) because France is arguably coming to terms with its Vichy past. For example, in 1995 President Mitterrand revealed his own links with Vichy. Moreover, the legal system was successful in finally making another eminent collaborator face charges in court in early 1997.[10]

Finally, *"Témoin Nº. 1"* and reality programming have been in the forefront of struggles with the French regulatory body for TV and radio, the CSA. The repeated problems with *"Témoin Nº. 1"* have created tension between TF1 and the CSA, which, along with other differences, caused doubt over the renewal of the channel's broadcasting license in March 1996 (Mamou 1996). The CSA continually intervenes in television and radio in order to safeguard standards and morals. Thus, the "commercial imperative" that has driven TF1's use of RP is meeting continued resistance, both in terms of "cultural standards" and in the form of competing products on the public service channels. The cultural defense of French identity, which was stimulated by the negotiation of GATT in the early 1990s, generated the establishment of quotas for French programs on French TV. The result was an explosion of inexpensive popular "national" programs such as *"Témoin Nº. 1."* Ironically, that program's success stimulated the production of French series and fiction programs that are beginning to recapture audiences from reality shows.

NOTES

1. A complementary aspect of the government's attempts to improve policing has been policies of urban renewal (*la politique de la Ville*) targeting run-down suburban areas and housing estates around France's major cities.

2. The 1995 film *La haine* (*Hate*), directed by M. Kassowitz is a well-known depiction of these tensions.

3. "I believe there is in our country today a climate whose presence means that the program we envisaged can no longer be made. . . . France is unwell. She is recovering from a great shock, and we should take this into account" (Etienne Mougeotte, cited in Claude 1990).

4. To place *"Témoin Nº. 1"* in the context of American television, it suffices to say that it is the gallic version of programs such as "Rescue 911," "Unsolved Mysteries," and "America's Most Wanted."

5. The 8:00 P.M. evening news programs are the "flagship" broadcasts of the main French TV channels. TF1 and France 2 compete intensely by screening high-profile programs before and after the news, by poaching each other's star presenters, and even by starting the programs a minute earlier than their rival!

6. This further complication for the ambiguous status of *"Témoin Nº. 1"* oc-

curred in spring 1993, when the judicial system and the police became even more closely involved in the program. Journalists involved in the program were requisitioned by the magistrates, and police officers participated live on air in the studio, responding directly to telephone calls to the studio switchboard.

7. "La télévision-providence fleurit sur les ruines du 'welfare state.' La télé dont vous êtes le héros: démocratie directe ou exhibitionnisme?"

8. "Dans 'Perdu de vue' comme dans 'L'amour en danger,' nous ne répercutons pas l'image des gagneurs qui avancent dans la société. Nous rompons avec tout ce qu'on nous a appris jusqu'ici: que les émotions sont une faiblesse, que pleurer c'est pas bien et craquer, pas beau. Nous brisons les tabous, nous explorons les terrains personnels, nous fréquentons les no man's land de l'intimité. Nous faisons donc des émissions qui distillent le doute."

9. "Mea culpa" (TF1), shown between 10:30 and 11:30 P.M. on May 27, 1993, attracted 7,250,000 viewers.

10. The trial of Maurice Papon, a senior public figure of the 1960s and 1970s, and former government minister, accused of deporting Jews from Bordeaux during the Occupation, was finally authorized and began in 1997, despite attempts since 1981 to shelve proceedings.

REFERENCES

Arrighi, Marie-Dominique. 1996. "Audience, la Une est au bout." *Libération*, December 13, p. 40.

Bourges, Hervé. 1993. *La télévision du public*. Paris: Flammarion.

Braudeau, Michel. 1995. "Carpentras, ville empoisonnée." *Le Monde*, November 11, p. 11.

Brocard, Véronique. 1997. "Plus dure est la chute." *Télérama* 2454(22, January):8–10.

Broussard, Philippe. 1996. "Controverse sur l'émission de 'Témoin N°. 1' consacrée à une affaire criminelle en cours d'instruction." *Le Monde* February 10, p. 27.

Cavender, Gray and L. Bond-Maupin. 1993. "Fear and Loathing on Reality Television: An Analysis of 'America's Most Wanted' and 'Unsolved Mysteries.'" *Sociological Inquiry* 63(3):305–17.

Chaniac, Régine and S. Dessault. 1994. *La télévision de 1983 à 1993: Chronique des programmes et de leur public*. Paris: INA.

Chemin, Ariane. 1994. "L'émission de TF1 'Témoin N°. 1' prend ses distances avec les magistrats." *Le Monde*, April 20, p. 11.

Claude, Patrice. 1990. "TF1 abandonne le projet de l'Emssion 'La Trace.'" *Le Monde*, May 18, p. 13.

Darge, Fabienne. 1995. "Les réalités de 'La preuve par l'image.'" *Le Monde*, September 18, p. 7.

Dumay, Jean-Michel. 1995. "Réalité des sentiments familiaux." *Le Monde*, June 12, p. 7.

Dutheil, Guy, et al. 1996. "Le temps de la provocation à la télé est terminé, entretien avec Etienne Mougeotte." *Le Monde*, April 25, p. 28.

Erhel, Catherine. 1993. "'Témoin Nº. 1': les gendarmes au bout du fil." *Libération,* May 23, p. 44.

Girard, I. 1993. "Reality shows: comme le porno, toujours plus hard!" *L'événement du jeudi,* February 26, p. 89.

Hare, Geoffrey. 1994. "The Broadcasting Media." Pp. 238–70 in *France Today,* edited by J. E. Flowers. London: Hodder & Stoughton.

Humblot, Catherine. 1996. "TF1 renonce à son nouveau magazine 'Enquête publique.'" *Le Monde,* January 20, p. 27.

Kerviel, Sylvie. 1995. "Jean-Pierre Elkabbach supprime 'La preuve par l'image.'" *Le Monde,* September 23, p. 31.

Kilborn, Richard. 1994. "'How Real Can You Get?': Recent Developments in 'Reality' Television." *European Journal of Communication* 9(4):421–39.

Lalanne, Bernard. 1997. "Où est passée la recette pour faire des recettes?" *Télérama,* January 22, p. 10.

Le Monde. 1993. "'Mea culpa,' maxi-dégâts." *Le Monde,* June 6–7, p. 16.

Mamou, Yves. 1993. "'Mea culpa' rejette toute culpabilité." *Le Monde,* June 13–14, p. 7.

———. 1995. "'Perdu de vue' a cinq ans." *Le Monde,* June 12, p. 1.

———. 1996. "Le renouvellement de la concession de TF1 sera examiné le 26 mars." *Le Monde,* March 25, p. 21.

Meney, Patrick. 1995. "Justice et Medias: 'Témoin Nº. 1.'" Proceedings of the British Institute in Paris conference on "Trial by Media," September 23–24, 1994. *Franco-British Studies* 42(3):26–39.

Nouvel Observateur. 1992. "La télé dont vous êtes le héros: démocratie directe ou exhibitionnisme?" *Le Nouvel observateur,* March 18, p. 40.

Porte, Guy. 1995. "Des témoignages réorientent l'enquête sur la profanation de Carpentras." *Le Monde,* October 19, p. 12.

Pradel, Jacques. 1992. "Démagogie? Non, hygiène social." *Le Nouvel observateur,* March 18, p. 43.

Psenny, Daniel. 1993. "'Témoin Nº. 1' fouille les impasses judiciaires." *Libération,* March 1, p. 45.

Schlesinger, Philip and H. Tumber. 1994. *Reporting Crime: Media Politics of Criminal Justice.* Oxford: Clarendon.

Working Group on the Fear of Crime. 1989. *Grade Report, Report of the Working Group on the Fear of Crime.* London: HMSO.

Biographical Sketches of the Contributors

G. Blake Armstrong is an associate professor in the Department of Communication Studies at the University of Oklahoma. His research interests include cognition and communication, media effects on social reality and social conflict, and mathematical modeling of communication processes.

Chris Brants is a criminologist and a freelance journalist who holds the chair of Criminal Law and Criminal Procedure at the University of Utrecht, the Netherlands. Her main fields of research are crime, criminal law and the media, and the internalization of crime and criminal justice. She has published in English on journalists, freedom of expression and the criminal law, on the convergence of adversarial and inquisitorial systems of criminal justice, and on policing and the prosecution service. She is currently working on *Criminal Law and the Limits of Personal Autonomy,* a comparative work in cooperation with the Law School of the University of Wales at Cardiff.

Dianne Cyr Carmody is assistant professor in the Department of Sociology and Criminal Justice at Old Dominion University. Her research interests focus on violence against women and crime in the media, particularly the criminal justice response to domestic assault, victims' self-protective strategies, and women's attitudes and fears concerning sexual assault.

Gray Cavender is a professor in the School of Justice Studies at Arizona State University. His teaching and research interests include crime, punishment, and media. He is co-author of *Corporate Crime Under Attack: The Ford Pinto Case and Beyond,* as well as several articles that analyze how crime is depicted in newspapers, on television, and in film.

Hugh Dauncey is a lecturer in the Department of French Studies at the University of Newcastle upon Tyne. His major research interests are French television and radio, particularly reality programming, political communication, and France's reactions to new media. He has published on French high technology policy and is writing a book on the history of the French Space program.

R. Emerson Dobash is Professor of Social Research at the University of Manchester, England. His current research interests include evaluation of programs for violent men, and homicide in Britain.

Russell P. Dobash is Professor of Criminology at the Violence Research Centre of the University of Manchester, England. His current research interests include men viewing male violence, evaluation of programs for violent men, and homicide in Britain.

Pamela Donovan is a doctoral candidate in Sociology at the City University of New York Graduate Center. Her dissertation is a study of the use and meaning of contemporary legends about crime.

Aaron Doyle is a Ph.D. candidate in Sociology at the University of British Columbia in Vancouver. A former journalist, he has also recently published research on news sources in prisons, and on the media, corporate public relations and the future of British Columbia's forests.

Mark Fishman is an associate professor in the Department of Sociology at Brooklyn College, City University of New York. In addition to his interests in the rise of reality programming and tabloid news, he has published articles on the nature of crime waves and crime news, and is the author of *Manufacturing the News*.

Paul Kooistra is an associate professor at Furman University. He has published articles in criminology, the sociology of sports, and media. He is the author of *Criminals as Heroes,* which examines how organizational needs of media and politicians shape images of criminality.

John S. Mahoney is a professor of sociology at Virginia Commonwealth University. His areas of interest are collective behavior, media, minorities and work organizations. He currently directs an off campus education program for a major U.S. corporation.

Mary Beth Oliver is an associate professor in Communication Studies at Virginia Tech. Her research explores media images of race, gender, and violence, and the ways that such images affect viewers' attitudes, beliefs and emotional responses.

Philip Schlesinger is Professor of Film and Media Studies at Stirling University, Scotland and Director of the Stirling Media Research Institute. He is also Professor of Media and Communication at the University of Oslo, Norway. He is presently researching public space, national identity and communication in the European Union, and is working on a study of men viewing violence, the sequel to *Women Viewing Violence.*

C. Kay Weaver lectures in the Department of Film and Television Studies at the University of Waikato, New Zealand. She is co-author of *Cameras in the Commons* (Hansard Society, 1990) and *Women Viewing Violence* (BFI, 1992). She has published articles on media representations of crime, violence and gender and is currently researching "prosocial" media advertising campaigns.

Saundra D. Westervelt is an assistant professor of sociology at the University of North Carolina at Greensboro. Her forthcoming book, *Offenders or Victims? The Redefinition of Responsibility in America,* is an analysis of the development of the "abuse excuse" in American law. Her most recent work examines the risk factors for wrongful conviction and post-conviction reversal.

Index

213